U0645835

Knowledge Building in Physics Textbooks
in Primary and Secondary Schools

中小学物理教科书的
知识建构

赵清丽 著

厦门大学出版社 国家一级出版社
XIAMEN UNIVERSITY PRESS 全国百佳图书出版单位

序

　　听到赵清丽博士即将出版她的著作《中小学物理教科书的知识建构》，我为她感到高兴。赵清丽2009年到厦门大学攻读博士学位。她还申请国家公派研究生的博士生联合培养项目，在澳大利亚悉尼大学语言学系 James Martin 教授的指导下开展研究工作。在完成博士学位论文的过程中，赵清丽博士能刻苦钻研，结合论文的选题广泛阅读有关功能语言学、多模态话语分析和教育社会学领域的论著，努力扩大自己的学术视野，锻炼自己的研究能力。

　　中小学物理教科书的语言是一种独特的语类，在学生由普通日常话语过渡到科学语言的过程中起着重要的作用，因此教科书语言得到了不少学者的关注，各种理论从不同角度对它进行了探讨。赵清丽博士选择从功能语言学的角度探讨中小学物理教科书的知识构建，重点研究中小学教科书物理知识的构建以及意义生成的语义特征和语类特征，探索语言、图像等意义表达资源在传递物理知识中的机制。为了探讨中小学物理教科书的知识建构，这部著作建立了自己的分析框架，把语类、实体和行为、图像、语义密度和语义重力作为分析对象，详细分析和讨论中小学不同层次物理教材在知识建构方式上的异同。因此，这部著作为研究物理教科书的知识建构提供了很好的参考，对英语物理教材的编写也有很好的指导作用。

　　这几年，赵清丽博士在功能语言学的研究上取得了可喜的成绩。我相信她在今后的教学和科研工作中能发表更多的研究成果，取得更大的成绩。

杨信彰

2013 年 6 月于厦门

前 言

知识是人类文明得以传承和发展的载体,各个学科都对其本质进行了不同角度的探讨,但是对科学语篇中知识的建构方式鲜有研究,尤其是从语言学视角进行的研究更是如此。作为一名语言教育工作者,笔者一直关注知识的建构问题,该研究的形成源于基金委资助的厦门大学和悉尼大学的国家公派联合培养博士生项目。笔者于 2010 年 11 月至 2011 年 8 月在悉尼大学留学期间,有幸定期参加悉尼大学的系统功能语言学专家与教育社会学学者联合举办的研讨会,其前沿的理论促进了本研究的顺利完成。

系统功能语言学对科学语言的研究始于韩礼德《物理的语言》这篇文章,其分析对象由正统的科学话语逐渐过渡到了教育话语。前人对科学话语中知识建构的研究聚焦于小句层面,尽管后来也开始从语义层进行研究,但是很少有研究强调新知识是如何通过话语来获得的,也很少有研究强调其他符号(诸如图像、数学符号等)的功能。此外,尽管系统功能语言学对科学语言的研究起源于对物理语言的研究,但是接下来以物理语言为样本进行的研究几乎没有,尤其以中小学不同阶段物理教程为语料进行的研究更少。同时,鉴于物理在科学中的基础地位,该方面研究很有必要。

基于系统功能语言学、多模态话语分析以及教育社会学的基本理论,本书选择澳洲中小学的物理教材为研究对象,旨在探究不同层次物理教材建构科学知识的特征。具体来说,包括以下两方面问题:

(1)知识在每一层次物理教材中的建构方式;换言之,知识建构和意义生成在每一层次物理教材中的显著特征是什么?

(2)在不同层次的物理教材中,语义波(语义密度和语义重力)具有什么样的特征,而语义波和语言资源间又是何关系?

通过对不同层次物理教材的语言以及其他符号进行细致的分析和深入的研究,本书发现了物理教材建构科学知识的基本方法和语言特点,揭示了其中的基本规律,以期在语言学的视角下,能为中小学开展科学理论教学活动带来一些启示。

本书共六章。第一章是引言,介绍了研究背景、目的、意义并对本书结构进行了概述。第二章是对前人相关研究的综述和简评,为下面章节内容奠定了理论基础。第三、四、五章是本书的核心,第三章建立了本研究的理论框架,第四、五章具体分析了中小学不同层次物理教材中的知识建构方式。第六章为本书的结论,阐述了本研究的发现、意义、不足以及对未来研究的展望。

相对于前人的研究,本书有以下三个方面的创新,可以为系统功能语言学研究者以及话语分析研究者提供参考。首先,本书以系统功能语言学和伯恩斯坦的教育社会学为理论指导,更为全面地阐释了中小学各个层次物理教科书中的知识建构。此外,语言学角度的语义密度和语义重力的研究模型在一定程度上整合了系统功能语言学和伯恩斯坦对知识的研究。其次,修正的实体分类模型,其具体的运用方法和步骤,区分语法隐喻和科技术语的标准以及修正的类别关系系统为分析科学话语中的语场和概念提供了具体的方法。第三,对实体、过程、语类和多模态进行的量化研究以及定性分析使我们更加深刻地理解了各个层次中小学物理教科书中的知识建构是如何层层递进的。将语言学角度的语义重力和语义密度展开模型运用于每个层次的物理教科书分析中,拓展了系统功能语言学和伯恩斯坦教育社会学的理论视野,从而进一步扩充了话语分析研究理论。

诚然,金无足赤,书无完书,由于从系统功能语言学、多模态话语分析、教育社会学以及其(Legitimation Code Theory 合法化编码理论)相结合的视角对中小学物理教材的知识建构进行分析还是首次,加之作者水平所限及一些其他因素的制约,书中难免有纰漏乃至错误之处,还望广大读者多提建议,不吝赐教。

本书承蒙我敬爱的导师,厦门大学外文学院杨信彰教授以及悉尼大学语言学系的 James Martin 教授悉心指导,特此感谢!

Contents

1

List of abbreviations

SE	Bernstein's sociology of education
GSP	Generic structural potential
LCT	legitimation code theory
MDA	multimodal discourse analysis
SD	semantic density
SF-MDA	systemic functional multimodal discourse analysis
SFL	systemic functional linguistics
SG	semantic gravity

List of Figures and Tables

6

Chapter 1　Introduction

This book addresses how knowledge is built up step by step in discourse through an analysis of Australian physics textbooks for primary and secondary schools from an integrated perspective of systemic functional linguistics (hereafter SFL) and Beinstein's sociology of education (hereafter SE). This chapter will start with the background and purpose of the current study, followed by a brief introduction to the methodology adopted in this project and finally the organization of this book.

1. 1 Research Background

Since Halliday's (1993c) influential article *On the language of physical science* — an exploration of the evolution of scientific language from Chaucer's time to the present day, SFL has been interested in the language of science because the attempt to map out the meaning potential of scientific discourse "gives us a better understanding of what is required in order to learn and control scientific knowledge" (Martin & Veel, 1998: 181).

The analysis of the language of science in SFL develops from canonical science discourses to educational science discourses (Halliday & Martin, 1993; Hasan & Williams, 1996; Unsworth, 1996; Christie & Martin, 1997) so as to facilitate students' learning. One of the difficulties in learning science lies in the language of science as argued by Halliday and Martin (1993). Therefore, it is assumed that students' familiarity with the scientific language can get rid of their alienation of science.

Some researchers (Lemke, 2004; Doran, 2010) insist that, besides the language of science, other non-linguistic semiotic systems such as mathematics and images may also alienate many people from physical discourses. In fact, more and more researches (Lemke, 1998b; Lemke, 2003; O'Halloran, 2003;

1

O'Halloran, 2007; O'Halloran, 2008; Doran, 2010) about knowledge construction in scientific discourse begin to consider other semiotics other than language, such as mathematical symbolism and images.

As to the researches into knowledge, Bernstein's SE provides us valuable insights. Paying great attention to school education, SFL and Bernstein's SE[①] have opened a long dialogue which developed via four phases (1960s-1980s, 1980s-1990s, 2000s and 2010s), as the following table shows:

Table 1.1 SFL and Bernstein's SE Dialogue (after Maton, 2011)

	Code theory[②]	SFL
1960s—1980s	coding orientation	semantic variation
1980s—1990s	pedagogic discourse	genre-based literacy
2000s	knowledge structure	field
2010s	LCT (specialization) [③]and LCT(semantics[④])	appraisal, grammatical metaphor, affiliation, individuation, and many others.

Among the four phases of dialogue between SFL and Bernstein's SE, the third one, that is, the field and knowledge structure negotiation, will be the focus of this study. SE's mapping of types of knowledge structures and SFL's concern with the discursive construction of knowledge stimulate these two disciplines to go deeper into the knowledge research in a two-way traffic, as Figure 1.1 shows.

As Figure 1.1[⑤] shows, both SFL and Bernstein's SE emphasize knowledge

---

① SR (social realism) is originally used here to replace Bernstein's SE. The term "social realism" has been proposed by Maton and Moore (2010) for the "coalition of minds". However, Bernstein's SE will still be used in this study for it familiarity and the purposes of this research.

② Bernstein's SE starts its study from the concept of code and continuously focuses on this idea, so it is sometimes called code theory.

③ Legitimation code theory abbreviated hereafter as LCT, is a new development of Bernstein'SE, which will be introduced in Chapter 3. Specialization is one of the dimensions in LCT, but it is not the focus of this study.

④ Semantics, including semantic density and semantic gravity, is another dimension in LCT and will be mainly discussed in Chapter 3.

⑤ The term "BBology" is coined by Martin (2011a) to provoke the broader coalition than the term "social realism" to name themselves.

two way traffic···   verticality
                                            grammaticality
                                            gravity
                                            density

            SFL   BBology

casality
technicality
information flow
instantiation
grammatical metaphor

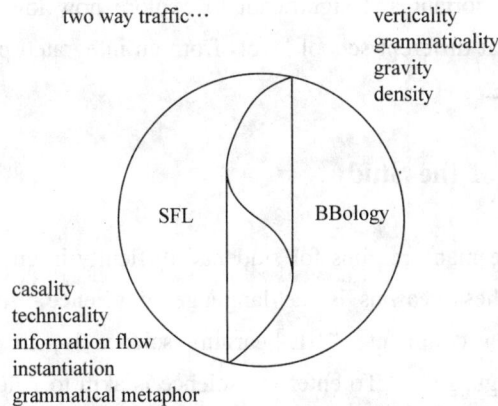

Fure 1.1   Parameters of Third Phase Field/Knowledge Structure Negotiation
(from Martin, 2011a: 53)

but from different perspectives. SFL takes knowledge as meaning and field as the basis of knowledge, focusing on the process of meaning-making by means of linguistic resources, such as causality, technicality, information flow, instantiation and grammatical metaphor, while Bernstein's SE emphasizes the nature of knowledge and explains its different dimensions, including verticality, grammaticality, semantic gravity (hereafter SG) and semantic density (hereafter SD)[1].

Physics is the basis of other science disciplines and is given a very important position in science curriculum, but most students feel it so difficult to learn this subject (National Curriculum Board, 2009). Therefore, it is expected that the analysis of ways of knowledge building in physics textbooks may facilitate their learning. However, researches in this aspect are lacking in SFL and Bernstein's SE. Halliday (1993d) has analyzed the language of physics in canonical discourses but not in textbooks. Martin (e. g. , 1993a, 1993c, 2002a) has studied textbooks, but paid less attention to physics. Bernstein's SE takes physics as the model of vertical discourse but gives no detailed explanation. In a word, few studies in SFL focus on physics textbooks across schooling, and less work specifically focuses on the way how new knowledge is gradually built in multisemiosis, and even fewer researches take both SFL and Bernstein's SE into consideration.

---

[1]   These four terms concerned with the development of knowledge structure will be discussed in Chapter 3.

Therefore, it is important and significant to explore how knowledge is built in physics textbooks at different school levels from an integrated perspective of SFL and Bernstein's SE.

1.2 Objectives of the Study

There must be many reasons for students' difficulty in entering the world of science. One of these reasons is the language of science. As Wellington and Iresong (2008: 3) comment, "[L] earning science is, in many ways, like learning a new language". "To enter the science is akin to Alice's passage down the rabbit hole into a new world" (Wellington & Iresong, 2008: 215). Alice is confused when she first read the book *Jabberwocky* as shown in the following.

> Twas brillg and the slithy toves,
> Did gyre and gimble in the wabe;
> All mimsy were the borogoves,
> And the mome raths outgrabe.
> Somehow it seems to fill my head with ideas—only I don't exactly know what they are! (Carroll, 1872: 191)

This is equally true of pupils' encounters with a new world of scientific discourses. When pupils are confronted by language and other semiotic resources in a science textbook or in a scientific prose on the blackboard, they may be as confused as Alice was when she first read the language of Carroll's poem *Jabberwocky*. In many ways, the language of science resembles the language of Carroll's poem.

Therefore, it is important for students to understand the features of physical language. Furthermore, it is important to explore how physics, by means of language and non-linguistic resources, builds its knowledge and develops its technicality across different levels of textbooks, and what the relationship is between knowledge building and the development of SD and SG. Specifically, this book is intended to address the following research issues.

First, the research is aimed to explore ways of knowledge building at each level of physics textbooks, that is, what the distinctive patterns of linguistic resources are in constructing knowledge and generating meaning across different levels of textbooks. Physics is a multisemiotic discipline which makes use of language, images and mathematical symbolism to construct knowledge for students. For students from primary to secondary schools, ways of building knowledge in their physics textbooks are different.

Second, this study is to investigate the patterns of semantic waves (that is, the development of SD and SG) at and across each level of textbooks, and the relationship between semantic waves and linguistic resources. Specifically, the relationship will be examined in terms of grammatical metaphor, technicality and semantics. In addition, the developing characteristics of technicality and its relationship with semantic waves will be studied across different levels of physics textbooks. Furthermore, it will be discussed how physics realizes its vertical knowledge structure.

The assumption behind these issues is that different levels of physics textbooks build knowledge in different ways because they are doing particular jobs. The semiotic resources used in these textbooks are therefore functional (in some way and for someone). Thus, the patterns of genres and the associated patterns of language will be determined by what the discourse is fundamentally trying to do and trying to get students to do. There is, of course, some overlap between different levels of physics textbooks, but each level tends to make different lexicogrammatical choices and has different developing patterns of SD and SG.

As students move through school science they also take a linguistic journey through the history of science (Martin, 1993). Through studying language development, everyday knowledge can be connected with educational knowledge. As Halliday (1990, 1994a) suggests, a language-based teaching/learning theory can be set up, seeing learning as a semiotic process.

1.3 Data and Methodology

The following section will explain the data and methodology adopted in this study in terms of data collection and data analysis.

1.3.1 Data Collection

Qualitative and quantitative methods will be applied to investigate how knowledge is built in physics textbooks. To achieve this goal, this research will focus on popular physics textbooks of primary and secondary schools for Years K-10 in Australia. There are four reasons for choosing these textbooks as the source of data in this project.

First, textbooks are chosen in this study for their importance in building disciplinary knowledge and introducing beginners to that field. As Halliday and Martin (1993e) claim, compared to spoken language, images and physical activity, historically written language has played a central role in the construction, production, reproduction and dissemination of scientific meaning in school science. Although there are radical changes in the physical appearance of written texts in recent years and the exclusive use of written textbooks has become unfashionable in classroom science teaching (Veel, 1997: 162), written language continues to play an important role in constructing scientific knowledge.

Textbooks state accepted knowledge and are the main basis for teaching. Many researchers in different fields pay attention to the important role of textbooks in school education. Wignell (1994: 358) argues that textbooks "are designed by practitioners in a field to introduce apprentices to that field" and "tend to represent the orthodoxy of their field". Sutton (1989: 151-152) emphasizes that "[T]here will always be a place for textbooks in science education" and "...the main purpose of a textbook is to define the fields anew, and to determine what shall count as part of it". Kuhn (1962) takes textbooks as the most obvious sign of paradigms — they are collections of concrete examples that shape scientific practice and thought. The important role of textbooks as carrier of knowledge in scientific education is further emphasized by Kuhn (1963).

In a word, textbooks play an important role in education. Therefore, their analysis will have some significant implications for science learning and teaching.

Second, the subject of physics is selected because of its basic role in scientific disciplines. Physics is referred to as the fundamental science because it describes phenomena in terms of their most basic underlying elements. Some physics textbook writers (Hewitt, 1998; Young & Freedman, 2004) emphasize the fundamental position of physics in science disciplines, from chemistry which studies the structure of molecules to paleontology which tries to reconstruct how dinosaurs walked. The principles of physics help to understand how human activities affect the atmosphere and oceans, and what alternative sources of energy are. Physics also plays an essential role in all engineering and technology. Engineers must first understand the basic physics principles before they design any kind of practical device.

In view of the basic function of physics in school science, it is very necesssay and important for students to learn it well. However, the fact is that most students feel it very difficult to learn. Therefore, textbooks selected in this research focus on physics with an aim to facilitate their learning in this subject.

Third, different levels of physics textbooks are chosen for the lack of researches in this aspect. Less work has specifically focused on the way new knowledge is acquired in discourse, which is of course of crucial importance for the study of textbooks. Meanwhile, less research has focused on textbooks across schooling. In addition, it is for the research purpose. The analysis of physics textbooks for primary and secondary schools may show whether there is a knowledge building gap, where and when it appears, and furthermore, what the development of technicality is.

Fourth, Australian versions of physics textbooks are examined for three reasons. The first reason is that Australian science education has a leading positon in the world. Findings of TIMSS (Trends in International Mathematics and Science Study) conducted by IEA (International Association for the Evaluation of Educational Achievement) in 1995, 1999, 2003, and 2007 show that Australian students' achievements in science are standing at the top world-level. The second reason is the higher quality of Australian textbooks, which are regarded as one of the famous versions in the world (佚名, 2012). The third reason is the convenience of data collection. When the author stayed in The University of Sydney, it was easy to find these textbooks in Fisher Library.

The data will be chosen with certain restrictions. First, textbooks will be chosen according to whether they include the contents prescribed by Australian science curriculum for different school levels. The textbooks are divided into three levels: textbooks of Level 1, textbooks of Level 2 and textbooks of Level 3. According *Shape of the Australian Curriculum: Science* (2009), textbooks of Level 1 (for Years K-2) are used for lower primary school students typically from 5 to 8 years of age, textbooks of Level 2 (for Years 3-6) for upper primary school students typically from 8 to 12 years of age, and textbooks of Level 3 (for Years 7-10) for junior school students typically from 12 to 15 years of age.

Second, textbooks should be popular and typical ones, three versions of which are chosen for each level of physics textbooks. The detailed information about these textbooks which have been chosen in this study is shown in Table 1.2.

Table 1.2 **Information About Physics Textbooks Used in This Study**

Level 1	Lower primary school (tpically for students from 5 to 8 years of age)		
Title	Forces and motion	Push and pull	Start science: forces and motion
Author	Angela Royston	Peter Riley	Sarah Nunn
Level 2	Upper primary school (tpically for students from 8 to 12 years of age)		
Title	Motion	Science: forces and motion	What are forces and motion
Author	John Farndon	Richardson Miriam	Eason Sarah
Leve3	Junior school (tpically for students from 12 to 15 years of age)		
Title	About Science	Exploring: forces and structure	Science Australia
Author	Brian Shadwick & Susan Barlow	Spiders Elizabeth	Mau Janet

Third, the analyzed texts should be about the same topic. In this project, the topic *force and motion* is chosen from physics textbooks for two reasons.

On the one hand, the topic *force and motion*, which is mainly based on Newton's ideas, is one of the fundamental concepts of physics. Newton's (1962) book on force and motion, the *Mathematical Principles of Natural Philosophy*, is uncontradicted by experiments for 200 years. All the everyday phenomena can be explained in terms of Newton's laws of motion, including circular motion and oscillations. Physicists use Newton's laws to interpret interactions at extreme length scales too, everything from sub-atomic particles to collisions of galaxies. Therefore, force teaching is a constant concern in physics in order to give real meaning to this abstract concept.

On the other hand, "[S]tudents' difficulties with *force and motion* have a long history in physics and science education research" (Brookes & Etkina,

2009). Therefore, the exploration of this topic is significant.

1.3.2 Data Analysis

This research draws on useful theories and practices available in SFL and other disciplines, such as systemic functional multimodal discourse analysis (hereafter SF-MDA), Bernstein's SE including Bernstein's ideas of hierarchical and horizontal knowledge structures within vertical discourses and Maton's notion of SD and SG in LCT, which will be used as a theoretical framework and analytical tools.

Both qualitative and quantitative analyses are adopted in the current project. This research will examine ways of knowledge building at different levels of physics textbooks in terms of language and visual images. The data analysis proceeds in three steps.

First, machine-readable versions of corpora are made. These original materials are scanned. Then verbal texts of these original materials are further electronized as a computerized Microsoft word corpus by the format-changing software.

Second, the data from different levels of textbooks will be analyzed. Each level of textbooks will be analyzed respectively in terms of genres, entities and activities, visual images, SD and SG. In the analysis, the author will resort to the above-mentioned theories.

The types of genres are identified and then their occurrences are counted for an analysis of their distribution at each level of physics textbooks. The different categories of entities and the different types of processes are manually identified and labeled in different colors (e. g. , yellow for generic entities and relational processes, red for the entities of technicality and material processes). For visual images, they are first analyzed qualitatively in two categories: ideational meanings realized by images themselves and ideational meanings realized by the interaction of language and images. Then their subcategories are given a quantitative analysis to find out their distributive characteristics. As to SD and SG, the occurrence of linguistic resources concerning with their variation is calculated and statistically analyzed. At the same time, their developing patterns are described qualitively.

Third, based on the statistic results, ways of knowledge building at each level of physics textbooks will be examined and compared. A conclusion will be drawn.

1.4 Terminology

In this section, several key concepts used in this book are explained: metafunctions, stratification, genre and field in SFL, intersemiotic relations in SF-MDA, knowledge structures in Bernstein's SE, and SD and SG in LCT.

SFL assumes that language has three metafunctions simultaneouly, namely the ideational, interpersonal, and textual metafunctions (Halliday, 1994). The ideational metafunction refers to the function of language to construe human experience of the world including both the internal and external world. It is the ideational metafunction that is concened with knowledge and will be the focus of this study. The interpersonal metafunction means the function of language used for interacting with other people, for establishing and maintaining relations with them, and for expressing their attitudes, feelings and judgements. The textual metafunction is the function of language to organize human messages into a coherent and unified text in ways which relate the ideational and interpersonal information to the context.

Stratification is another important notion in SFL. Language consists of three levels, namely lexico-grammar, discourse and social context, which are known as the strata of language. There is a relationship of redundancy among them, that is, lexico-grammar realizes discourse which in turn realizes social context.

As to social context, there are two sub-strata: context of culture realized by genre at the higher level, and context of situation including field, tenor and mode. In this study, the concept of genre follows Martin and Rose's (2008) definition and is seen as a recurrent configuration of meanings which enact the social practices of a given culture. In a working definition, Martin and Rose (2008: 6) take genres as "staged, goal oriented social processes".

Field, as one of the variables in context of situation, is related to the ideational meanings of language, that is, the "content" meanings of language. Thus, field is regarded as the basis of knowledge building in SFL. The concept of field has been developed through several phases in SFL, and it is treated in this research as a generalization of "what is going on" across genres and modalities (Martin, 2011b).

Intersemiotic relations refer to the interactional meanings among different semiotics (language, images, etc.) occurring simultaneously in a text.

The concept of knowledge structures, which refers to the nature of knowledge in creating theories in different discourses, is adopted from Bernstein. Bernstein (1999) distinguishes two kinds of knowledge structures in vertical discourse, hierarchical knowledge structures and horizontal knowledge structures. A hierarchical knowledge structure develops the knowledge by means of integration and subsumption of existing ideas within more generalising propositions, while a horizontal knowledge structure develops through accumulation of languages. Physics is the typical example of hierarchical knowledge structures.

Semantics, including SD and SG, is an important dimension in LCT. They are concerned with the development of knowledge. SD is about the condensation of knowledge and SG is related to the abstractness of knowledge from the context.

SG and SD can be stronger or weaker along a range of strengths, and the shift of semantic strength between weak and strong degree is just like a wave. The excerpt in Table 1. 3 illustrates how a semantic wave functions in constructing knowledge.

Table 1.3　Introducing the concept "force" in physics textbooks of Level 1

[*Push and Pull*] (**from Riley, 2001: 26—27**)
1. You use a force every time you move something, change its direction. or change its shape.
2. You push a pram/swing.   You pull a brush through your hair/a book from your bag.
3. A push/a pull is a force.

As the above text shows, three steps are needed in the introduction to the physical concept "force": introducing a conceptual term, unpacking the term, and repacking the term. There is a shift of semantic strength from the conceptual concept "force" (weak SG, hereafter SG – & strong SD, hereafter SD +) to everyday examples unpacking the term (strong SG, hereafter SG + & weak SD, hereafter SD –) and to a definition repacking the term (SG – & SD +), as Table 1.4 shows.

Table 1.4   Three Steps of a Semantic Shift

Step 1 (SG – & SD +)	Step 2 (SG + & SD –)	Step 3 (SG – & SD +)
Introducing a conceptual term	*unpacking the term into everyday language, including example from everyday life*	*repacking of descriptions into a definition*
"a force"	*"push a pram/swing; pull a brush/a book"*	*"a push/pull is a force"*

This semantic shift in introducing the physical concept "force" is represented as a wave diagrammed in Figure 1.2.

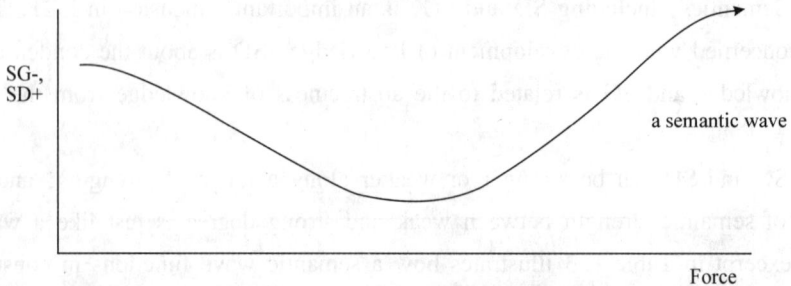

Figure 1.2   A semantic wave

In a word, the construction of knowledge depends on the waving of SG and SD.

1.5 An Overview of the Book

The book includes six chapters. The specific contents of each chapter are described as follows.

Chapter 1 is an introduction to the study. It first presents the background, and then introduces the objectives of the current study and specifies the significance of studying knowledge building in physics textbooks. It also describes the data collection and the methodology of the study, and presents an overview of the organization of the book.

Chapter 2 is the literature review. It briefly summarizes the major academic works on knowledge and scientific discourses especially from the perspectives of SFL and Bernstein's SE. This review first describes how knowledge is interpreted differently in different research fields, especially focuses on how knowledge interpretation diverges and converges in SFL and Bernstein's SE. It then examines the studies on scientific discourses. Those in pragmatics and English for Special Purpose (hereafter ESP) are briefly reviewed, and those in SFL and SE are reviewed in detail. This review generalizes SFL's researches into scientific discourses. These researches go from canonical scientific discourses to educational scientific discourses, and their focus develops from language to other semiotic resources. What is reviewed in this chapter also includes the studies on scientific discourses in Bernstein's SE, the studies on scientific discourses in China, researches into science textbooks and the concept *force and motion* from the linguistic perstpective.

Chapter 3 first proposes a theoretical framework with which ways of knowledge building will be analyzed. Then three theories from which the analysis framework mainly comes are discussed: SFL, SF-MDA, and a theory of knowledge structures in Bernstein's SE. SFL theories are first presented. To be specific, the theoretical considerations are of three aspects, namely, strata, metafunctions, and especially field. The analytical tools of entities and activities in the field are discussed. The discussion then proceeds to SF-MDA which is explained in detail to provide a theoretical basis for the analysis framework of visual images. In later sections, Bernstein's knowledge structures and Maton's semantics are explored to explain the nature of knowledge building in physics textbooks. Finally, the analytical model for an exploration of SD and SG from the linguistic perspective is given, which is followed by the summary of this chapter.

Chapters 4 and 5 apply the theoretical framework established in Chapter 3 to study ways of knowledge building in physics textbooks, with a view to operationalize the model and prove its applicability.

Specifically, Chapter 4 examines different linguistic ways of knowledge building across three levels of physics textbooks, the analysis of which is made in terms of genre, field and images. The realization of genres in physics textbooks shows different features at various school levels. Besides the two types of genres, **explanation** and **report**, which are typical in scientific discourse, other two types of macro-genres need to be given more attention, the first of which is **picture commentary** predominating at the first physics level and the second of which is **experimental procedure** occurring at all the three physics levels. In addition, story occurs with different percentages and various subtypes at different levels of physics textbooks. For each genre, a sample text is selected from the textbooks, and its generic structure is discussed. Field is construed by various kinds of entities and activities, which are analyzed in terms of their patterns and their frequencies across three levels of physics textbooks to show the variation in knowledge building. In the last section of this chapter, ways of knowledge building in physics textbooks are further investigated in terms of images and the interaction between images and verbal texts.

Chapter 5 does a linguistic exploration of the development of SD and SG in physics textbooks in two aspects. On the one hand, the study explores the variation of SG and SD by giving a quantitative analysis of linguistic resources in physics textbooks, showing the vertical nature of physical knowledge, that is, hierarchical knowledge structure of physics. On the other hand, the study makes a qualitative analysis of various patterns of SG and SD in introducing technical concepts at each level of physics textbooks. For each level of textbooks, a typical text explaining a physical concept is selected, the development of SD and SG is analyzed, and relevant SD and SG waves are drawn. Finally, the development of SD and SG is generalized across the three levels of physics textbooks.

Chapter 6 draws the conclusion of the study, specifies its significance, shows the limitations and provides suggestions for future work.

Chapter 2   Literature Review

This chapter conducts a literature survey so as to depict a general picture of how knowledge building is explored in previous studies.

Adopting an integrated perspective of SFL, SF-MDA and Bernstein's SE, this book is interested in how scientific knowledge is constructed by language and other semiotics in physics textbooks and in what the nature of physics knowledge is. Therefore, the following literature review will focus on the previous studies on knowledge, scientific discourses and what textbooks of science have done and not done with an aim to set up the theoretical background for the current project.

2.1 Knowledge Interpretation

Knowledge is investigated and interpreted differently in various research fields. In the traditional view of philosophy, knowledge often refers to justified true beliefs and is reserved for universal, or absolute, truths (e. g. , Klein, 1971, 1976; Sellars, 1975; Chisholm, 1989; Moser, 1992; Feldman, 2003). Knowledge is addressed as an epistemological issue (e. g. , Russell, 1940; Rozeboom, 1973; Goldman, 1986; Hussey, 1990). Therefore, gaining knowledge involves the subject's exercise of intellectual abilities or powers (Sellars, 1963; Reid, 1764, 1785; Kant, 1781), e. g. , perceptual knowledge is gained in virtue of exercising human perceptual abilities.

This use of the term knowledge in philosophy contrasts with its use in the field of cognition, where knowledge refers to an individual's personal stock of information, skills, experiences, beliefs, and memories. Cognitive psychology usually deals with knowledge in terms of concepts represented in long-term memory, organized by a taxonomic system of categories, prototypes, scripts and other schemas (e. g. , Collins & Loftus, 1975; Schank & Abelson, 1977). In this point of view, knowledge is idiosyncratic and encompasses what a person knows or believes to be true, whether or not it is verified as true in some sort of objective or external way. van Dijk and Atienza (2011: 91) adopt a sociocognitive approach and "practically define as knowledge of an epistemic community the beliefs that are presupposed in the public discourses of that community".

Some researches (Exline, 1984; Eugene, 1993; Good, 1993; Brookes & Etkina, 2007, 2009; Wellington & Ireson, 2008; Iran, 2010) in science education examine knowledge in terms of language from the cognitive point of view, that is, knowledge construction is how people acquire and use scientific language of some discipline. Bazenman (1990) emphasizes the close relationship between language and knowledge. Bazenman (1990) takes language as the medium of knowledge accomplishment, considering the construction of scientific language as part and parcel of the human construction of social modes of investigation and knowledge production. In Bazenman's (1990) opinion, the special features of scientific language have developed to meet the rise of science activities.

In view of the reseach objectives, this study is not to engage those literatures in the field of philosophy and cognition, but to focus on literatures that are socially oriented. In fact, this study is interested in SFL and Bernstein's SE. SFL regards knowledge as meaning and Bernstein's SE examines the nature of knowledge. SFL and Bernstein's SE provide us new insights different from the above approaches into what knowledge is, which are concerned with the objectives in this research and will be given a detailed review in this section.

2.1.1 SFL's Understanding of Knowledge

SFL interprets knowledge from the linguistic perspective, regarding its construction as inseparable from language. The construction of knowledge cannot do without language which serves as its building materials. In fact, scholars in SFL have long been concerned with the language of science and explain how scientific knowledge is construed in a new perspecive. In order to understand knowledge from this point of view, an investigation must be given of a close interrelationship among knowledge, language, grammar, experience and meaning. Knowledge, experience and meaning are not completely different phenomena in SFL's perspective, and the relationship among them is intermediated by the lexicogrammar of language.

16

　　Halliday (1998a: 25) has discussed the relationship between language and knowledge, assuming knowledge as "prototypically made of language". The texts which construct common-sense knowledge tend to use clauses expressing processes, while those which build educational and technical knowledge resort to nominal groups showing entities. For individuals, moving from common-sense knowledge into educational knowledge and then into technical knowledge demands much on one's powers of language, which means learners' ability to construe different discourses.

　　Halliday and Matthiessen (2008) contend that the conception of "knowledge" cannot exist as something independent of language, and may be then coded or made manifest in language. They (2008) take all knowledge as constituted in semiotic systems, with language as the most central, claiming that all such representations of knowledge are constructed from language in the first place. Hence when the knowledge is considered enshrined in a particular school subject, e. g. physics, the ways of physical knowledge building can be understood by examining its language and other semiotic resources.

　　The construal of human experience depends on language. Adopting a constructivist view, Halliday and Matthessien (2008: 3) define experience in linguistic terms as "the reality that we construe for ourselves by means of language". The close relationship among language, experience and meaning has been elaborated by Halliday (1998a) clearly. Language provides human beings with "the power of transforming experience into meaning" (Halliday, 1998a: 25). An experience is not internalized until it is transformed into meaning. Once an experience is internalized, it has the potential for being worded, that is, it already exists as a virtual text. However, the same experience comes to be construed in very different ways as children mature and as they get into various contexts.

　　Halliday (1998b: 51) emphasizes the role of grammar in transforming human experience into meaning. In his opinion, when construing a universe of things and relations, grammar imposes categories on our perceptions of phenomena. In other words, grammar sets up a theory of experience and models the immensely complex interaction between the human organism and its environment. That is to say, the construal of experience as meaning or the building of knowledge cannot do without language. The lexicogrammatical forms for construing

17

the same experience change with individuals' language development, that is, "[E]xperience is first construed clausally, and only later is it reconstrued in nominalized form" (Halliday, 1998b: 89). "[...] the individual experience is one of **growth**, not evolution, and follows the typical cycle of growth, maturation and decay" (Halliday & Matthiessen, 2008: 17).

Grammar is the powerhouse to construe experience through meaning into knowledge. Language, as a system of meaning potential, functions through its lexicogrammatical system. For individuals, the development of their language is in fact a process of learning new ways or grammatics of (re)construing experience through meaning. According to Halliday (1998a), there are three radical grammatical transformations for children's language development, that is, the move from protolanguage to language, the move from everyday spoken grammar to the grammar of literacy, and the move from the grammar of written language to that of the language of the subject disciplines. In terms of knowledge, the three critical moments that lexicogrammatical transformations occur are the moves into commonsense knowledge (age 1-2), into educational knowledge (age 4-6) and into technical knowledge (age 9-13, childhood to adolescence). Halliday (1998a: 27) summarizes these moves as follows:

(1) generalization: from "proper" to "common" terms (individual to general);
(2) abstractness: from concrete to abstract elements;
(3) metaphor: from congruent to metaphorical construals.

Each of these moves "is enacted through a critical progression" (Halliday, 1998a: 27). Generalization enables the child to construe experience, while abstractness and metaphor enables the child to reconstrue experience.

On the whole, the language development of an individual is in fact a developing process from his common-sense knowledge to educational knowledge and then to scientific and technical knowledge, that is, "knowledge" enshrined in a particular discipline is understood as something dependent on language and is "constituted in semiotic systems, with language as the most central" (Halliday & Matthiessen, 2008: 3).

There is a close relationship between knowledge and meaning. Knowledge is taken as the outcome of semiotic transformation from human experience into meaning by means of lexicogrammar in natural language. As Halliday (1995: 11) states, "[U]nderstanding, and knowing, are semiotic processes — processes of the development of meaning in the brain of every individual; and the powerhouse for such processes is the grammar". In other words, understanding is considered as a process of transforming experience into meaning through grammar. Knowledge is the outcome of this transformation of something into meaning. In other words, understanding or knowing something is transforming it into meaning.

That is to say, "knowledge" and "meaning" are not considered as two distinct phenomena but "different metaphors for the same phenomenon, approaching it with a different orientation and different assumptions" (Halliday & Matthiessen, 2008: 3). Knowledge is meaning, the construal of experience through the lexicogrammatical system of language. Knowledge construction, which is transformed from human experience, cannot do without the lexicogrammatical system of language, which is "a **theory** of human experience" (Halliday, 1999: 119). Different lexicogrammatical features result in different forms of knowledge, that is, common sense knowledge and educational knowledge, showing us two different worlds.

Common sense knowledge is construed by the grammar of spoken language, showing us a fluid and transitory world without very clear boundaries. Clauses are taken as the main form of the grammar of spoken language, expressing processes — doing and happening, sensing, saying and being. By contrast, educational knowledge is construed in nominal groups which are the typical grammatical form of written language, expressing a nominalized world that is solid, lasting and clearly bounded. According to Halliday (1999), the world of common sense is just as speaking itself is fluid, transitory and without very clear boundaries, and the nominalized world of educational knowledge looks like a written text.

Scientific knowledge is constructed by means of special lexicogrammatical features of its language, that is, the language of science. The scientific language contributes to construe human experiences in a scientific field and construct a nominalized world of events and objects. There are many systemic functional researches into the most general sources for grammatics in building scientific knowledge (Halliday, 1985/94; Davidse, 1991; Martin, 1992, 1993a; Eggins, 1994; Matthiessen, 1995). On the whole, these researches focus on the ideational meaning of language because it is the 'content' meaning that is related with knowledge. Therefore, field is the main basis of knowledge building.

In a word, knowledge is meaning, depending on language as the most central semiotics for its construction. Thus, the investigation of knowledge building needs to explore how meaning is realized by lexicogrammar.

2.1.2 Interpretation of Knowledge in Bernstein's SE

Although knowledge is claimed to be very important in every aspect of social life, a theory of knowledge as an object of study is lacking. In fact, over recent decades, what studies of education have tended to address is knowing or knowers rather than knowledge itself. In other words, many approaches in studies of education discuss knowledge, but do not take knowledge itself as their real research object. For example, psychologically-informed approaches have typically focused on generic processes of learning; and sociologically-informed approaches have typically focused on how relations of power shape learning. In contrast to other researches, which pay less attention to knowledge itself, Bernstein's SE, focusing on "the transmission of knowledge" (Maton & Muller, 2006), begins to make the study of knowledge visible and develops over time from code theory through pedagogic device to knowledge structures. The following section offers a review of how knowledge is interpreted in Bernstein's SE.

Bernstein (1996, 1999, 2000) has shown his ongoing concern with knowledge, the study of which develops into three phases as Figure 2.1 illustrates.

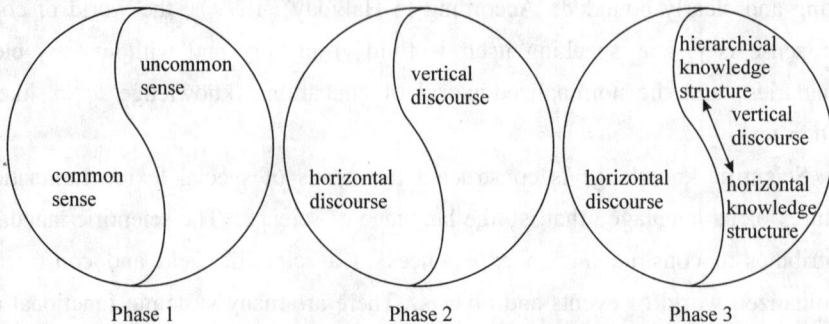

Phase 1   Phase 2   Phase 3

Figure 2.1   Bernstein's Ongoing Concern with Knowledge (from Martin, 2010: 10-13)

At the first phase of Bernstein's researches into knowledge, common-sense and uncommon-sense categories, that is, everyday and educational knowledge, are divided. The division of knowledge into these two categories starts from his concepts of codes to explore how differently valorised and rewarded forms of knowledge are differently distributed in society. The conceptualization of "restricted code" and "elaborated code" not only gives a good explanation of the failure of some students in school education, but leads Bernstein to introduce his pedagogic device which more closely focuses on knowledge.

Maton and Muller (2006: 10) give a clear explanation of Bernstein's pedagogic device. According to this pedagogic device, a society circulates its various forms of knowledge through three fields of practice: a field of production, a field of recontextualisation and a field of reproduction. The first one is where "new" knowledge is constructed and positioned, the second one is where discourses from the field of production are selected, appropriated and repositioned to become "educational" knowledge, and the third is where pedagogic transmission and acquisition takes place.

At the second phase of his study on knowledge, Bernstein (1996, 2000) focuses on production of knowledge, and distinguishes "horizontal discourse" from "vertical discourse", the former producing everyday knowledge and the latter formal knowledge.

Bernstein (2000: 207-208) emphasises the importance of generalisation and hierarchy for knowledge acquisition. In line with his early distinction between elaborated and restricted codes, formal knowledge which consists of a semantic structure can (to a greater or lesser extent) elaborate the relation between ideas and thus control the possible range of correlations between concepts and empirical phenomena. On the other hand, the meaning potential of informal knowledge is restricted in that it depends on a local context. As a result, its capacity to generalize in extended time and space is weak.

At the third phase of his study about knowledge, to account for the different forms taken by vertical discourses, Bernstein (2000) makes a further distinction between hierarchical knowledge structures and horizontal knowledge structures.

Hierarchical knowledge structrures are exemplified by disciplines in natural sciences, a prime example of which is physics. On the other hand, a horizontal

21

knowledge structure describes the disciplines of humanities and social sciences, which are characterized by weak semantic development and weak internal coherence. These disciplines can be further classified into two types: strong (e. g. , mathematics and linguistics) and weak disciplines (e. g. , sociology). For a weak discipline, it is not capable of constructing precise explanations about empirical phenomena, and each of its theories (or 'specialised languages') exists as a discrete system with "its own criteria for legitimate texts" (Bernstein, 2000: 162). That is, the form of its development is fragmented. To use Bernstein's example, in sociology the langugages refer to its wide array of competing theoretical approaches including functionalism, post-structuralism, postmodernism, Marxism, etc, and within each broad category or language, there are specific theories (Bernstein, 1999a: 162).

The classification of knowledge structures has provided us with insights into the nature of disourses, but offered no tools for doing specific analysis. Therefore, Muller (2006, 2007) has highlighted the two dimentions introduced by Bernstein, verticality and grammaticality, which are used as tools of describing knowledge structures in different fields. These two attributes play a role in determining the capacity of a particular knowledge structure to progress.

The theory of knowledge structure is for the purpose of education. In fact, many researches (e. g. , Halliday & Martin, 1993; Christie & Martin, 1997; Unsworth, 2000) contribute a lot to the study of the relationship between knowledge structures and their corresponding curriculum structures. In Maton and Muller's (2006) opinion, a knowledge structure is not necessarily a curriculum structure or pedagogic structure, and the relations between them is a key area for future exploration. Maton (2007) explores how to integrate analyses of knowledge structures and of curriculum structures within the same conceptual framework. As Maton and Muller (2006: 37) state, "analyses of textbooks or curriculum guidelines are studies of recontextualised pedagogic discourse rather than of knowledge structures".

The reason for students' difficulities in learning vertical discourses lies in the nature of knowledge structures. Shalem and Slonimsky (2010: 769) claim that, "[A]cdamic practices are constituted through de-contextualised knowledge and dis-embedded language". It is these features of all vertical discourses which compound students' difficulties in acquiring the rules that structure academic knowledge. Therefore, students can only act.and make sense of their experiences on the basis of their existing knowledge, and the recognition and realisation rules they have developed through their participation in previous social practices.

LCT develops Bernstein's ideas of knowledge structure. It integrates insights from the approaches of Pierre Bourdieu, Basil Bernstein, critical realist philosophy, SFL, Karl Popper and many others. LCT currently comprises five principal dimensions: autonomy, density, specialisation, temporality and semantics, offering a powerful and sophisticated toolkit for conceptualizing the forms taken by knowledge practices and exploring their roles in education. Muller (2006, 2007) has introduced two variables, verticality (subsumption and integration) and grammaticality, to describe knowledge structures in different fields. Maton (2008b), unpacking verticality, considers the form taken by theories and knowledge structures along two dimensions: SD and SG, which are closely related to meaning in SFL and is about to be explored deeply in this study.

In epistemological terms, this distinction of SD and SG can be shown to draw on Bernstein's restricted and elaborated distinction about orientations to meanings. In both, the classification refers to the kind of context (epistemic or empirical) to which a unit of meaning is attributable and to the degree of integration with other meanings it displays.

From the perspective of pedagogy of knowledge transmission, Maton (2008b) goes further. Two steps in Maton's distinction are relevant for this study. First, the distinction denotes what counts as a horizontal/vertical ordering in students' production. A lengthy description of empirical details, substitution of examples for explanation, and the listing of specifics without a structure, demonstrates weak SD (ideas do not integrate relationally) and strong SG (ideas are context bound and not generalisable). When an idea 'has more meaning condensed within it' (Maton, 2008a: 8)-that is, the idea subsumes and integrates more propositions (SD +)-it is decontextualised or its semantic gravity is weaker (SG –). Thus, a strong proposition is one that is integrated with other propositions (SD +) and can be shown to be connected to its empirical detail logically rather than contextually or ideologically. Second, Maton's distinction shows that the kind of pedagogy is necessary if one is to move an acquirer from a restricted

23

to an elaborated code. Pedagogical relations must oscillate between integration (SD +) and specificity (SG-), and thus students need to be taught to see the traces of a strong proposition in the empirical detail.

The strenghthening or weakening of semantics is necessary for knowledge building. According to Maton (2009), weaker SG is one of the conditions for building knowledge or understanding over time. Shalem and Slonimsky (2010: 769) emphasize that academic practices are constituted through de-contextualised knowledge and dis-embedded language. In Maton's (2009) argument, hierarchical and horizontal curriculum structures can be distinguished according to whether a unit of study (lesson, module, year, etc.) builds upon the knowledge imparted in previous units through integration and subsumption or through segmental aggregation.

2.1.3 The Complementarity of Knowledge Interpretation Between SFL and SE

Both SFL and Bernstein's SE focus on knowledge, but they are exploring it from different points of view. As Muller (2007: 66, original emphasis) points out, SFL primarily focuses on "*knowledge as meaning*", describing "the universal semantic building blocks that enable transition from one form to the other", that is, it aims to "uncover the most basic universal processes and hence to reveal the ideal underlying unity of semiosis". On the other hand, Bernstein's SE is primarily interested in "*knowledge as distributed social goods*", describing "the way both forms have distributive rules which are in turn conditioned by discontinuities in semiotic structure that mirror, sustain and reproduce inequalities in society", that is, its task "is to delineate the social limits to distributive equality" (ibid).

However, the two projects have something in common which makes it possible to find a bridge for them. First, although their points of view on knowledge are different, their research objects are similar. The different insights may lead to a more complete understanding of knowledge and stimulate each other's research forward. For linguists, LCT's semantics (SD & SG) provides a useful theoretical tool for explaining the existence of some special linguistic features in certain discourses. For example, why grammatical metaphor and technicality are two linguistic resources indispensable in scientific discourses lies in the fact they are

connected with higher verticality. On the other hand, for Bernsteinain researchers, linguistic ananlysis of discourses offers more concrete and specific evidence
for their explanation.

Second, both include context in their research. Muller (2007: 66-67)
makes a fundamental distinction between what Bernstein calls horizontal and vertical discourse. The vertical discourse is integrated at the level of meanings allowing decontextualization, while the horizontal discourse at the level of (culture-
ally specialized) segments binds the language to context. Martin (2007) makes
the same point when he makes a division between everyday and scientific taxonomies.

Third, like Bernstein, Halliday (1995: 19) pays attention to common-sense
and uncommon-sense knowledge, focusing on the language features in construing
them. Uncommon-sense knowledge develops in two phases, the first phase of
educational knowledge and the second phase of technical knowledge. According
to Halliday (1995: 14), "written knowledge" that children will learn in school
is better called "educational knowledge" because this kind of knowledge doesn't
actually depend on being written down. Educational knowledge is accociated
with writing and depends on abstractness, while technical knowledge, the discourse of the specialized disciplines, depends on grammatical metaphor which is
the wholesale recasting of the relationship between grammar and semantics.

Fourth, both Bernsteinain scholars and systemic functional linguists recognize and appreciate the long-term cross-disciplinary dialogue between them. Maton and Muller (2006: 1) point out that the cross-disciplinary dialogue between
Bernstein's sociology and SFL "has been ongoing since Bernstein in his early
work adapted the linguistic notion of 'code' to his own sociological purposes".
As Maton and Muller (2006) state, Bernstein often shows his appreciation of
systemic linguists such as Francis Christie, Michael Halliday and Ruqaiya Hasan.
It is their ideas that contribute both to the development of this phase of the code
theory and his thinking more generally.

On the other hand, SFL also assimilates the insights developed in
Bernstein's sociology. As Martin (2007) suggests, knowledge structures are re-
conceptualized in social semiotics as the register variable of field on the context
plane (i. e. , activity and subject matter), which comprises patterns of linguistic

and multi-semiotic patterns.

In a word, the linguists in SFL and researchers in Bernstein's SE may complement each other, with the former engaged in establishing what the building blocks of hierarchy are, and the latter engaged in establishing how hierarchy is distributed.

2.2 The Researches into Scientific Discourses

The following section will review previous studies on scientific discourses in three aspects: researches in pragmatics, researches in ESP, and researches in SFL.

2.2.1 In Pragmatics

The researches into scientific discourses in pragmatics vary from exploring the usage of expressions to clauses and to investigating organizational structures of the texts.

Pragmatic force modifiers (pragmatic force modifier refers to expressions such as *in fact*, *sort of*, or *you see* when they are used to modify) have been widely examined in academic prose including scientific research articles (Myers, 1989, 1990; Bloor & Bloor, 1993; Hyland, 1996, 1998), medical discourse (Salager-Meyer, 1994), and textbooks (Holmes, 1988a; Myers, 1992a; Hyland, 1994, 2000). Recently, pragmatic force modifiers are explored in the British Academic Spoken English lecture corpus (Lin, 2010). This study finds no definite correlation between forms and functions. For instance, both intensifiers and softeners are associated with positive politeness and the formation of effective argumentation patterns.

Lindwall and Lymer (2011) examine thirty hours of video-recorded and transcribed interaction taken from a lab course in a teacher education program to investigate the positioning, use, and interactional significance of utterances that include "get it", "understand", or any of their conjugations.

Some studies (Myer, 1992; Bloor & Bloor, 1993; Dahl, 2008) have the linguistic realisation of new knowledge claims as their main focus. Knowledge claims refer to what the academic author in a discipline is offering as new knowledge when contributing to the academic "conversation". For example, claims in economics may be signalled by expression such as "The key message is...". Myers (1992b) primarily conducts an investigation of knowledge claims in a natural science discipline, molecular biology, but it also makes comparisons with linguistics. Bloor and Bloor (1993) deal with knowledge claims in economics. Dahl (2008) attempts to identify knowledge claims in the introduction section of 50 English research articles in economics and linguistics. The claims identified will also be considered in terms of hedging, a phenomenon that has been linked to the nature of the knowledge represented by the disciplines in question as well as to the author's stance towards the knowledge (cf. Hyland, 1998).

Loock (2007) explores non-restrictive relative clauses, which are collected from different registers including specialized texts mostly from the fields of psychology and medicine, and suggests a taxonomy of non-restrictive relative clauses. The taxonomy is based on "syntactic, semantic, and above all, pragmatic criteria, following Prince's (1981, 1992) definitions of given/new information and Sperber and Wilson's relevance theory (1986)" (Loock, 2007: 336).

Myers (1989) extends studies of the pragmatics of politeness from conversational data to some genres of written texts. Taking a corpus of articles by molecular geneticists, Myers (1989) assumes a simple model of a two-part audience and focuses on two kinds of impositions: claims and denials of claims. With this framework, one can see politeness strategies in regularities of scientific style such as the use of pronouns and of passives that are usually explained in terms of conventions. The analysis explains some otherwise unexplained stylistic features, such as the use of adverbs in establishing solidarity, and the use of personal attribution in hedging.

It is now established that a significant part of the rhetorical structure of research articles, that is, the attempt to make it persuasive, is shaped by employing metadiscourse (Hyland, 2005). By analyzing metadiscourse from the genre of research articles in science, Abdi et al. (2010) introduce a tentative model based on Gricean cooperative principle that is hoped to help the multilingual members of academic discourse community in the use of metadiscourse markers. This practical framework leads to a new classification of metadiscourse and adds two new metadiscourse strategies of collapsers and disclaimers.

The studies about scientific discourses in pragmatics are concerned with the function of short linguistic expressions, interactional principles and rhetorical structures of the texts. Few researches focus on the "content" knowledge expressed in the discourses, especially in textbooks of different school levels.

2.2.2 In ESP

The researches in ESP explore scientific discourses aiming to bring some pedagogical implications. These studies focus on the features of scientific discourses such as ways of text organization, functions of hedges, and use of questions.

Drawing on a large corpus of research articles, Hyland (2007) explores how academic texts construct their arguments by reformulation (restating information) or exemplification (providing examples). His analysis reveals that elaboration is a complex and important rhetorical function in academic writing, and that both its use and meanings vary from discipline to discipline.

It is now often stated that hedging, "the expression of tentativeness and possibility" (Hyland, 1996: 433) in the form of modal expressions, is a common feature in academic discourse (Crystal, 1988; Crismore & Farnsworth, 1990). It is frequently claimed that instead of saying "I know", members of academia should rather assume or suggest when they address other scholars. Similarly, in the place of saying how things are, one should sometimes preferably say how things might be, or how things perhaps are.

Academic writing is rich in hedged propositions since "[H] edging is a significant communicative resource for academics since it both confirms the individual's professional persona and represents a critical element in the rhetorical means of gaining acceptance of claims" (Hyland, 1996: 433). The use of hedging in academic writing has received more and more attention. Hyland (1994) discusses the importance, functions, and expression of epistemic modality in scientific discourse in order to evaluate the treatment given to hedging devices in a range of ESP writing textbooks. Analyses of written academic corpora have revealed some of the characteristics of hedging in molecular biology (Hyland, 1996), textbooks (Myers, 1992a), economic forecasting (Pindi & Bloor, 1987), science digests (Fahnestock, 1986), abstracts (Rounds, 1982), medical discourse (Salager-Meyer, 1994; Varttala, 1999), and molecular genetics articles (Myers, 1989).

Because hedging in scientific discourse is a necessary and vitally important

28

skill, these researches often present some pedagogical implications such as the use of sensitization, translation and rewriting exercises in ESP courses.

The exploration of questions in scientific discourses is another focus of researches in ESP. Hyland (2002) explores the distribution and use of questions in research articles, textbooks and L2 student essays, suggesting that questions underline the essentially dialogic nature of academic writing between writers and their readers in the discourse. Hoey (1983) investigates the use of questions to underpin textual coherence in written discourse, and Webber (1994) studies questions in academic writing on medical journals. Kirszner and Mandell (1987: 67) recommend questions as a means of creating interest in student essays, and Swales (1990: 156) observes that questions are a "minor way of establishing a niche" in research article introductions, but they are generally seen as strategies to be avoided (e. g. , Swales & Feak, 1994: 74).

According to Hyland (2004), metadiscourse offers a way of understanding the interpersonal resources writers use to present propositional material and therefore a means of uncovering something of the rhetorical and social distinctiveness of disciplinary communities. Adopting Swales's (1990, 2004) framework of move analysis, Loi (2010) investigates the rhetorical organization of the introduction sections of English and Chinese research articles in the field of educational psychology. The study shows that some similarities and differences exist between English and Chinese research article introductions in terms of the employment of moves and steps. It is suggested that the rhetorical differences reflect some of the distinctive characteristics of the two different cultures, English and Chinese.

Like the researches in pragmatics, those in scientific discourses in ESP focus less on the "content" knowledge expressed in the discourses, especially in textbooks of different school levels.

2.2.3 In SFL

SFL contributes a lot to discourse analysis. Halliday (2004: F41) states clearly that "[T]he aim has been to construct a grammar for purposes of text analysis" and that "[A] discourse ananlysis that is not based on grammar is not an analysis at all, but simply a running commentary on a text". As a linguistic phenomenon, scientific discourses have aroused the interests of systemic functional linguists at the beginning of their research. The scientific language has appeared to meet the need of science research, not only recording and spreading knowledge but also creating new knowledge. According to Martin and Veel (1998), the study of scientific language gives us a better understanding of what is required in order to learn and control scientific knowledge.

The researches into scientific discourses in SFL have developed in two lines. First, there is a change of scientific discourse types in their researches, that is, from canonical scientific discourse to educational scientific discourse. Second, their study of semiotic resources which realize scientific knowledge varies from language to other forms. Based on the two dimensions of researches in scientific discourses in SFL, this section gives a review in three aspects: researches from canonical scientific discourses to educational ones, researches in scientific discourses from language to other semiotic resources, and studies on scientific discourses in China.

2.2.3.1 From Canonical Scientific Discourse to Educational Scientific Discourse

"Language is as it is because of what it has to do" (Halliday, 2001: 19). It is true of scientific language which develops its characteristics to construe scientific knowledge that is different from everyday language. SFL has begun its long interest in mapping out the meaning potential of scientific discourses since Halliday's (1993c) exploration into the language of physical science which is the basis of canonical scientific discourses.

It is commonly recognized that the origin of scientific language stems from the language of the physics. It is physicists who lead the way in creating the discourse of science. Halliday (1993d: 217) agrees that it is in the context of the physical sciences that "the new conception of knowledge was first worked out" and that "the leading edge of scientific language was the language of the physical sciences, and the semantic styles that evolved were those of physical systems and of the mathematics that is constructed to explain them".

In one of his most influential paper *On the Language of Physical Science*, Halliday (1988) sets out to identify, describe and explain a typical syndrome of grammatical features in the register of scientific English. He explores from a historical perspective how and why this pattern of prototypical syndrome of features that characterizes scientific English has evolved over the past four to six centuries to become the dominant grammatical motif in modern scientific English. Halliday begins his analysis of the language of science from Chaucer's *Treatise on the Astrolabe* (c. 1390) to Newton's *Treatise on Opticks* (published 1704; written 1675-1687) and then to Priestley's *The History and Present State of Electricity, with Original Experiments* (published in the 1760s). He identifies two kinds of grammatical features of which scientific writers use resources to build their scientific knowledge and theory: nominal elements and verbal elements. Nominal elements fulfill two functions, that is, to form technical taxonomies, and to summarize and package representations of processes. Technological categories, methodological categories and theoretical categories are three types of technical taxonomies organizing concepts. The construction of concepts, which is realized through processes, is packaged into information in the form of nominal elements and distributed by backgrounding (given material as Theme) and foregrounding (rhematic material as New). Verbal elements may signal that the nominalized process happens, or they may show a logical relationship between two processes, either externally to each other (*a* causes *x*), or internally to our interpretation of them (*b* proves *y*).

These relevant grammatical features in the scientific writings of Chaucer and Newton can be summarized in Table 2. 1.

Table 2.1　Some Grammatical Features in the Scientific Writings of Chaucer and Newton (from Halliday, 1990: 172)

Grammatical Features		Typical Contexts
Chaucer: treatise on the astrlabe		
1: nominal	nouns noun roots nouns derived from verbs and adjectives nouminal groups (with prepositional phrase and clause Qualifiers)	technical terms: technological (parts of instrument) astromnical and mathematical mathematical expression
2: clausal	material and mental; imperative relational("be","be called"); indicative	instmctions("do this""observe/reckon that" observations; names and their explanations

续表

Grammatical Features		Typical Contexts
Newton: Opticks		
1: nominal noun	nouns	technical terms:
	roots	general concepts;
	nouns derived from verbs and	experimental apparants
	adjectives nouminal groups(with	physical and mathematical
	prepositional phrase and clause	mathematical expressions
	Qualifiers) * nominaliz ations	
	of processes & propertics	
2: clausal	terial and mental indicative	logical argumentation explanations and con-
	relational("causc", "prove";	clusions description of experiment ("I did
	indicative	this","I saw reasoned that") logical argu-
		mentation explanations and conclusions

Then in his another important paper *Some Grammatical Problems in Scientific English*, Halliday (1989: 162) discusses seven difficulties that are characteristic of scientific English: interlocking definitions, technical taxonomies, special expressions, lexical density, syntactic ambiguity, grammatical metaphor and semantic discontinuity. Although it is problematic and alienating for learners, scientific language "has construed for us the vast theoretical edifice of modern knowledge" (Halliday, 1997: 182), and "[T]he language of science is, by its nature, a language in which theories are constructed" (Halliday, 1993d: 207).

Grammatical metaphor has appeared to meet the need of constructing scientific knowledge. Grammatical metaphors can construe for scientists a still world, or one consisting only of things, or even new, virtual realities. As one of the important features of scientific language, grammatical metaphor is further explored by Halliday (1995, 1998a, 1998b, 1999) in a series of papers.

In the disciplines of science and mathematics, grammatical metaphor is considered to be a significant feature in the construction of scientific and technical knowledge (Halliday, 1987; Martin, 1993e). Certain kinds of grammatical metaphors appear to be difficult for young children to use and interpret (Halliday, 1993b).

Jane and Harman's (1997) study also proves the important role of grammatical metaphor in literacy development of pulpils. Adopting the assumption that what is regarded as knowledge is constructed intersubjectively through language, Jane and Harman (1997) examine how scientific knowledge is taught and explore certain linguistic features in the discourse of two Year 1 teachers and their students. They analyze one teacher's strategies for developing her students' understanding of scientific register. The study finds differences in the nature and extent of the grammatical metaphor used by the teachers, describing two pieces of evidence for the construction of a proto-scientific discourse in classroom. First, some abstract lexical items in the discourse signal a scientific register, e. g., technical, concept, information, specific, observation, spiracle, sustenance, fluid. Second, the presence of ideational grammatical metaphor, especially nominalizations, plays an important role in making the discourse scientific. On the whole, this study proves that the development of the ability to access abstract knowledge, which is constructed by means of abstract lexical terms and grammatical metaphor, is an essential aspect of language and literacy development after the commencement of formal schooling.

As the researches into scientic discourses progress, the idea about grammatical metaphor, which is about the meaning shift between language strata, motivates O'Halloran's (1999, 2000) interests in semiotic metaphor. Semiotic metaphor is about the shifts in semiotic codes. In studying the multisemiotic nature of mathematical discourses, O'Halloran (1999) notices the phenomenon of semiotic metaphor. The interactions between the semiotic resources of mathematical symbolism, visual display and language means that experiential metaphor, which is confined to lexical and grammatical metaphor at the beginning, may expand to the shifts in meaning caused by movements between lexicogrammatical systems in the different semiotic codes. In O'Halloran's (1999) opinion, semiotic metaphor, that is, the shifts in semiotic codes in mathematical discourse, is conceptually related to grammatical metaphor in that both refer to shifts in the functions of elements, but it is distinct because the shifts in meaning for semiotic metaphor take place in the different semiotic codes. According to O'Halloran (1996, 2000), these metaphorical shifts are one major cause of teaching and learning difficulties in mathematics.

Attempting to show how grammar is at work to create meaning in scientific discourse, Halliday (2002a) expands his analysis of scientific language from phys-ics to biology. Halliday (2002a) adopts Charles Darwin's *The Origin of Species* as a sample for an analysis of the language of science, finding out that the text is characterized by three prominent linguistic features. First, very simple clause com-plexes are used and the favoured structural pattern is one of embedding rather than taxis (hypotaxis or parataxis). Second, there is a higher lexical density (lexical words per ranking clause). Third, much more nominalization and more use of grammatical metaphor occur. With such an anlysis, Halliday (2002a) shows us clearly how knowledge and value are constructed in the grammar of scientific dis-course through their textual functions of Theme (in Theme-Rheme) and New (in Given-New), around a small number of distinct but interlocking motifs.

In a word, the language of science starts its origin from physical discourses, later extends to "compass other, more complex kinds of system: first biological, then social systems" (Halliday, 1993d: 217), and finally takes over as the lan-guage of literacy.

Halliday (2002a: 87) realizes the alienating feature of "scientific English" which has to reconcile the need to create new knowledge with the need to restrict access to that knowledge (that is, make access to it conditional on participating in the power structures and value systems within which it is locatied and defined).

Taking cognizance of the way science is construed in language may throw some light on making science more accessible in approaches to science education.

2.2.3.2 Researches in Scientific Discourse from Language to Other Semiotics

Scientific knowledge is not construed through language alone. Other non-linguistic semiotics also play important roles in building scientific knowledge. Many researches (Ainsworth, 1999, 2006; de Jong et al. , 1998; Dolin, 2001; Lemke, 1998; Russell & McGuigan, 2001; Gee, 2002; Jewitt, 2003; Gonzalez et al. , 2003) in science education notice the co-function of multimodal represen-tations in learning concepts. However, they explore multimodality from the cog-nitive perspective, and few of them focus on the analysis of these semiotic re-sources themselves. Compared with these multimodal researches in science from the cognitive perspective, SFL studies multi-semiotics which include both lan-guage and other non-linguistic meaning-making resources, and provides some useful implications for science learning and teaching from the linguistic point of view. Therefore, the multimodal analysis in this research will be done from the perspective of SFL and will be reviewed in the following section.

With slight differences in nomenclature, many SFL-influenced social semioticians have effectively established a mapping of the SFL metafunctions across modalities, as summarized in Table 2.2.

Table 2.2　Metafunctions in Verbiage and Image (from Martin, 2002: 1)

Metafuntion: Modalities:	Naturalizing Reality	Enacting Social Relations	Organizing Text
Verbiage			
Halliday (1994):	ideational	interpersonal	textual
Image			
Kress and van Leeuwen (1996):	representation	interaction/modality	composition
O'Toole (1994):	representational	modal	compositional
Lemke (1998b):	presentational	orientational	organizational

Corresponding to Halliday's (1994) three metafunctions of language, ideational metafunction, interpersonal metafunction and textual metafunction, three similar metafunctions of image are described respectively as representation, interaction/modality and composition by Kress and van Leeuwen (1996), as representational, modal and compositional metafunctions by O'Toole (1994), and as presentational, orientational and organizational metafunctions by Lemke (1998b).

Based on Halliday's (1994) systemic functional model of language, a series of researches begin to investigate other semiotic systems. O'Toole (1990, 1992, 1994, 1995) demonstrates a systemic model for the visual forms of painting, architecture, and sculpture. Kress and van Leeuwen (1990, 1996) develop a functional approach to visual images, and O'Halloran (1999) explores the multisemiotic nature of mathematics, which is construed through the use of semiotic resources of mathematical symbolism, visual display in the form of graphs and diagrams, and language.

Within multisemiotic genres, Lemke (1998b: 92, original emphasis) argues that, "meanings made with each functional resource in each semiotic mo-

35

dality can modulate meanings of each kind in each other semiotic modality, thus *multiplying* the set of possible meanings that can be made".

Lemke (2009) explains how the multimodal genres of natural science and technology were born at the beginning in the seventeenth century with the rise of scientific printed publications, pointing out that scientific research reports today contain not only the running text, but typically one or more graphs, charts, tables, or other specialized visual displays per page. Lemke (2009) analyzes brief specialized technical research reports in the prestigious journal *Science*, finding out that there is an average of no less than six non-textual visual displays per article, normally accompanied by extensive captions and references to the figures in the main text.

It is now widely accepted that language is not the only mode to construe meaning in literacy and literacy pedagogy. With the development of technology, images begin to play an increasing role from the latter part of the twentieth to the early part of the twenty-first century in science textbooks (Kress & van Leeuwen, 1995; Kress, 1997) and particularly in science books for children in the pre-teenage years (Parkinson & Adendorff, 2005). Typically in such books the double page layout, of which the images occupy a very significant portion, is often used for young children as illustrated in Figure 2.2.

Figure 2.2   Double Page Spread in a Physics Textbook for Students of Years K-2
(**from Nunn, 2003: 4-5**)

Images play prominent roles in constructing knowledge in physics textbooks especially for younger students. Figure 2.2 provides students with a lot of familiar common-sense activities which may facilitate their understanding of the forces that make things moving. However, as Roth et al. (2005) note, students generally neither receive instruction in critical analysis of photographs nor are provided with opportunities for participating in the associated practices. Furthermore, previous studies have noted the confusing nature of some images and the difficulty students experience in interpreting images in science texts (Unsworth, 1992; Henderson, 1999).

More recently attention has been drawn to interpreting the interrelations between image and verbiage in constructing meaning in school science materials (Kress, 1997, 2003a; Lemke, 1998a, 1998b, 2002; Unsworth, 1997, 1999a, 1999b, 2004). These researches into multimodality develop in two stages. In the first stage they recognize the functions of different modes in meaning-making such as verbiage and images, but focus more on their independent meanings. In the second stage, they pay more attention to the interaction of language and image in construing meaning.

At the beginning of multimodal researches, the independent functions of language and image are emphasized. Kress (1997, 2000b, 2003a, 2003b) and Lemke (1998b) have drawn attention to what they call the "functional specialization" of language and image. Following Lemke (1998b), knowledge in scientific discourses is constructed commonly by language and other semiotics together, and each semiotic system is uniquely functional in its contribution to meaning construction. Linguistic resources are most suitable for representing sequential relations and making categorical distinctions, while images are most apposite for representing spatial relations and topological relations (Lemke, 1998b: 87). That is, semantic commonalities may occur, but the meanings realized by one type of semiotics cannot be exactly replicated by another type.

Lemke (2004) has explored this specialization principle further. Natural language primarily realizes typographical modalities or categorical descriptions and is much better at showing relations among categories, while "topological semiotics" are much more powerful at expressing topological and therefore quantitative meanings, which is extremely important for science and science education.

37

Kress (1997, 2000a, 2003a, 2003b) has explicated the functional specialization principle. Kress (2003b: 197) shows the different functions between language and diagrams by an example. The language which is expressed in relatively simple sentences (one or two clauses) is about events, while the diagrams represent the core information of the teaching contents.

Although both Lemke and Kress provide a detailed discussion of the meaning-making resources including image and text, they do not develop a system of intersemiotic relations that would explicate the kinds of interactions between images and verbiage.

In addition to making meanings separately, language and images combine to make more meanings than the sum of the parts in new ways, which can be illustrated by an example of the appreciation of an image accompanying the text. When you respond at first sight, often in a diffuse way, to the image, you will have an impression on it. After that, when you reframe this image after reading the text, your gaze may be directed to certain qualities in the image. Then when you return to the image, there is more meaning than before-a third semantic domain which is more than the sum of the parts. It is the interactive meaning between image and verbiage. Therefore, in order to get the full meaning in a multimodal text, researchers begin to explicate an intersemiotic framework of image/verbiage relations.

Later, Thibault (2000: 362) points out that it is through contextual relations between different semiotic choices that the meaning of multimodal discourse is created. Following O'Halloran (1999), Lim (2004) classifies the contextualization relations into co-contextualization and re-contextualization. When the two semiotic resources share co-contextualization, the meaning of one modality seems to reflect the meaning of the other through some type of convergence. On the other hand, if the semiotic resources share re-contextualization relations, the semantic relationship between two modalities is one that diverges, that is, the meaning of one modality seems to be at odds with or unrelated to the other. However, further attention needs to be paid to the nature of contextualization relations in multimodal discourse. O'Halloran (1999, 2005, 2007b) formulates the theory of semiotic metaphor to account for the nature of two contextualization relations in multimodal discourse. According to O'Halloran (1999, 2005,

38

2007b), a parallel semiotic metaphor results in co-contextualization while a divergent semiotic metaphor gives rise to re-contextualization.

Roth et al. (2005) give an analysis of the role of photographs in Brazilian science textbooks, claiming four image-text functions which relate photographs and their captions to the main text — the *decorative*, *illustrative*, *explanatory* and *complementary* functions. Their claim of four image-text functions is very useful in drawing attention to the need for a multimodal conceptualization of reading comprehension of science textbooks, but again does not provide a sufficiently precise intersemiotic framework for explaining the interrelations between photographs with captions and texts. On the whole, these previous researches only give partial accounts of image/verbiage relations in science texts.

Aiming at the intersemiotic framework between image and text, Unsworth (2006) presents his discussion about the intermodal construction of ideational meaning in school science materials in the form of books and websites, describing emerging functional semiotic accounts of image-text relations and their implications for approaches to multimodal literacy education. Unsworth (2006) argues that an agenda of ongoing research in image-verbiage interaction is needed for the development of a pedagogy of multiliteracies in school science education.

Like Martinec and Salway (2005), who have proposed a system of logico-semantic relations between images and text in new (and old) media, Unsworth (2006a) derives his initial framework from Halliday's (2004) account of logico-semantic relations, as shown in Figure 2.3. The logico-semantic relations have been shown to recur throughout the grammar and have been extended by Martin (1992) to model relations between discourse units.

Unsworth (2006b) elaborates his framework of image-language relations and presents two types of projection: the projection of an image by the verbiage and the projection of verbiage within image, emphasizing that the main text can project images such as photographs and drawings in picture story books for children. However, Unsworth (2006b) emphasizes that, the situation with science materials remains unclear. The following figure shows his elaborated framework for analyzing ideational meanings at the intersection of language and image.

```
                                 ┌ clarification
                                 │ expositon
                    ┌ concurrence┤                  ┌ image instantiates textcomplementarity
                    │            │ exempilfication  └ text instantiates image
                    │            └ homospatiality
    EXPANSION ┤                  ┌ manner
                    │            │ condition
                    └ enhancement┤ spatial
                                 │ temporal
                                 └ causal
                    ┌ verbal
    PROJECTION ┤              ┌ perception
                    └ mental ┤ cognition
                             └ cognition
```

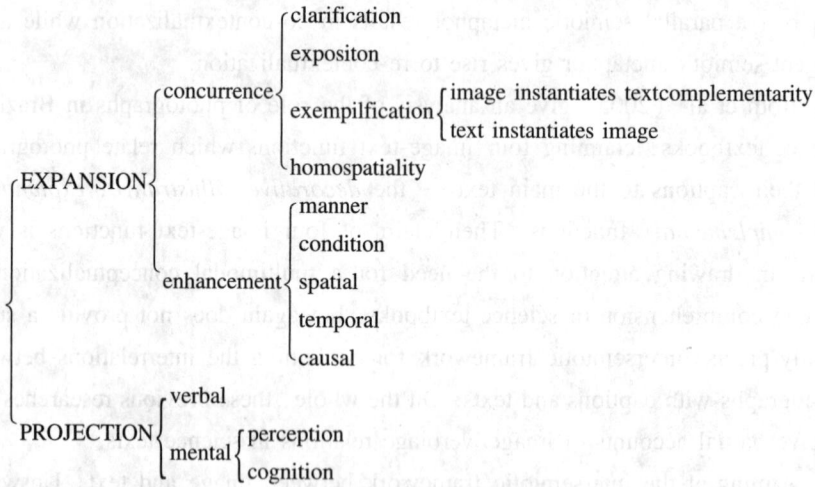

Figure 2.3   Towards a Framework of Image-language Relations in the Construction of Ideational Meaning (from Unsworth, 2006a: 1175)

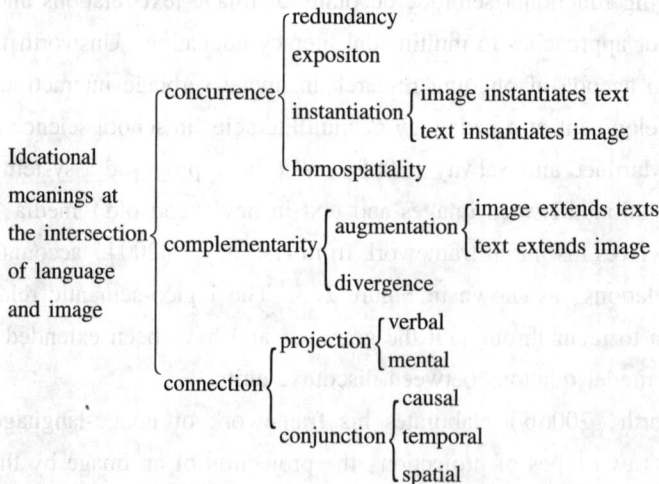

```
                                         ┌ redundancy
                                         │ expositon
                            ┌ concurrence┤                ┌ image instantiates text
                            │            │ instantiation ┤ text instantiates image
                            │            └ homospatiality
    Idcational              │                             ┌ image extends texts
    mcanings at             │            ┌ augmentation ┤ text extends image
    the intersection ┤ complementarity ┤ divergence
    of language              │                             ┌ verbal
    and image                │            ┌ projection ┤ mental
                            │            │              ┌ causal
                            └ connection ┤ conjunction ┤ temporal
                                         │              └ spatial
```

Figure 2.4   Ideational Meanings at the Intersection of Language and Image (from Unsworth, 2006b: 67)

Although Halliday and Hasan (1985:4) focus on language, it is realized at the beginning that this is only one semiotic system among many other modes of meaning in any culture, which might include both art forms and other modes of cultural behaviour that are not in the form of art. All these bear meaning in the culture and a culture can be defined "as a set of semiotic systems, as a set of systems of meaning, all of which interrelate" (Halliday & Hasan, 1985:4).

Based on the SFL metafunctional hypothesis, many researchers have explored image-text relations in their work (Lemke, 1998a, 1998b, 2002; Royce, 1998, 2002, 2007; Baldry, 2000; Martin, 2002c; Macken-Horarik, 2003, 2004; O'Halloran, 2004; Baldry & Thibault, 2006). Similar extrapolations from the metafunctional basis of SFL have provided social semiotic descriptions of "displayed art" (O'Toole, 1994), music and sound (van Leeuwen, 1999) and action (Martinec, 1999, 2000a, 2000b). These studies focus on grammatical descriptions (e. g, Martinec & Salway, 2005; Unsworth, 2006) to account for image-text relations. Based on the discourse-based approach, Liu and O'Halloran (2009) make a further exploration of the logical relations across language and images, providing their complementary framework as the following figure shows.

Logical Relations		Meaning
Comparative	Gemerality ↗ ↘ Abstractiom	Simiarity
Additive		Addition
Consequential	Consequence ↗ ↘ Contingency	Cause Purpose
Temporal		Successive

Figure 2.5　Intersemiotic Logical Relations (from Liu & O'Halloran, 2009: 384)

Liu and Owyong (2011) propose a social semiotic approach and demonstrates how meaning is multiplied through the use of three closely related cross-modal mechanisms in chemical discourse — intersemiotic correspondence, intersemiotic trans-categorization and inter-semiotic metaphor, arguing that the semiotic transition from language to symbolism expands the meaning potential of chemical discourse, re-construes everyday experience as scientific knowledge and creates hierarchical knowledge structures in chemistry.

Wells (2007) argues that, language is at the heart of all forms of education, whether in the informal learning and teaching that occurs in everyday activities in the home and local community, or in the more formally organized activities through which the curriculum is enacted in the classroom.

Every written genre has always been multimodal, deploying not only the signs of the linguistic system but also those of the visual-spatial meaning systems associated with orthography, typography, and page layout.

Lemke (1994, 2004) pioneers the application of systemic functional theory to multisemiotic discourses such as science and mathematics. According to Lemke (2004), language of words has evolved its specialized characteristics as "scientific language" for the need of constructing scientific knowledge, but words alone can never express what scientists want to say. As noted by Lemke (2004), the integration of these different modes is a key feature of the development of scientific and mathematical knowledge, where drawings and gestures are much more powerful at expressing topological and therefore quantitative meanings, while verbal language is much better at reasoning about relations among categories. Science does not speak of the world in the language of words alone, and in many cases natural language is very limited in its ability to describe scientific concepts and scientific language. Therefore, the expression of scientific concepts must resort to a synergistic integration of words, diagrams, pictures, graphs, maps, equations, tables, charts, and other forms of visual and mathematical expression, and all these semiotic resources co-function in building scientific knowledge.

As Lemke (2009) points out, genre theory is extended to include multimodal genres even as simple as those that are mainly textual-graphical. Therefore, models will need to be developed of multi-linear or functional meaning relations among elements that may constrain the sequence of viewing and interpreting (e.g., how far apart text and related image can be), but do not strictly sequence them. His other works (Lemke, 1998b, 2002a, 2002b) on hypertext semantics and organization suggest that representations of branching options in flowchart models of speech genres (Ventola, 1987) offer one direction for dealing with the organizational parallelism of multimodal genres. As Kress (1997) and Lemke (2004) have shown, the texts of science are increasingly produced with a multi-semiotic mode of communication.

As the basis of science, physics has used different modes to meet different needs in constructing its scientific knowledge. It is especially true of physics textbooks since language sometimes fails to express some scientific concepts.

2.2.3.3 Researches on Scientific Discourse in SFL in China

Recent researches about scientific discourse from the perspective of SFL in China can be divided into three categories: those focusing on language, those focusing on multimodality, and those focusing on educational discourse.

In terms of those researches focusing on language, both qualitative and quantitative ones are found. Qualitative studies in this aspect are often general overviews and sometimes with examples. Guo（郭建红, 2010）uses typical examples to probe into the notion of nominalization, its discourse functions and cognitive effects of nominalized metaphor in scientific English texts. Zeng（曾蕾, 2007）explores the role of grammatical metaphors in constructing the deeper, complicated meanings and functions of "projection" in academic discourses. It is found that grammatical metaphor can help to provide further explanations as to what syntactic and semantic features of "projection" are used for in academic discourses. Lin（林芳, 2002）makes a comparative study of grammatical metaphor types in both English and Chinese scientific languages, showing that the grammatical metaphor in Chinese and English is not only agreeable in types but also strikingly similar in function. Jiang and Zhao（姜亚军, 赵刚, 2006）introduce three linguistic approaches to academic discourses, that is, genre analysis, multi-dimensional analysis and Hallidayan linguistics, and tries to integrate the different methods used in them. Zhao（赵英玲, 1999）explores three kinds of hedges in scientific English discourses: accuracy-oriented hedges, writer-oriented hedges and reader-oriented hedges. Li（李努尔, 1992）gives a general analysis of three register variables（field, tenor and mode）in scientific English.

Other researches, which focus on the language in scientific discourses, are quantitative. These studies are explored in two aspects. On the one hand, they study the functions or characteristics of linguistic phenomena, such as nominalizations, hedges, specificity and delicacy. On the other hand, they explore the relationship between linguistic resources and metafunctions.

Some scholars examine the functions or characteristics of linguistic phenomena. Yang（杨信彰, 2011）explores, in terms of clausal patterning, nominalization and technicality, how lexicogrammar constructs scientific knowledge in popular science text and thus finds out show some of the major differences between science text and popular science text. Wang (王晋军, 2003) finds that the frequency of nominalization occurrence in a text is concerned with the type of the text. The higher the frequency of nominalization occurrence is in a text, the more formal the language of the text. Yang and Yan (杨蕾, 延红, 2012) examine 45 academic articles chosen from international journals and investigate the pragmatic characteristics of hedges in scientific English used by Chinese scholars, showing that propositions tend to be stated in an objective way. Tang (唐青叶, 2007) distinguishes specificity and delicacy under the two theoretical frameworks. Through an analysis of medical texts, she proposes that the distinction in specificity is reflected in register with a cline. The result of her study illustrates the features of knowledge construction.

Other researchers explore the relationship between linguistic resources and metafunctions. Based on the appraisal theory, Yao and Chen (姚银燕, 陈晓燕, 2012) analyze the engagement of concessive connectives in 40 English academic reviews from 8 linguistic journals in SAGE. This study describes the interpersonal metafunction of concessive connectives, especially their role in English academic reviews. It is found that concessive conjunctions and concessive conjuncts account for most of the concessives in the corpus, while the association of attitudinal disjuncts and concessive conjunctions or concessive conjuncts bears more interpersonal meanings. The analysis of this study may give some enlightenment to the writing of English academic reviews. Taking written and spoken English academic texts as data, Zeng and Liang (曾蕾, 梁红艳, 2012) explore how tense patterns construct knowledge in academic text and explains the metafunctions of tense patterns in achieving certain academic meanings.

Recent studies on scientific discourses in SFL in China turn to multimodal discourse analysis (hereafter MDA), but most of them provide only macro-introductions. Zhang (张德禄, 2012) investigates the important theoretical concept — design in MDA. Design is the process of selecting appropriate modes and mode sets according to their discourse meanings. In his opinion, design is constrained by context of culture, context of situation, communicative purpose, genre and discourse meaning. The designer selects modes from the available resources to meet these factors, and can also create new meanings and use new modes to meet communicative needs. The redesigned is the multimodal discourse. Wang (汪燕华, 2010) explores the image-text relation in multimodal discourse. She discusses the impasse in this practice, the causes of this impasse, and the feasibility of systematic functional exploration on the image-text relation in multimodal discourse, and argues that analysis and evaluations of the image-text relation can only be achieved through empirical studies incorporating both text type and image type. Yang (杨信彰, 2009) discusses the nature of multi-modality and illustrates the role of systemic theory in MDA. He points out that, in multimodal discourse, different modes interact with and complement each other to create meaning in context. Zhu(朱永生, 2007) elaborates the theory and methodology of MDA. He discusses four issues which are closely related to MDA: the origin of multimodal discourse, the definition of multimodal discourse, the nature and theoretical basis of MDA, and the content, methodology and significance of MDA.

Some researches in SFL in China are concerned with educational discourses. Zhu (朱永生, 2011) discusses the impact of Bernstein's theory of pedagogic sociology, especially his code theory and knowledge structure theory, on the development of SFL in the past five decades. He points out the responsibilities which should be taken by the systemic functional linguists in China. Zhang and Wang (张德禄, 王璐, 2010) investigate the synergy of different modes in multimodal discourse and their realization in foreign language teaching. With a comparison of two cases of college English classroom teaching, it is found that oral language is the main mode of discourse in classroom teaching, and other modes mainly complement and highlight it. Finally, six suggestions are proposed for the teacher to improve his teaching. Yang (杨信彰, 2007) discusses the necessity and significance to study educational texts from the perspective of SFL.

In summary, these studies on scientific discourses from the perspective of SFL in China follow the international research fashion. However, there are few quantitative researches in mulitimodal and educational scientific discourses, especially physics textbooks. In addition, these studies of knowledge construction lack an integrated perspective of Bernstein's SE and SFL.

2.2.4 From an Intergrated Perspetive of SFL and LCT

Nowadays many researches are beginning to do discourse analysis from the perspective of both SFL and Bernstein's SE, especially one dimension in the new development of SE — LCT, that is, SD & SG.

Martin and Matruglio (2011) interpret SD and SG by a detailed analysis of linguistic resources in history discourse. They investigate how participants and their activities are generalised, organised into phases, named as eras, and axiologically charged with moral values in relation to what can be termed "-isms", such as "colonialism".

By analyzing the school history discourse, Maton and Matruglio (2009) show that students' ability to strengthen and weaken both SG and SD has a great influence on the cultivation of students' legitimate historical "gaze". In other words, students need to be able to move from the specifics of certain historical events or personages to wider issues of how to interpret these historically and understand the way they contribute to the construction of historical principles. These types of shifts in SG and SD are essential to students' apprenticeship into the community of historians and are often referenced explicitly in the classroom.

Matruglio et al. (2011) make use of Coffin's six categories for construing time (sequencing, segmenting, setting, duration, phasing, organising) in the analysis of history writing and composing in the classroom. By analyzing the different ways of construing time in history, Matruglio et al. (2011) show how to move people through time and enable them to get beyond their current contexts. They conclude that cumulative learning depends on mastering the ability to move up and down SG and SD. Moving down SD, namly the weakening of SD, grounds knowledge in examples and concrete particulars. On the other hand, moving up SG, that is, the strengthening of SG, enables the already known out of context and everyday language to transfer knowledge across contexts.

2.3 Researches into Science Textbooks

Educational scientific discourses have some similarities to canonical scientific discourses in that they both belong to the activities of scientific community,

46

but school science is somehow different from canonical science in terms of their purposes which are realized by different linguistic resources. Bernstein (1990, 1996) points out that what learners are learning is not science as it is produced and practiced in the field of economic production, but science that has been re-contextualised in the education field as pedagogic discourse.

Textbooks are one of the important forms of educational scientific discourses and their importance has drawn many scholars's attention. In Swales' (1995: 4) words, introductory textbooks are usually "conservative encapsulations of pre-vailing paradigms", and all the features of appearance, arrangement, certitude, and style make them examples of "canonizing discourse". Taken as a genre, textbooks have been the subject of many studies (e. g. , Tadros, 1989; Love, 1991, 1993; Myers, 1992a), especially with particular attention to secondary school textbooks within the systemic functional tradition (e. g. , Martin, 1993a; Wignell et al. , 1993). The following review will divide the researches in science textbooks into two groups: non-SFL perspective and SFL perspective.

2.3.1 From a non-SFL Perspective

In earlier researches, there have been a great number of investigations with respect to the levels of reading difficulty of textbooks and instructional materials in the field of science. One of the major ones in earlier researches is explored by Curtis (1938), who summarizes the results of one hundred investigations in the problems of vocabulary related to the teaching of science. He draws four important conclusions about vocabulary problems in science textbooks. First, many technical and non-technical words are unfamiliar to students. Second, provision is insufficient for repetition of difficult scientific terms. Third, too many difficult words are non-scientific or non-technical. Fourth, newly-introduced scientific terms are seldom defined.

Among these scientific materials, those in the field of physics have received great attention. Allinson et al. (1952) have investigated the degree of reading difficulty at different levels of high-school physics textbooks, assuming that the reading difficulty depends on the number of words in the sentences, the relative number of personal references (I, you, etc.), and the number of affixes and suffixes (syllabification) to the words.

Studies of textbook discourses have so far been largely restricted to introductory texts in standard undergraduate fields such as physics (Kuhn, 1970), genetics (Myers, 1992a), geology (Love, 1991, 1993), and economics (McCloskey, 1985; Tadros, 1985; Henderson & Hewings, 1990). These studies provide us with useful insights into a wide range of textbook characteristics: their organization (e. g. , Love, 1991), the contractual nature of the author-student reader bond (e. g. , Tadros, 1985), the paucity of hedging, the diminution of human agency, and the use of abstract nominalization as subjects of processes (e. g. , Hewings, 1990; Myers, 1992a; Love, 1993), the deployment of prevailing metaphors (e. g. , Mason, 1990), and the mediation and the marketing of difficult material (e. g. , Tadros, 1985; Swales, 1993).

Indeed, many researchers focus on the differences between the "primary" genres of papers and research articles and "secondary" ones of textbooks and lectures. Myers (1992a: 8) has argued that, "authors of textbooks try to arrange currently accepted knowledge into a coherent whole, whereas authors of journal articles try to make the strongest possible claim for which they can get agreement".

Roth et al. (1999) investigate the differences in graph-related reading and interpretation practices between scientific journal articles and high school biology textbooks, showing that those inscriptions used most frequently by scientists [e. g. , tables with statistics, histograms, various Cartesian graphs (scatter plots, scatter plots with points connected, scatter plot with best fits, scatter plots with graphical models, and graphical models with scales), and equations] are those least used by textbook authors. Conversely, textbooks heavily draw on photographs, drawings, diagrams, and unlabeled graphical models which are little used in scientific literature.

Many researches in recent years suggest that science teaching is dominated by textbooks and whole-class instruction (Swales, 1995; Jetton & Alexander, 1997; Spor & Schneider, 1999; Wade & Moje, 2000; Langer, 2001; White, 2001; Alvermann, 2002; Osborne & Dillon, 2008).

Tobin (1990) emphasizes that, high school science is dominated by textbook-oriented approaches to teaching and learning. To explore what degree science textbooks introduce students to the literary practices of science, DiGisi and Willett (1995) make a survey of 149 teachers, showing that biology students have to read, depending on academic level, between 10 and 36 pages per week from their textbooks. Little science education research has addressed the quality of curriculum materials, particularly textbooks, although Good (1993) suggests that "[F] ar more research should be done to provide consumers (e. g. , science teachers and principals) with better information about curriculum materials".

Chiappetta (1993) overviews some problems associated with science textbooks such as covering far too much subject matter in a superficial, bad quality in presenting the nature of science and failing to present important topics (such as evolution and sex) in a thorough manner for fear of offending special interest groups.

Lemke (1982) points out that the sentences in physics textbooks tend to make reasonable sense even if taken out of context, and that for textbooks their immediately relevant contexts are constructed by the text itself with the signals of repetitions of words, intersentence reference, predictable patterns of argument, etc.

All the above researches are made from the perspective of the layout or organizing structures of scientific textbooks, but not from the perspective of linguistic resources realizing the meaning.

2.3.2 From a SFL Perspective

Systemic functional linguistists have contributed a lot to researches into scientific textbooks by means of analyzing specific linguistic recources. Halliday and Hasan (1985) have mentioned that the original aim of SFL is for education, that is, the study of linguistics should be able to be applied in teaching or learning practice. As Halliday (2006) states, his aim is to construct an "applicable linguistics". His followers inherit his idea and turn the study of scientific language from canonical scientific discourses to educational scientific ones.

As a pioneer in studying science textbooks, Martin contributes a lot to this field. Martin and Rothery (1986) have a discussion of writing in primary schools. Martin (1993c: 167) notes that textbooks are the main models of written science for schoolchildren. Martin (1993a) documents the construal of technicality in the context of science textbooks, observing that children "naturally"

49

cope better with factual texts than with narratives. Martin (1993b: 212) points out, nominalization is also important in classifying phenomena and in distilling meaning in technical terms.

Veel (1997: 161) discusses the roles that textbooks (as opposed to lab science) construct for the reader and participants. He notes that school science differs from lab or applied science in the genres it emphasizes (considering genre from the perspective of the Australian tradition). In school science, explanations and descriptive and taxonomic reports are the most common genres (Veel, 1997: 167). While in lab and applied science, exposition and discussion are the most common genres (Veel, 1997: 168). Veel (1997: 168) argues that this recontextualization of lab and applied science makes school science abstract, impersonal and disconnected from the processes leading to its formation. Veel's (1998: 121) study of environmentalist texts for children notes that these reflect romantic anti-industrialism as well as scientific/rationalist influences, allowing emotive and scientific meanings to be construed together. Working within the system developed by Kress and van Leeuwen (1996) for the analysis of visual images, Unsworth (1997: 37) notes the use of four different coding orientations in illustrations in science books for children: naturalistic (e. g. , colour photographs), realistic (e. g. , colour paintings), scientific (e. g. , schematic line drawings), and fantasy (e. g. , cartoon characters).

According to Halliday (1998b: 223), children favour congruent rather than metaphorical expression of meaning in the process of their language development. Halliday (2003) has pointed out the two crucial roles grammatical metaphor plays in scientific discourse: packaging the argument and theorizing the argument, which enable the meanings to be densely packed. Ravelli (1985) has investigated the relation between lexical density and grammatical metaphor. Love (1991, 1993) examines some lexico-grammatical features of an introductory geology textbook, particularly the use of grammatical metaphor and the associated features of verb types, subject-noun phrases, and choices of thematization. These features are then discussed in relation to the schematic organisation of information in the textbook, which suggests that the text is made up of a series of discourse "cycles" based on the interaction of geological "process" and geological "product". Later, a comparison is made by the author with a second textbook, and the contribution of these lexico-grammatical features to a model of the epistemology of geology is discussed. Suggestions are made for supporting ESL students in their efforts to process information in a new subject.

Therefore, it is also important to provide scaffolding for reading factual texts as advocated and illustrated in Unsworth (1997). Parkinson and Adendorff (2005) also do a research of science books for facilitating children's reading. Parkinson and Adendorff (2005) make an analysis of science books in terms of *human participants*, *organization of the message* (*passivization* and *nominalization*), *hedging* and *evaluation*, and claim that there are similarities in science books for children and science textbooks because both genres assume that the reader is a member of or seeks access to a broadly defined science discourse community.

Motivated by the research initiated in the field of SFL by Australian researchers (e. g. , Eggins, Wignell, & Martin, 1993; Veel &Coffin, 1996; Unsworth, 1999a, 1999b; Coffin, 1997, 2004; Martin, 1997, 2002a, 2002b), Achugar and Schleppegrell (2005) explore patterns of language that construct causal reasoning in history textbooks used in the U. S. from systemic functional perspective, analyzing the genres that students encounter when learning history and the linguistic features that characterize these genres. In this work, they see the deployment of prediction as the main organizational strategy to construct the explanation. A macro-Theme at the beginning of a text frames the coming discourse and predicts the logical organization.

Researches into scientific textbooks gradually move from the analysis of specific lexico-grammar to that of discourse and genre. Recent work in genre analysis has paid attention to the relationship between lexico-grammatical features and specific genres, or to the differences in distribution of features in different sections of a particular genre. For example, Davies (1986) has pointed out the differences in verb process types in different text types. Eggins et al. (1987) have reported on lexico-grammatical features that are characteristic of geography and history textbooks at junior secondary level. MacDonald (1992) compares the degree of abstraction or particularism involved in sentence subjects, both between academic subjects and in different parts of academic articles. Gosden (1992) traces the "flow" of different types of marked theme through the stages of research papers. All these writers are concerned with relating lexico-grammatical features to the schematic structure of genres. Particularly, they are concerned with linking these features to the main concerns and methodologies of particular academic disciplines. As MacDonald (1992) comments, most work on disciplinary writing focuses on the text level, with the amount of work at the sentence level relatively slim.

Sriniwass (2010a, 2010b) provides an indispensable cross-disciplinary ways to analysing and interpreting clause complexing relations in the genre of chemistry textbooks. He offers a comprehensive view of the analysis, application and development of SFL outlined by Halliday and Matthiessen (2004) to uncover how the systems of taxis and logico-semantic relations intersect to construct knowledge in these textbooks. Furthermore, he also explores the manner in which the distinction between parataxis and hypotaxis emerges as a dominant grammatical strategy for guiding knowledge construction in the same genre, demonstrating the distribution, range and functions of the congruent forms of language which have received little attention in SFL studies on scientific texts. It is hoped that the findings will make textbook knowledge more accessible to learners and reduce their sense of alienation.

As the above review shows, although the previous researches into scientific textbooks have focused on a large range of topics, few explore the school physics and fewer make an intergrative study of both language and images in this kind of discourse. In addition, much fewer explain knowledge building from the intergrated perspective of both SFL and Bernstein's SE.

2.4 Researches into Force and Motion

More science education researches begin to pay attention to linguistic contributions and focus on the important role of language in science, but there are few researches into physics, especially into its important concept *force and motion*. Only Brookes and Etkina (2007, 2009) explore this topic from a linguistic point of view, which is reviewed in the following.

Brookes and Etkina (2009) introduce a linguistic framework, which derives from the theories of cognitive linguistics and systemic functional grammar. Using

52

this framework, one can interpret systematically students' understanding of and reasoning about force and motion. Brookes and Etkina (2009: 010110-3) first present an analysis of the force and motion literature, claiming that Talmy has done the most complete analysis of everyday language about motion and its causes, and that "our everyday conceptual understanding of motion and its causes is far more sophisticated (as indicated by our language) than may initially appear from studies of physics students".

Then Brookes and Etkina (2009: 010110-11) discuss the implications of their findings for physics instruction and argues that, "[I]f learning physics involves learning to *represent* physics, then learning physics must involve a refinement of terminology and cases in language" (original emphasis).

Brookes and Etkina (2007) introduce a theory about the role of language in learning physics. The theory is developed in the context of physics students' and physicists' talking and writing about the subject of quantum mechanics. The findings show that physicists' language encodes different varieties of analogical models through the use of grammar and conceptual metaphor. In this study, Brookes and Etkina give a hypothesis that students categorize concepts into ontological categories based on the grammatical structure of physicists' language, and that students over-extend and misapply conceptual metaphors in physicists' speech and writing. In addition, they show how, in some cases, students' difficulties in quantum mechanics can be explained as difficulties with language.

2.5 Comments on the Previous Studies

This chapter has conducted a literature review of studies about how knowledge is built in scientific discourses mainly from the perspectives of SFL, SF-MDA and Bernstein's SE. In addition, the previous researches in scientific textbooks are also reviewed from the field of science education. It should be borne in mind that each approach, despite its limitations in either theoretical or practical consideration, has its peculiar contribution to the present project. Therefore it is of vital significance to sum up the contributions and limitations of the previous studies so that light will be thrown upon the current investigation.

The interpretation of knowledge as meaning in SFL and SF-MDA offers a new insight into ways of knowledge building in scientific discourses, and the analysis of canonical and educational scientific discourses presents us an easy understanding of how knowledge is constructed by means of language and other semiotic meaning-making resources. These researches provide implications for school science teaching and learning. Students' alienation to science may be lessened by raising their consciousness of scientific language.

However, there are several limitations in SFL and SF-MDA in terms of the explanation of knowledge and the analysis of knowledge building in scientific discourses. First, although language and other non-linguistic semiotics, which function as the realizing forms of knowledge, are explored in detail, the nature of knowledge is unclear. Second, it is shown that the previous researches into scientific language started from physics but few continued to explore physical data, especially physics textbooks although physics is the basis of science. Third, previous researches into knowledge building in scientific discourses focus on the clause level and then on the semantic level, but few focus on the level of context. Fourth, many studies in scientific textbooks begin to pay attention to the functions of other semiotics, such as images, mathematical symbols, but the previous researches rarely adopt an integrated perspective on both language and images in this kind of discourses.

Bernstein's SE makes the nature of knowledge visible and contributes a lot to knowledge building in scientific discourses. Furthermore, the description of SD and SG shows the principles of knowledge accumulation: the construction of any knowledge must experience a wave of SD and SG. These researches bring in pedagogical implications for school science. Teachers' ways of instruction may be improved by understanding the nature of knowledge. On the other hand, the demerit of Bernsteinain researches in knowledge building in scientific discourses lies in the lack of explanations of how the different types of knowledge are realized in visible semiotic resources, which can be complemented by ideas in SFL and SF-MDA.

As to science education researches, although they begin to pay attention to linguistic contributions and focus on the important role of language in science, there are few researches in physics, especially its important concept *force and motion*. Fewer researches of this topic are conducted from a linguistic point of view.

Overall, the previous studies provide a general understanding of how knowledge is built in scientific discourses mainly from perspectives of SFL and SE repectively, including both canonical discourses and science textbooks. However, few researches investigate knowledge building in physics textbooks from an integrative perspective of both SFL and Bernstein's SE. Adopting an integrated perspective of SFL and Bernstein's SE, the current book aims to explore the ways of physical knowledge building and the nature of physical knowledge in physics textbooks.

2. 6 Summary

This chapter has primarily reviewed previous studies on knowledge and knowedge building in scientific discourses. The importance of knowledge is indisputable in human history, and many research fields pay attention to this topic. Both Bernstein's SE and SFL take knowledge as their research focus although from different points of view. Bernstein's SE makes the knowledge itself as the focus of its research, studying knowledge structures and the devices for its building such as SD and SG. SFL assumes what is regarded as knowledge is constructed intersubjectively through language. In other words, knowledge taken as meaning must be transmitted by means of semantic building blocks from one form to another. For example, "grammatical metaphor 'engenders' the 'drift' from spoken to written discourse, from horizontal to vertical discourse" (Muller, 2007: 66; original emphasis). In the perspective of SFL, there is an inextricable connection between human cognitive development and his linguistic development, because "language is at the same time a part of reality, a shaper of reality, and a metaphor for reality" (Halliday, 1993a: 8). Therefore, if these knowledge-building blocks in science can be delimited, the sense of apprentices' alienation of science may be reduced.

That is why SFL has paid attention to the language of canonical science from the beginning of their research. Halliday (1997) describes his approach as focusing more on the "micro" aspects of scientific forms of discourse, that is, the grammar of the scientific clause, which is where the meaning is made.

On the whole, previous researches into knowledge building in scientific discourses focus on the clause level and then on the semantic level, but few on the functions of other semiotics, such as images, mathematical symbols. Later, linguists in SFL expand their research fields from canonical science discourses to school science textbooks because SFL has never ignored its educational application, and at the same time they begin to focus on the functions of multisemiotics in constructing scientific knowledge.

Textbooks play an indispensable role in setting up a discipline, providing important teaching materials and guidelines for teachers' classroom teaching and making science accessible to apprentices. In Bernstein's term, science textbooks exist as a field of knowledge recontextualization which bridges the gap between knowledge production by scientists and knowledge reproduction in classroom. Therefore, the analysis of knowledge building in physics textbooks will make textbook knowledge more accessible to learners and reduce their sense of alienation.

These previous investigations, taken together, are handicapped in the following ways. First, the nature of knowledge and the semiotic realization of knowledge are explored separately. Second, studies in semiotic realization of knowledge are rarely explored from the integrated perspective of both language and images in scientific discourses. Third, the observation and understanding of knowledge building in physics textbooks has received insufficient attention. To date, not full-length monographs or books are devoted to the nature and patterns of knowledge building in physics textbooks with respect to context consideration. In addition, the further analysis is needed from an integrated perspective of Bernstein's SE and SFL.

The next chapter will establish a framework to analyze the nature and patterns of knowledge building in physics textbooks, which is followed by a description of theories of SFL, SF-MDA, Bernstein's SE, SD and SG in LCT. In the subsequent chapters of this book, knowledge is taken as meaning and seen as constructed by verbiage and non-linguistic resources together. Knowledge building across physics textbooks will be explored from an integrated perspective of SFL and Bernstein's SE. In addition, based on these meaning resources, the development of SD and SG will be investigated in this book.

Chapter 3   Theoretical Framework

Previous studies on knowledge building, as reviewed in Chapter 2, have not systematically approached this topic from an integrated perspective of Bernstein's SE and SFL. Meanwhile, researches about the realization of knowledge have not focused on the level of context in SFL, in particular in terms of genre and field. Furthermore, studies on the interaction of language and image in knowledge construction are also lacking in previous researches about physics textbooks. Taking these into consideration, this book takes the argument one step further by examining the ways of knowledge building in physics textbooks in terms of genre and field from the perspective of SFL, investigating the interaction between language and image in constructing physical knowledge, and exploring the nature of physical knowledge and the patterns of knowledge building from the perspective of Bernstein's SE and semantics in LCT.

This chapter unfolds with the framework the present project establishes for the purpose of analyzing ways of knowledge building in physics textbooks. It further outlines the theories from which the theoretical model of this research comes- SFL, SF-MDA, a theory of knowledge structure developed by Bernstein and semantics including SD and SG in his followers' LCT, which are necessary for readers to understand the analysis and conclusions of this research.

3.1 The Framework for the Analysis of Knowledge Building

The focus of this study is on knowledge building across three levels of physics textbooks from the lower primary school level through the upper primary school level to the junior high school level. Ways of knowledge building in physics textbooks can be analyzed based on the framework proposed in this research, as shown in Figure 3.1.

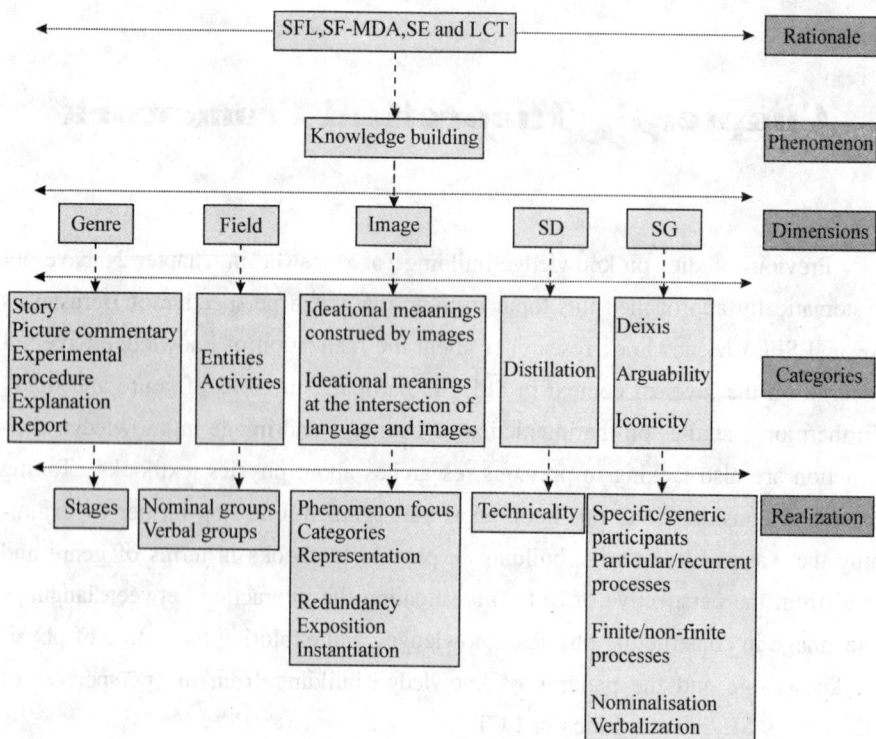

Figure 3.1　The Framework for Analyzing Knowledge Building

As Figure 3.1 shows, ways of knowledge building will be approached from the perspectives of SFL, SF-MDA, SE and LCT. SFL and SF-MDA interpret the semiotic realization of knowledge, while SE and LCT provide explanations for the patterns of knowledge building. On the whole, knowledge building in this research will be analyzed in terms of five dimensions: genre, field, image, SD and SG. Each dimension of knowledge building will be examined from its own categories, which may be realized by relevant linguistic features. As to genre, it includes five categories, namely, story, picture commentary, experimental procedure, explanation and report, which are realized by stages in texts. For field, it consists of two categories, that is, entities and activities. Entities are realized by nominal groups and activities by verbal groups. In terms of images, they are analyzed from two categories: the ideational meanings construed by themselves, and interactional meanings between images and language. The ideational meanings construed by images themselves are realized by phenomenon focus, categories and representation, and interactional meanings between images and language are realized by redundancy, exposition and instantiation. For SD, it is analyzed by means of distillation which is realized by technicality in physics textbooks. As for SG, it is investigated through three categories of linguistic resources: deixis realized by specific/generic participants or particular/recurrent processes, arguability realized by finite or non-finite processes, and iconicity realized by nominalization or verbalization.

The following sections will introduce the relevant notions in the above framework and explain techniques necessary for the detailed analysis of knowledge building in the subsequent chapters.

3.2 SFL

In profiling ways of knowledge building in physics textbooks, this book resorts to a great deal of researches within the SFL theory, which forms part of the analysis framework in this study. The following section will examine some notions concerned with this framework, that is, stratification, metafunctions, field, grammatical metaphor and technicality.

3.2.1 Stratification

Strata is one of the important perspectives for looking at the phenomena of discourse. There are three strata of language: grammar, discourse, and social context. As is shown in Figure 3.2, language itself as a system of meaning-making resources plays its function through three inter-related strata: discourse semantics, lexicogrammar and phonology/graphology. Discourse semantics is realized by lexicogrammar which is realized by phonology/graphology in turn.

Discourse semantics, the most abstract level of language, is most closely related to and realizes social context which can be divided into two levels: register and genre, with the former referring to "context of situation" and the latter "context of culture". Genre, which maps our culture, stays at a higher level and is realized by register. Register, consisting of field, tenor and mode, is closely interacted with discourse semantics.

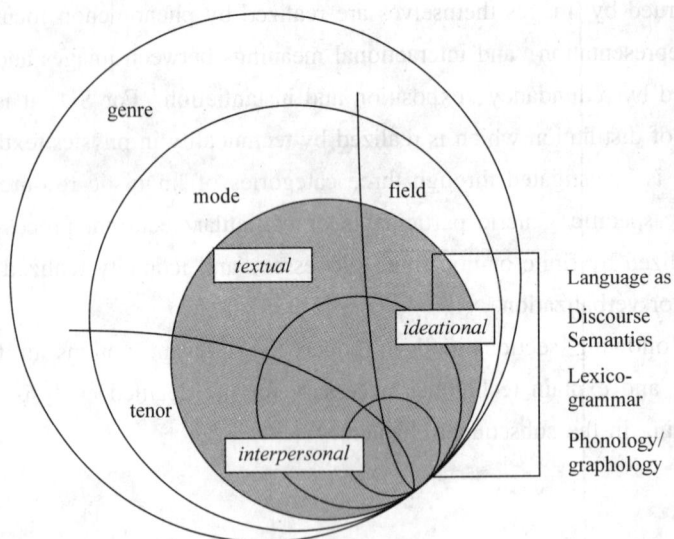

Figure 3.2   Modelling of Language in Context（after Martin & White：2005）

Genre and register are two main theoretical constructs used by functional linguists to model context, and they are concerned with knowledge building. The following section will explain genre, register and the relations between them mainly from the perspective of SFL.

3.2.1.1 Genre

There are three traditions of genre studies, ESP, rhetorical tradition and SFL. The concept of "Genre" in all the three approaches takes account of the culture of the discourse community that uses the genre, but each approach has its own focus.

In ESP, genre studies（Swales, 1981, 1986, 1990; Bazerman, 1988; Bhatia, 1993, 1997a, 1997b, 1999; Thompson, 1994; Askehave & Swales, 2001）is aimed at analyzing and teaching language in academic and professional settings. Swales（1990：58）has defined genre as "a class of communicative events which share some set of communicative purposes".

Genre studies in rhetorical tradition is mainly headed by Miller（1984, 1994）and Freedman（1993）. According to Miller（1984：27）, genre should "be limited to such a type of discourse classification based on rhetorical practice and thus open and organized in situation actions（that is, pragmatic, rather than

60

syntactic or semantic)". For Freedman (1993: 222), genre is considered in the light of social action, where 'action' refers to the social purposes that a genre fulfils.

Genre studies in SFL is divided by two groups. One is headed by Halliday and Hasan, and the other is led by Martin. Halliday and Hasan (Halliday & Hasan, 1976; Hasan, 1977, 1985a, 1985b; Halliday, 1978) have provided some influential and inspiring ideas about genre. However, there are some drawbacks in their perspectives of genre. As Lai (2011: 36-37) points out, "Halliday's uncertainty concerning the status of genre in his theory" reflects his inconsistency in positioning of genre and "Hasan's theory of genre also has some drawbacks" which are characterized mainly by the following two features: linearity of Generic Structural Potential (hereafter GSP), realization of GSP exclusively by language. Martin's approach to genre studies, which has developed from a long-term genre-based literacy program (cf. Martin, 1993, 1999), is aimed for school discourse analysis, which will be the main framework of this study and thus will be elaborated in detail in this section.

The genre theory headed by Martin has been developing for quite a long time. The term genre, since it is first defined by Martin (1984: 25) as "a staged, goal-oriented activity in which speakers engage as members of (their) culture", has been developing on different occasions (Painter & Martin, 1986; Marin, 1992, 1993d, 1997; Martin & White, 2005) to its more complete sense (Martin & Rose, 2008; Martin, 2011b).

According to Martin and Rose (2008: ix), genre has been theorized as "part of a functional model of language and attendant modalities of communication". As a working definition, genres are characterized as "staged, goal oriented social processes" (Martin and Rose, 2008: 6), which is explained in detail as follows.

> As a working definition we characterized genres as staged, goal oriented social processes. Staged, because it usually takes us more than one step to reach our goals; goal oriented because we feel frustrated if we don't accomplish the final steps (as with the aborted narrative [1:9] above); social because writers shape their texts for readers of particular kinds. (Martin and Rose, 2008: 6)

In functional linguistics terms, Martin and Rose (2008: 6) define genres as "a recurrent configuration of meanings" and point out that "these recurrent configurations of meaning enact the social practices of a given culture". In other words, how individual genres relate to one another need to be considered.

In simple terms, genres refer to a taxonomy of text types and reconfigurations of meaning. They are recurrent global patterns used to distinguish one text type from another. Within genres there are recurrent local patterns which are recognised as **schematic structures** to distinguish stages within a text. That is to say, one text type is classified as a kind of genre in that these texts have some recurrent patterns. Each type of genre has its typical schematic structures including optional and obligatiory ones. For example, the distinction between reports and explanations is made by whether the phenomena focused on are entities or activities. The schematic structures in explanations should include at least two obligatory stages, phenomenon and explanation.

According to Martin and Rose (2008), there are mainly four families of genres in science: **reports**, **explanations**, **procedures** and **procedural recounts**. Reports are used to classify and describe entities, explanations are used for explaining activities in sequences of causes and effects, procedures serve for observing and experimenting, and procedural recounts report on observations and experiments.

Scientific reports can be subclassified into three types, descriptive reports, classifying reports and compositional reports. Descriptive reports are characterized by two stages, classification of a phenomenon and description of its features. Classifying reports are realized also by two stages, classification systems and types of phenomena. Compositional reports, which discribe the components of an entity, usually include two obligatory stages, i. e. , classification of entities and classification of components, and an optional stage of definition. Genre options in scientific reports and its stage realization can be shown in Figure 3. 3.

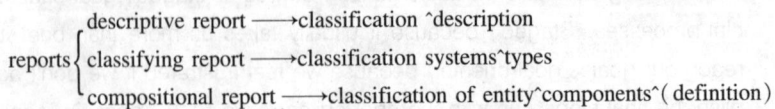

descriptive report ——→classification ^description
reports ⎰ classifying report ——→classification systems^types
compositional report ——→classification of entity^components^(definition)

Figure 3.3　Genre Options in Scientific Reports and Its Stage Realization

Explanations are about explaining how processes happen, which implies a kind of logical patterns termed implication sequence (Wignell et al. , 1993). This means a sequence of causes and effects: process x occurs, so process y results, which in turns causes process z, and so on. Martin and Rose (2008) describe four subtypes of scientific explanations: sequential explanations, factorial explanations, consequential explanations, and conditional explanations. A sequential explanation consists of a simple sequence of causes and effects, while a factorial explanation involves multiple causes. As to a consequential explanation, it may involve multiple effects. When the effects vary depending on variable conditions, a conditional explanation appears.

The typical schematic structure of explanations includes two obligatory stages, the one at which the phenomenon to be explained is specified at the beginning, and the other that is about the explanation of the phenomenon. Sometimes an optional stage of extension or definition occurs in the end. The stage of definition is important in science textbooks, as Martin and Rose (2008: 148) state, "[I]n science textbooks, reports and explanations may finish with a technical definition" and "[T]he definition distills the detailed information presented, becomes part of the taxonomic organisation of the technical field".

Genre options in explanations and its stage realization can be shown in Table 3.1.

Table 3.1   Genre Options in Explanations and Its Stage Realization

Types of explanation	Schematic structures of explanation
sequential explanation	
factorial explanation	phenomenon^explanation^(extension)^(definition)
consequential explanation	
conditional explanation	

Reports and explanations are concerned with genres that describe and explain the world, and procedures and procedural recounts are about those that direct us how to act in it. Martin and Rose (2008: 182) take procedures as "pedagogic texts in that they teach the reader how to perform a specialised sequence of activities in relation to certain objects and locations", and analyze five types of proce-dures, i. e., everyday procedures, operating procedures, cooperative proce-dures, conditional procedures and technical procedures. Everyday procedures ac-company an activity in which "[T] he pedagogic relation is direct, personal, here and now (see Gamble, 2004 on craft pedagogies)". Operating procedures explicitate steps in special activities, cooperative procedures assign responsibility in teamwork, conditional procedures are to make choices, and technical proce-dures apply technicality to technology. Procedures, which conduct science exper-iments and observations in schools, "typically include the stages **Equipment & materials** and **Method**" (Martin & Rose, 2008: 185, original emphasis).

Step-by-step procedures are rarely occurring on their own in scientific field, and are usually followed by procedural recounts in the form of technical notes by technical officers, research articles by scientists and experiment reports written by school science students. The staging of these forms of procedural recounts is summarized in Table 3. 2 as follows:

Table 3. 2   Staging of Procedural Recounts (from Martin & Rose, 2008: 200)

Technical Note	Introduction	(Method)	Investigation	Conclusion & Recommendation
Research Article	Introduction	Method	Results	Discussion
Experiment report	Purpose, Equipment & materials	Method	Results	(Conclusion)
Text[5:13]	1 Issue & 2 Background	3 Field trip: observation information	4 Identify what is happening	5 Develop a plan

An outline of main genres in science is presented in Figure 3. 4. A network diagram is used here to show relations between genres in science in terms of the role of time in their structuring, which are shown as a series of choices. The first choice between genres is time-structured or not. The second choice is further made in time-structured or not-time-structured gentres themselves. For not-time-structured genres, the choice of report and argue is made; for time-structured genres, the choice is given along two dimensions: consequential-time-structured ones and temporal-time-structured ones. Each choice is indicated by an arrow leading to further options.

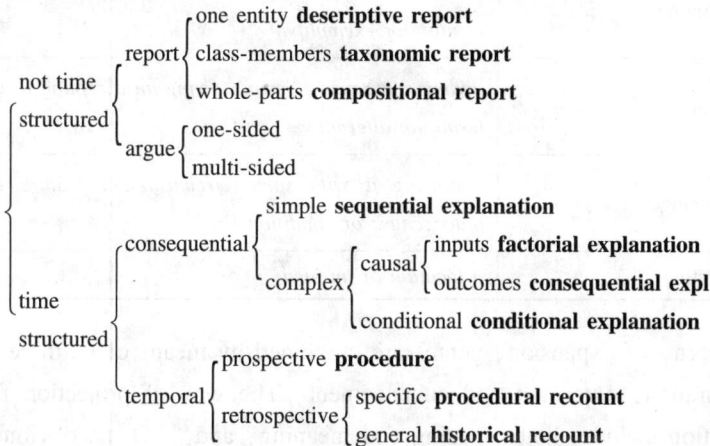

```
                          ┌ one entity deseriptive report
                  report ┤  class-members taxonomic report
   not time               └ whole-parts compositional report
   structured
                         ┌ one-sided
                  argue ┤  multi-sided

                                 ┌ simple sequential explanation
                consequential ┤          ┌ inputs factorial explanation
                                 │ complex ┤ causal ┤
                                 │          └ outcomes consequential expl
   time                          └ conditional conditional explanation
   structured
                         ┌ prospective procedure
                temporal ┤          ┌ specific procedural recount
                         └ retrospective ┤ general historical recount
```

Figure 3.4   A typological Perspective on Relations Between Genres in Science
(from Martin & Rose, 2008: 167)

As Figure 3.4 shows, explanations, procedures and procedural recounts are time-structured genres, while reports are not-time-structured genres.

Reports, explanations, procedures and procedural recounts are short types of genres, many of which are extracts from longer texts. In studying the relations between short genres that go to make up larger texts, the term "macrogenres" is introduced and explored to deal with texts which combine familiar elementary genres (Martin, 1994, 1995, 1997, 2001a; Christie, 2002; Martin & Rose, 2008). In simple terms, macrogenres can be called genre complexes. Based on Halliday's logicosemantic relations for the analysis of clause complexes, macro-genres are modeled as "serial structures" to be employed for investigating the re-lations of the elementary genres. The model of logicosemantic relations devel-oped by Halliday (2004), as is shown in Table 3.3, is used to describe how genres are connected in series in textbooks. Projection and expansion are two ideational strategies for the development of macregenres.

Table 3.3   Types of Logicosemantic Relations

(from Halliday, 2004: 220)

Type	Symbol	Subtypes
Elaborating	=	*restating in other words, specifying in greater detail, commenting or exemplifying*
Extending	+	*adding some new element, giving an exception to it, or offering an alternative*
Enhancing	×	*qualifying it with some circumstantial feature of time, place, cause or condition*
projecting	'	*a locution or an idea*

In terms of expansion, genres are combined by means of its three subtypes — elaboration, extension and enhancement. The way of projection for genre combination includes both wording and meaning, and "[O]ne obvious way in which genres combine through projection is for a character in one genre, a story let's say, to project another genre by verbalising it (telling another story for example, or writing a letter)" (Martin & Rose, 2008:256).

Martin (e.g., 1997) defines contextual metaphor as the process whereby one genre is deployed to stand for another. Like grammatical metaphor, contextual metaphor arises from the meaning shift between strata at the level of context, that is, the tension between genre and register. In other words, every genre has its congruent realizations by some typical register patterns, but when it is realized metaphorically by other register patterns which should realize another type of genre congruently the contextual metaphor will happen. For example, a recount genre may be standing for a scientific explanation, and a procedure for a hortatory exposition. "There may in fact be more than one layer" in contextual metaphors which are "offering readers a literal 'surface' reading implicating one genre, but providing in addition 'other genre' indicators signalling the presence of a 'deeper' genre lurking behind" (Martin & Rose, 2008: 248). Therefore, students should be directed to realize the deeper genre for better reading comprehension. The following example in Text 1 in Table 3.4 illustrates how contextual metaphors help us gain valuable insights into the meaning expansion.

Table 3.4   Text 1 (from Martin and Rose, 2008: 249)

Yesterday I went to the library and found a book about dolphins. I had seen dolphins on TV and I was ubterested in them. I wanted to find the answer to the question, why are dolphins so interestiong to humans?

The book said that dolphins were sea mammals. I bet you didn't know that dolphins have to breathe air! If they don't breathe air, they will die.

I have ofen wondered what dolphins like to eat, so I looked in the book for information about this. Do they eat other fish, I wondered? I found out that they do.

I suppose you know what dolphins look like, of course. I found out some interesting things, such as what that dorsal fin is for and how they keep warm. Why do we humans like dolphins so much, I often wonder. I searched in the book for the answer to this question, but could not get down to the real reason. The book talked about their tricks and stunts and their general friendiliness. As I thought about it, I came to the conclusion that it had something to do with the fact that they, like us, are mammals.

The above text, which is about a trip to the library, is literally a personal recount. However, it may also be taken as "a recount (about a trip to the library) standing for a report (about dolphins)" by using "projection to mould a second field which is concerned with dolphins", as Text 2 in Table 3.5 shows.

Table 3.5   Text 2 (from Martin and Rose, 2008: 249)

The book said	that dolphins were sea mammals.
I bet you didn't know	that dolphins have to breathe air!
I have often woundered	what dolphins like to eat,
I wondered	do they eat other fish
I often wonder	why do we humans like dolphins so much
I came to the conclusion	that it had something to do with the fact that they, like us, are mammals.

In addition, the text might be construed as an argumentative genre since it "unfolds dialogically though a question and answer format", as Text 3 in Table 3.6 shows.

Table 3.6   Text 3（Martin & Rose, 2008：249）

I wanted to find the answer to the question, why…?

—The book said that…

I have often wondered what…

—so I looked in the book for information about this.

Do they…I wondered?

—I found out that…

I suppose you know what…of course.

—I found out some interestiong things, such as what…and how…

Why do we…so much, I often wonder.

—I searched in the book for the answer to this question, but could not get down to the real reason. The book talked bout…As I thought about it, I came to the conclusion that…

As the above analysis shows, the text exists as "a recount standing for a report standing for an argument" (Martin & Rose, 2008：250).

3.2.1.2 Register in SFL

In Halliday's (1978：110) definition, "[T]he register is the semantic variety of which a text may be regarded as an instance". It is defined as "the configuration of semantic resources that the member of a culture typically associates with a situation type", in other words, "the meaning potential that is accessible in a given social context" (Halliday, 1978：111). In SFL, register is organized by metafunction into three dimensions：field, tenor and mode. The tenor, field and mode of a situation together constitute the register of a text. As its register varies, so too do the kinds of meanings in a text. Because they vary systematically, tenor, field and mode are referred to as register **variables**.

The dimension of field is concerned with the social activity of interactants; that of tenor is concerned with relationships between interactants; that of mode is concerned with the role of language. Halliday and Hasan (1985) provide a clear and detailed explanation of these three dimensions of a situation.

Field refers to what is happening, to the nature of the social action that is taking place: what it is that the participants are engaged in, in which language figures as some essential component.

Tenor refers to who is taking part, to the nature of the participants, their statuses and roles: what kinds of role relationship obtain, including permanent and temporary relationships of one kind or another, both the types of speech roles they are taking on in the dialogue and the whole cluster of socially significant relationships in which they are involved.

Mode refers to what part language is playing, what it is that the participants are expecting language to do for them in the situation: the symbolic organization of the text, the status that it has, and its function in the context. (Halliday & Hasan, 1985: 12)

As language realizes its social contexts, so each dimension of a social context is realized by a particular metafunction of language, as the following table shows:

Table 3.7   Metafunction and Context

METAFUNCTION	CONTEXT	
interpersonal	tenor	kinds of role relationship
ideational	field	the social action that is taking place
textual	mode	what part language is playing

As far as genre is concerned, field, tenor and mode can be thought of as resources for generalizing across genres from the differentiated perspectives of ideational, interpersonal and textual meaning.

3.2.1.3 The Relation Between Genre and Register

There are two perspectives on the relationship between register and genre. One is proposed by Hasan and her colleagues, who model it on the "axial" relationsip between system and structure. Another is developed by Martin (1992), who argues a model of inter-stratal relationship between register and genre.

Hasan (1995, 1999) and her colleagues argue an axial realization relationship between register and generic structures. In this model, generic structure consists of both obligatory and optional elements. The obligatory elements of genre structure appear to be determined by field, and the presence of optional ones by tenor and mode. The distinction among genres is thus a variation of the field, tenor and mode selections that genres do and do not share.

This contrasts with the inter-stratal model developed by Martin (1992), where choices among genres form a system above and beyond field, tenor and

69

mode networks at the level of register. Martin's model has certainly been influenced by the work in educational linguistics where mapping relationships among genres across disciplines has been a central concern (Mattheissen, 1993; Martin & Plum, 1997; Martin, 1999, 2001, 2001d, 2002a, 2002b; Martin & Rose, 2005, 2007).

The main difference is that register analysis is metafunctionally organized into field, tenor and mode perspectives whereas genre analysis is not. Register and genre are different ways of thinking about context. Similar to the relationship between language and context, and among levels of language, the relationship between the register and genre perspectives is treated as an inter-stratal one, with register realizing genre.

In Lemke's (1995) term, there is a relationship of "metaredundancy" between register and genre, that is, genre is a pattern of register patterns. However, the relation between register and genre is not a hierarchy of control but realizational. Genre does not determine register variables including field, tenor and mode. Rather a genre is construed as a dynamic configuration of these register variables, which are in turn construed as unfolding discourse semantic patterns.

On the whole, relations among genre, register, discourse and grammar tend to be predictable for members of a culture, but at the same time they are independently variable. These complementary features make language and culture capable for both stability and change.

3.2.2 Metafunctions

Metafunctions are another important perspective for looking at the phenomena of discourse.

3.2.2.1 Ideational, Interpersonal and Textual Metafunctions

SFL model of language in social context recognizes three general social functions of language as ideational, interpersonal and textual metafunctions. Ideational metafunction is "the content function of language" (Halliday, 1978: 112), that is to say, language is used to construe experience around us, including both our external experience and internal experience. It refers to what's going on, including who's doing what to whom, where, when, why and how and the logical relation of one going-on to another. Interpersonal metafunction refers to "the participatory function of language" (Halliday, 1978: 112), that is, language is concerned with doing things and negotiating social relations: how people, with feelings, are interacting with each other. Textual metafunction shows "the relation of the language to its environment, including both the verbal environment—what has been said or written before—and the nonverbal, situational environment" (Halliday, 1978: 113).

These three systems of language respectively relate to three register variables at the context level, i. e. , field, tenor, and mode. Given the focus of the current investigation on scientific knowledge building in physics textbooks, field and discourse semantic systems realising ideational meanings are particularly relevant. At the discourse semantic level, field can be examined through the analysis of ideation, which is the basis for knowledge and will be focused on in this research. Ideation, one of the five major systems (appraisal, ideation, conjunction, identification and periodicity) in discourse analysis is introduced by Martin and Rose (2003) as follows:

> **Ideation** focuses on the content of a discourse-what kinds of activities are undertaken, and how participants undertaking these activities are described and classified. These are ideational kinds of meaning, that realize the field of a text. (Martin & Rose, 2003: 16-17)

3. 2. 2. 2 Ideational Meaning System

Ideational base mainly shows content meaning, that is, what is going on. It is the important basis for construing human experience and knowledge. The following section will give a simple description of the ideational base and show how it may be expanded through the deployment of grammatical metaphor.

The ideation base is about "how the phenomena of our experience are construed as categories and relationships of meaning" (Halliday & Matthiessen, 2004:48).

Sequence, figure and element, the phenomena of experience of three orders of complexity, are typically realized in lexicogrammar by clause complex, clause and group/phrase accordingly, as Figure 3. 5 and Figure 3. 6 show (Halliday & Matthiessen, 2008: 49):

phenomenon
- Sequence (complex)
- figure (configurational)
- Element (elementary)

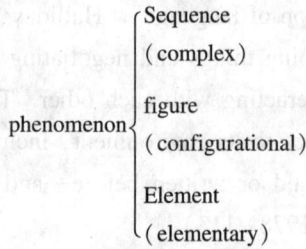

Figure 3.5　Types of Phenomenon（from Halliday & Matthiessen, 2008: 49）

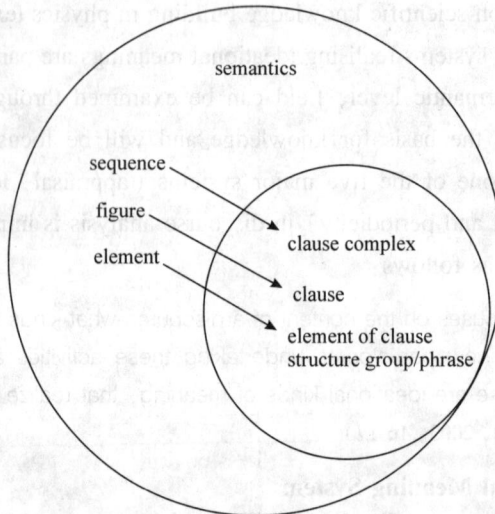

**Figure 3.6　Typical Realization of Sequences, Figures and Elements
（from Halliday & Matthiessen, 2008: 49）**

3.2.3 Field in SFL

One of the merits of SFL is its connection with context which consists of three variables, field, tenor and mode. Field tends to "determine the content of what is said or written" (Halliday, 1978: 225) and is the basis of knowledge. Its interpretation in SFL develops through two stages: Halliday's elaboration, the idea of field developed by Martin.

3.2.3.1 Halliday's Elaboration of Field

The elaboration of field cannot be separated from the context theory in SFL, to which Halliday has made a great contribution. Halliday (1978: 110) delimits out the semiotic structure of a situation type, which consists of three dimen-tsions: "field"—the ongoing social action in which the text is embedded, "ten-or"— the role relationships involved, and "mode"— the symbolic or rhetorical channel.

There is a close relationship between the semiotic components of the situa-tion (field, tenor and mode) and the functional components of the semantics (ideational, interpersonal and textual). In terms of field, it is related to "the ideational component, representing the 'content' function of language" (Halli-day, 1978: 123). Field, corresponding to type of social action, is associated with experiential meaning, that is, "the field determines the selection of experi-ential meanings" (Halliday, 1978: 143).

3.2.3.2 The Idea of Field Developed by Martin

Halliday initiates the idea of field which inspires the following researches, but it is too much a macro theory to be used as a specific tool in discourse analy-sis. Martin has defined field on different occasions in detail to make it more ap-plicable in practice.

Martin (1992) treats field as a set of activity sequences oriented to some global institutional purpose, alongside the taxonomies of participants involved in these sequences (organized by both classification and composition).

Later, field is related with genre, which is described by Martin and Rose (2007: 306) as a dimension of register "concerned with generalising across genres according to the domestic or institutional activity that is going on". It is elaborated as follows:

> By definition a field is a set of activity sequences that are oriented to some global purpose within the institutions of family, local community or society as a whole. The activity sequences, the figures in each step of a sequence, and their taxonomies of participants create expectations for the unfolding field of a discourse. (Martin & Rose, 2007: 306)

On this basis, activities which are construed by processes, and entities which are construed by participants, are needed to be considered when fields are identified.

Recently, the concept of field is further related to modalities. As Martin (2011) comments, since field is construed through a complementarity of modalities and genres, it ultimately needs to be treated as a generalization of "what is going on", across genres and modalities (Martin, 2011). This is illustrated in Figure 3.7:

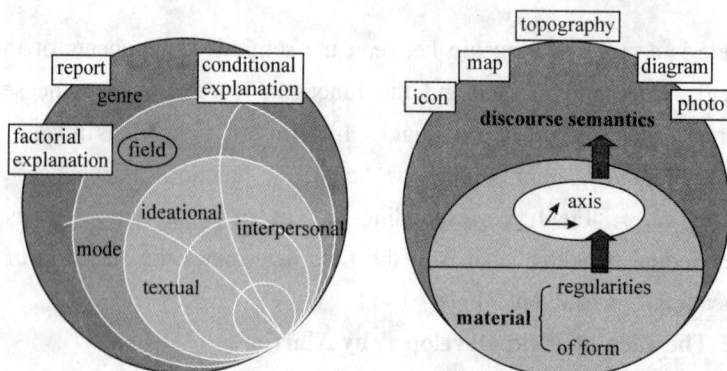

Figure 3.7 Field as a Generalization of "What Is Going on", Across Genres and Modalities (from Martin, 2011b: 98)

As Figure 3.7 shows, field, as a generalization of "what is going on" alongside the taxonomies of participants, is associated with ideational metafunction. The construing of a field is concerned with different types of genres, such as report, condiontional explanation, and factorial explanation, and with different forms of modalities, such as icon, map, topography, diagram and photo. In a word, when field is explored, besides entities and activities, genres and modalities also need to be considered. In the perspective of SFL, field is the basis of knowledge. Therefore, the examination of ways of knowledge building must involve not only entities and activities, but also genres and modalities including language and image.

3.2.3.3 Acivities and Entities in the Field

The above definitions show that there are two main components in the field of experience, activities realized by processes and entities by participants. These two main components of the field will be discussed in the following part.

Activities are realized by processes. Halliday (1994) has described six types of processes: material, mental, relational, behavioural, verbal and existential, the first three of which are the principal types in English grammar and the last three of which are subsidiary types. Material processes are those about what people do or what happens. Mental processes are those of feeling, thinking and sensing. Relational processes are those of being, "to ascribe qualities to people and things, to classify them as one thing or another, to name their parts, or to identify them" (Martin & Rose, 2003: 76). Behavioural processes, sharing characteristics of both material and mental, are those of "(typically human) physiological and psychological behaviour, like vreathing, coughing, similing, dreaming and staring" (Halliday, 1994: 139). Verbal processes, having features of mental and relational, are those of saying. Existential processes, possessing characerics of relational and material, are those showing that something exists or happens.

According to Halliday and Matthiessen (1999), the process is at the core of each figure which refers to the arrangement of process, participants and circumstances. Martin and Rose (2003) describe four kinds of figures, which are labeled as "doing", "saying", "sensing" and "being". Figures of "doing" focus on activities, figures of "saying" and "sensing" can project another figure, and figures of "being" are concerned with entities. Figures of "saying" and "sensing" are further grouped together as "signifying" in that both can project, and figures of "being" include qualities, classes, parts, identities and existence, as shows in Table 3.8:

Table 3.8   Types of Figures (from Martin & Rose, 2003: 82)

doing	middle	he was working
	effective	five policemen viciously knocked me down
signifying	saying	I can't explain the pain
	sensing	I saw what was left
being	quality	he was popular
	class	he was an Englishman
	part	goannas have flattish bodies
	identity	the narrator was Helena
	existence	there is the penalty

Besides activities, entities are also important in construing field. Like processes, participants, which include things and people, are also important components of figures. They are forming different classes of entities when seen from the field, which will be elaborated in the following section.

Ideational analysis at the discourse semantic level may provide some insight into the field. For example, the analysis of chains of relations between lexical elements in a text, known as "taxonomic relations", can help us construe a picture of people and things in its fiels as the text unfolds (Martin & Rose, 2007: 73). There are five types of relations between lexical items: repetitions, synonyms, contrasts, classes and parts. They consist of a taxonomic relation system, as Figure 3.8 shows:

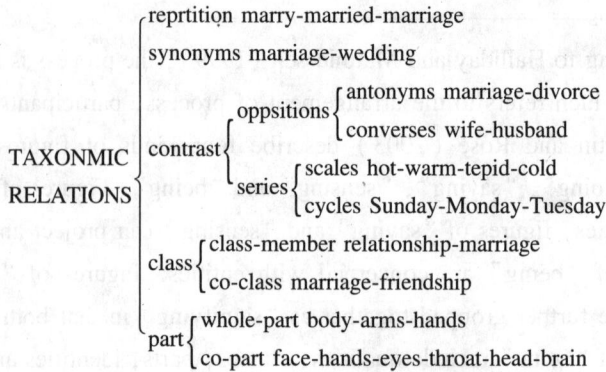

reprtition marry-married-marriage

synonyms marriage-wedding

TAXONMIC RELATIONS

contrast

oppsitions { antonyms marriage-divorce / converses wife-husband

series { scales hot-warm-tepid-cold / cycles Sunday-Monday-Tuesday

class { class-member relationship-marriage / co-class marriage-friendship

part { whole-part body-arms-hands / co-part face-hands-eyes-throat-head-brain

Figure 3.8   Taxonomic Relation System (from Martin & Rose, 2007: 81)

Martin and Rose's (2007) taxonomic relation system provides us a good starting point for analyzing how field is construed in terms of entities. According to Martin and Rose (2007: 81), "[E]ach lexical item in a text expects further lexical items to follow that are related to it in one of these five general ways. A lexical item initiates or expands on the field of a text, and this field expects a predictable reange of related lexical items to follow".

3.2.3.4 Entity Classifying Model and Taxonomic Relation System in This Study

The entity classifying model and the taxonomic relation system presented by Martin and Rose (2007) offer us a good understanding of how things and people help us construe the field as a discourse unfolds, but some adjustments are needed to make the models more suitable for analyzing scientific discourses.

Two previous entity classifying models in SFL, Martin and Rose's (2007)

and Humphrey and Hao's (2010), will be discussed before the adapted one in this study is presented.

When participants, that is, things and people are seen from the field, they are themselves classes of entities. The analysis of entities may provide a whole picture of things and people in the field as the text unfolds. Martin and Rose (2007) have distinguished four kinds of entities: concrete entities, abstract entities, metaphoric entities, and indefinite pronouns. The first three types are further divided into some subcategories. For concrete types of things, their meaning can be learnt by pointing to them and using them. They may belong in everyday activities, such as *man*, *girlfriends*, *face*, *hands*, or in specialized occupations, such as *mattock*, *lathe*, *gearbox*. Abstract entities refer not to concrete objects, but to abstract concepts, including technical, institutional, semiotic and generic ones. Metaphoric entities are classified into two types: process and quality. Metaphoric process entities are the metaphors derived from processes (e. g. , relationship, exposure), and metaphoric quality entities are those derived from qualities (e. g. , justice, truth). The model of entity types is shown as Table 3. 9.

Table 3. 9　Kinds of Entities (from Martin & Rose, 2007: 114)

indefinite pronouns		some/any/no thing/body/one
concrete	everyday	man, girlfriend, face, hands, apple, house, hill
	specialized	mattock, lathe, gearbox
abstract	technical	inflation, metafunction, gene
	institutional	offence, hearing, applications, violation, amnesty
	semiotic	question, issue, letter, extract
	generic	colour, time, manner, way, kind, class, part, cause
metaphoric	process	relationship, marriage, exposure, humiliation
	quality	justice, truth, inegrity, bitterness, security

Martin and Rose's detailed and fundamental classification of types of entities in fields of activity in modern cultures provides a good starting point for this research, but there is something more to be added to this entity framework. For example, Humphrey and Hao (2010) point out that the boundary between "concrete" and "abstract" categories is problematic because some technical entities in biology are "concrete" rather than "abstract" (e. g. , *algae*, *cell wall*) , suggesting to distinguish only the subordinate categories, particularly "specialised", "technical" and "generic" sub-categories in order to avoid confusion. Humphrey and Hao's model of entity types is summarized in Table 3. 10:

Table 3.10   Summary of Entity Types in Undergraduate Biology

(from Humphrey & Hao, 2010: 23)

specialised	experimenter	we, I, student
	material	microscope, glove, loop, glass slides, filter paper
technical	sensible: trained gaze	zebrafish, algae, fungi, leaflet, petiole
	sensible: technologically enhanced gaze	cell, cell wall, nucleus, cytoplasm
	inferable	plasmid, molecule, protein, pathogen
	dead metaphor	drug resistance, colicin production, metal tolerance
	method	turbidimetric method, plate count method, oxidase test
	Problem (from other field)	disorder, disease, hypoxia
generic	classification	organism, species, kingdom, genus
	method	method, approach, way
	cause	determinant, factor, reason
semiotic		question, study, research
metaphoric		occurrence, presence, investigation, consideration

Based on the two entity classifying models, Martin and Rose's (2007) and Humphrey and Hao's (2010), the author puts forward the adapted entity classifying model in this study which is more suitable for the analysis of entities in scientific discourses.

To express the difference of entities between everyday fields and scientific fields, a general classification is needed. Since entities are participants seen from the angle of field, the distinction of entity types may be made based on various fields. According to Martin and Rose (2007), there is a fundamental division in fields of activity in modern cultures between the everyday activities of family and community, and the "uncommon sense" fields of technical professions and social institutions such as law, medicine or education. Therefore, in this research entities are classified into common sense ones and uncommon sense ones especially for the following reasons.

Firstly, physics textbooks play an important role in training apprentices into the real scientific field. They serve as the intermediate from the everyday common sense field to the uncommon sense field. Physical knowledge in textbooks needs be recontextualized to be transmited to students. Therefore, kinds of entities in physics textbooks, that is, people and things, will be included in both common sense and uncommon sense.

Secondly, both common sense and uncommon sense entities include concrete and abstract subcategories. Although some specialized entities, such as *pulley* and *lever*, are concrete entities, they imply the meanings in the uncommon sense field. At the same time, generic and semiotic entities (e. g., way, time, colour) belong to abstract ones, but they are also used in everyday activities. For example, *people* and *animals* are generic entities, but they belong to the common sense field.

Thirdly, some specialized entities, such as *radar waves* and *returning waves*, are not concrete but abstract, therefore, the concrete specialized in Martin and Rose's model will be put into the category of specialized entities in the uncommon sense field. Some physical units, such as speed, mass, kilometres, pascal and newton, are also classified into this category.

Fourthly, together with technical terms, physical and mathematical symbols will be classified into the category of technical entities in that physical and mathematical symbols belong to the highest level in the taxonomies of the words of science (Wellington & Ireson, 2008: 217).

In addition, "personal pronouns" and "proper nouns" do not receive attention in Martin and Rose's entity model. The first and the second personal pronouns, such as *we* and *you*, will be grouped together with indefinite pronouns because they do not have definite meanings in physical textbooks. Other personal pronouns, such as *he* or *she*, refer to the previous common nouns or proper nouns, and they will be put in the category of concrete everyday in the statistic analysis. Proper nouns are included in the category of concrete everyday entities.

Concrete entities refer to those which can be pointed to and sensed directly.

Based on the above reasons and criteria, this research will adapt the entity model by Martin and Rose (2007) a little, as shown in Table 3.11.

Table 3.11　Adapted Entity Classifying Model in This Study

pronouns (indefinite/personal)		some/any/no thing/body/one we, you (he, she unanalyzed)
common sense	concrete everyday	Paul, The earth, Moon, Tower of Pisa, France face, hands, apple, house, hill, Man, girlfriend
	generic	colour, time, manner, way, kind, class, part, cause people, animals
	semiotic	question, issue, letter, extract
uncommon sense	technical	**Technical terms**: force, gravity, gene **Physical and mathematical symbols**: F, m, a
	specialized	mattock, lathe, gearbox, gear, pully
	metaphoric process	relationship, marriage, exposure, humiliation
	metaphoric quality	justice, truth, integrity, bitterness, security

As Table 3.11 shows, entities in scientific fields are divided into three major categories: pronouns, common-sense entities and uncommon-sense entities. Pronouns include indefinite pronouns and the first and the second personal pronouns. Common-sense entities include three sub-types: concret everyday, generic and semiotic ones. Uncommon-sense entities consist of four sub-types: technical, specialized, metaphoric process and metaphoric quality.

The entity classifying model used in this research provides a useful criterion for analysing entities in physics textbooks. When this model is applied in the analysis, two steps are needed: identifying entities in texts, and then analysing them in texts.

(A) Identifying entities in texts. Before classifying them into different categories, entities must be identified. Entities in field are realized by participants in semantic strata which experientially are construed in turn by a group of nouns (common nouns, proper nouns and pronouns) in lexico-grammatical strata. Therefore, to pick out entities is necessary for analysing out these types of nouns. As Martin et al. (2010: 166) state, like a clause, a nominal group embodies all three metafunctions, that is, experiential, interpersonal and textual metafunctions, again the first of which is concerned with knowledge and is focused on in this research.

(B) Analysing entities in texts. The author puts forwards three steps in analysing entities in texts.

First, adopt multivariate structures in the nominal group analysis. Nominal groups can be analysed in terms of multivariate structures and univariate structures. Having "**Thing**" as a must function, the multivariate structure of nominal groups also includes several optional parts functioning as **Deictic, Epithet, Post-deictic, Numerative, Classifier** and **Qualifier**. The following example shows the multivariate structure of a nominal group.

Table 3.12　**The multivariate structure of the nominal group**
(**after Martin et al. , 2010: 166**)

function	Deictic	Post-deictic	Numerative	Numerative	Epithet	Epithet	Classifier	Thing	Qualifier
examples	those	famous	first	two	dreadful	long	maths	sums	in the exam

In the univariate structure of a nominal group, **Head** and **Thing** may be conflated or not. For example, **Head** and **Thing** are conflated in "her yellow dress" ("dress" is **Head** and **Thing** respectively in these two structures, but not in "the side of the house" ("side" as **Head** and "House" as **Thing**). When these two structures are out of phase, that is, **Head** and **Thing** are not the same, it is still **Thing** that is focused on in the analysis of this study because "the Head is a noun that does not represent a thing in its own right but rather an elaboration or extension of another thing" (Martin et al. , 2010: 169). Therefore, in this research, the analysis of entities adopts the multivariate structure to pick out the "**Thing**" for convenience.

Second, focus on "things" or "classifier + things" in nominal group. "The **Thing** provides the basic general class in terms of which the participant is construed. It thus locates it in some particular domain of experience, such as the domain of conscious beings or the domain of abstractions" (Martin et al. , 2010:

167). **Classifier** specifies the subtype of **Thing**, answering the question *what kind/subclass*? It may display various types of meanings such as role, accompaniment, location, extent, and manner (Martin et al., 2010: 168). Therefore, in deciding entities in nominal groups, only "things" or "classifier + things" are analyzed. For example, "tennis ball" will be taken out as an entity in "a light tennis ball", and "cases" in "each of the following cases".

However, for nominal phrases construing technical entities (e. g., "**effects** of the forces", "the **motion** of objects", "the **mixture** of the two the control of the aircraft"), **Head** is focused on in the analysis, the reason of which lies in that nominalization is the focus of experience. Furthermore, in appositive phrases, such as "**Newton's Laws of Motion**", "**a bed** of nails", "the **oars** of a boat" and "your **model** of a penguin's wing", the **Head** is again focused on. Martin et al., (2010) assimilate the appositive nominal groups with the classifying type of focus nominal groups (where **Thing** and **Head** are out of phase), regarding **Focus** as similar to **Head**.

Third, group entities into their own categories. Common nouns and proper nouns usually construe the entities visually and are put into the category of concrete everyday. Indefinite pronouns (someone, nobody, nothing, etc.) and the first and the second personal pronouns are classified into the category of pronouns. For personal pronouns in physics textbooks, only the first and the second personal pronouns are regarded as separate entities because they do not refer to previous entities. Other pronouns will not need to be analyzed as separate types of entities because they are recurring entities which have been analyzed in the previous text. For example, "another" in the sentence "[T]he Law of Conservation of Energy tells us that energy cannot be created or destroyed but it can be changed from one form to another" (Janet, 1999: 21) refers to the generic entity "form" in front of it, so it is still included into the generic entity category same as "form".

The classified entities present features of participants in the field. In order to have a whole picture of participants as the discourse unfolds, the taxonomic relations of lexical items construing participants must be provided. Technicality, the subtype of uncommon-sense entities, plays an important role in building scientific knowledge in physics textbooks. Therefore, an adapted taxonomic relation system for analysing technicality is put forward in this study.

Based on Martin and Rose's (2007) taxonomic relation system, the author examines all the technical terms and finds out that, besides the five types of taxonomic relations suggested above, there is another relation type between technical lexical items in school science texts. This is a relation of causation including two subtypes: cause-effect and factor-effect. Therefore, the taxonomic relation system is adapted to meet the analysis of this research, as shown in Figure 3.9.

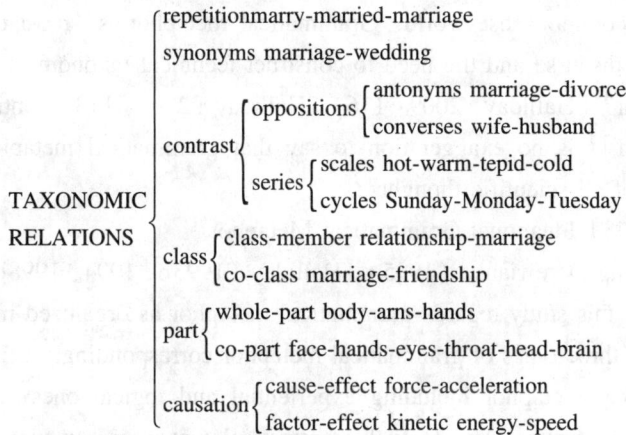

```
                      ┌ repetitionmarry-married-marriage
                      │ synonyms marriage-wedding
                      │                 ┌ antonyms marriage-divorce
                      │      ┌ oppositions ┤
                      │      │          └ converses wife-husband
                      │ contrast ┤
                      │      │          ┌ scales hot-warm-tepid-cold
                      │      └ series ┤
 TAXONOMIC            │                 └ cycles Sunday-Monday-Tuesday
 RELATIONS ───────────┤        ┌ class-member relationship-marriage
                      │ class ┤
                      │        └ co-class marriage-friendship
                      │      ┌ whole-part body-arns-hands
                      │ part ┤
                      │      └ co-part face-hands-eyes-throat-head-brain
                      │           ┌ cause-effect force-acceleration
                      └ causation ┤
                                  └ factor-effect kinetic energy-speed
```

Figure 3.9　Taxonomic Relations System in Scientific Texts in This Study

3.2.4 Grammatical Metaphor and Technicality

Grammatical metaphor is the main powerhouse for constructing scientific knowledge, as Halliday and Matthiessen (2004) point out:

> The ideation base with its framework of sequences, figures and elements serves well enough for construing the experience of daily life, and for organizing and exchanging commonsense knowledge. But it proves inadequate to meet the semiotic demands of advanced technology and theoretical science. In the construction of scientific knowledge, the system needs to invoke the power of metaphor on a more global scale. (Halliday & Matthiessen, 2004: 225-226)

Technicality is the carrier of scientific knowledge in its field. There is a close relationship between technicality and grammatical metaphor, which will be discussed in the following section.

3.2.4.1 Grammatical Metaphor

Grammatical metaphor is an important concept in SFL. Halliday (1994: 342) takes grammatical metaphor as "variation in the expression of a given meaning". If a given semantic configuration is not realized in its unmarked congruent lexicogrammar, it is considered as realized metaphorically. Grammatical metaphor is in fact a decoupling and recoupling between the semantic stratum and the lexico-grammar stratum, which opens a semantic space to construe something beyond our commonsense world. Grammatical metaphor is "most characteristic of scientific disourse and the need to construct technical taxonomies and sequential argument" (Halliday, 2009: 116). Halliday (2009: 118) continues to emphasize, "[I]t is no exaggeration to say that grammatical metaphor is at the foundation of all scientific thought".

3.2.4.1.1 Ideational Grammatical Metaphor

Following Derewianka (1995), Halliday (1993b, 1994, 1998b) and Martin (1992), this study regards grammatical metaphor as organized metafunctionally, and so three types of grammatical metaphor correspondingly exist: ideational grammatical metaphor including experiential and logical ones, interpersonal grammatical metaphor, and textual grammatical metaphor. In views of the research purpose, this research will focus on experiential grammatical metaphors that most commonly occur in the form of nominalization.

Nominalization occurs when a grammatical class or structure of process, circumstance, quality or conjunction is turned into another grammatical class, that of a nominal group or an object, as shown in Figure 3.10.

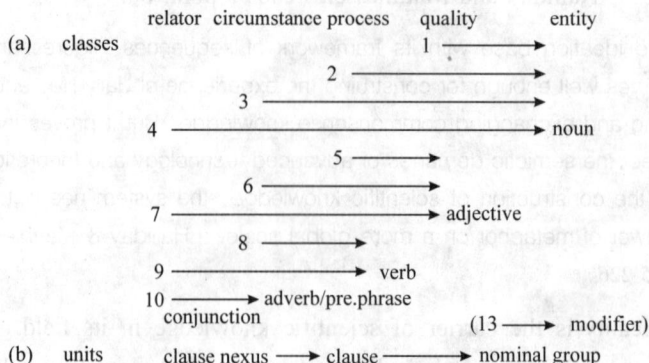

Figure 3.10   The "General Drift" of Grammatical Metaphor (after Halliday, 1998b: 76)

3. 2. 4. 1. 2 Functions of Ideational Grammatical Metaphor in Science

Martin (2011c) shows the three functions of ideational grammatical metaphor in sciences: explaining, defining and classifying.

(A) Explaining

In congruent realization of experience, it is often the case that explanation of experience is construed by means of processes leading on to processes (between clauses), e. g. , "High, white, wispy clouds appear and so (we know that) a warm front is approaching". On the other hand, in scientific fields, the explanation of experience is through grammatical metaphors in the following two ways. First, the explanation is given inside a clause. For example, the clause "The *approach* of a warm front is heralded by the *appearance* of high, white, wispy clouds" performs its function of explanation in the form of "nouns affecting nouns (inside a clause)". Second, the explanation is realized within clauses. Consider the following examples (from Martin, 2011c) in which a relationship of causality is construed metaphorically respectively by a noun, an adjectival, a prepositional and a verb.

(1) This rising air becomes cooler "for the reasons" mentioned earlier. (noun)

(2) The "resulting" clouds are usually of the cumulous type. The front edge of the cold air mass is known as a cold front. (adjectival)

(3) Much of the rain that falls in Australia occurs "as a result of" cold front conditions. (prepositional)

(4) Figure 7. 7 shows how a cold front "causes" uplift and condensation in a warmer, humid, air mass. (verb)

(B) Defining

One of the typical characteristics of scientific texts lies in the need of defining many technical terms, some of which occur in the form of nominalization as the following examples (from Martin, 2011c) shows:

(5) The amount of water vapour present in a sample of air is called the humidity.

In this definition, two things are presented: "the amount of water vapour"' and "humidity", which are related to each other. The first "thing" is in congruent expression and the other is realized in metaphoric expression. The metaphoric form of "humidity" functions as a technicality. In other cases, both sides of a definition may involve nominalization, as the following sentence displays:

(6) This *curving* of the waves which is called diffraction

In this definition, two things, "curving of the waves" and "diffraction" is used as a technical term.

(C) Classifying

Another important role of nominalization in scientific discourses is its classifying attribute, which can be shown by the example of "ability". "Ability" as a verb (can or can't) pocesses only negative or positive polarity, and cannot be classified, as the examples (from Martin, 2011c) show:

(7) Substances can carry electricity

(8) Substances can't carry electricity

However, "ability" as a noun in metaphoric form may play the role of entity and thus can be classified in various degrees, such as "a low ability to carry electricity", "an intermediate ability to carry electricity" and "a high ability to carry electricity".

3.2.4.2 Technicality

Technicality plays a very important role in construing scientific knowledge and it is often related to grammatical metaphors. The following section will discuss it in detail.

3.2.4.2.1 The Definition of a Technicality

Wignell et al. (1993: 160) refer to technicality as the use of terms or expressions (but mostly nominal group constituents) with a specialized field-specific meaning. For example, the term duck means differently for the cricketer (e. g. , out for a duck) as opposed to the bridge player (e. g. , to duck a trick), or the haberdasher (e. g. , a kind of cloth); and none of these meanings will be equivalent to the commonsense vernacular meaning (a bird with webbed feet and a flat beak).

Technicality plays two functions, as a field-creating process or to distill or compress meanings. Technical terms include different types. Some are seemingly familiar ones (sound, weight, etc.). Most of them can be classified into abstract ones (e. g. , particle, force, speed) and nominalization (resistance, motion, etc.). Although a few of technical terms are realized by verbs (e. g. , condense, melt), most of them "are nominal group constituents, usually things or Classifier^Thing compounds" (Wignell et al. , 1993: 161).

　　Two processes are needed for something to become a technicality: distillation and transcendence of the text. Distillation refers to technical language's ability to compact and change the nature of everyday words (Martin, 1993c: 172). As Doran (2010: 30-31) explains, the technicality is not simply renaming other terms, it is encapsulating the meaning of all the previous entities and their relations into a single nominal group, and as such it is changing the nature of everyday words.

　　After distillation, transcendence is needed for a term to become technicality. Transcendence means technical lanuage's ability to represent the meanings it encapsulates throughout many texts within the field. A distilled term doesn't mean that it will become a technicality immediately. To become part of the knowledge of its field itself, the distilled term must also transcend the text. If the term does not do this, and can only be recovered from the text it is introduced in, it is said to be instantial (Martin, 2006: 13). Instantial namings cannot be called technicalities because they are recoverable from the text, but not beyond; while a technicality is recoverable from the field itself. However, a technicality can be seen to transcend the text if it can be presumed without any introduction within other texts (Doran, 2010: 31).

　　3.2.4.2.2 Ways of Introducing a Technicality

　　Some technicalities can be introduced without using grammatical metaphor, such as the introduction of a technical term directly in an identifying definition or by previous technical terms, but most of them depend on nominalizations. Defining and naming are two ways of setting up technical terms. "Introducing technical terms means placing a Token in relation to its Value, and this entails relating meanings in the grammar as participants" (Martin, 1993e: 249).

3.2.4.3 Identifying Grammatical Metaphor and Technicality

　　Technicality is not equal to grammatical metaphor. Sometimes there is a clear distinction between them. Grammatical metaphor is the accumulation of the value and technicality is the distillation of the value. An technical term, with its semantic status as that of an abstract theoretical entity, belongs to the theory; a grammatical metaphor, the nonimalized form, retaining its semantic status as original, is only "a temporary construct set up to meet the needs of the discourse" although "such 'instantial' technicalizations may in time evolve into technical terms; but there is still a difference between the two" (Halliday & Martin, 1993: 14).

Sometimes the boundary between them is ambiguous since some grammatical metaphors stand for an instant technicality and some grammatical metaphors die immediately to evolve into a technical term. In other words, grammatical metaphor helps building technicality, but once technicality is built the grammatical metaphor ceases to be a grammatical metaphor. In this case, it is important and necessay to distinguish instant grammatical metaphors and distilled grammatical metaphors (technicalities) in discourse analysis. Some linguistic resources can be used as criteria to distinguish a grammatical metaphor from a technicality. The following criteria are proposed in this study by the author for distinguishing any grammatical metaphor as a technical term:

(a) With a classifier (e.g. *air/water resistance*)

(b) In a definition (e.g. *Motion* is the change in position and orientation of an object.)

(c) With a focus (e.g. the value of *the surface tension*)

(d) With an elaboration (e.g. The simplest movement of this kind is *linear motion*, which means the object moves in a straight line.)

(e) Without introduction (e.g. *All circular motion* from an orbiting planet to spinning bicycle wheel is acceleration.)

In other words, if a grammatical metaphor occurs with a classifier, in a definition, with a focus, with an elaboration or without introduction, it can be taken as a technicality. These criteria for identifying grammatical metaphors and technicalities are useful in the analysis of entities since they are two main subtypes.

3.3 SF-MDA

Language plays a very important role in constructing knowledge in science textbooks, but there are other semiotics, such as visual images and mathematical symbols, which also present their indispensable contribution to knowledge building. Language and other semiotics cannot replace each other in that they construe their own special meaning independently. In addition, they complement each other in meaning-making since the whole meaning in a multimodal discourse is more than the sum of meanings construed by each type of semiotics. Therefore, it is necessary to provide a description of the framework for analyzing these extra-linguistic meaning-creating resources and to explore the interactive device between written language and visual images. This section will focus on the theories of SF-MDA advocated especially by O'Halloran, Kress and van Leuveen, and some other researchers.

3.3.1 SF Framework for Mathematical Symbolism

Mathematical semiotics, including mathematical symbolism and mathematical visual images, takes a very import place in building knowledge in physics field. O'Halloran (2005) has studied mathematical discourses and set up a SF model for mathematical symbolism, as Table 3.13 shows:

Table 3.13   SF Model for Mathematical Symbolism
(after O'Halloran, 2005: 98)

Plane	MATHEMATICAL SYMBOLISM
	Stratal realization
Content	**Discourse Semantics**
	Inter-statemental relations
	Grammar
	Statements (or clause complex)
	Clause (// //)
	Expressions (([[...]])
	(rankshifted participants of the clause which are the result of mathematical oprations)
	Components
	(the functional elements in expressions)
Display	**Graphology and Typography**

The mathematical symbolism model includes two planes: content plane and

89

display plane. The display plane corresponds to the "expression plane" for language in the model and is renamed because a new grammatical rank of "expression" is introduced for mathematical symbolism.

The content stratum for mathematical symbolism consists of discourse semantics and grammar strata. Parallel to the lexicogrammatical ranks of clause complex, clause, word group/phrase and word for language, grammar strata in mathematical symbolism has the following ranks from higher to lower in order: statement (clause complex), clause, expression and component. That is, components realize the rank of expressions which realize that of clauses which again realize that of statements, which can be exemplified by the following equation illustrating the law of Conservation of Momentum.

$$mv = m_1 v_1 + m_2 v_2$$

As the lowest rank, components refer to the individual symbols within equations such as m, v, m_1, v_1. Expressions, realized by components, are made up of configurations between participants and operative processes (such as x, +, −, ÷−). Two examples are $m_1 v_1$ and $m_2 v_2$ in the above equation. If two full expressions are related to by a single relational process such as =, <, ⩾, it is a clause as the above equation $mv = (m_1 v_1) + (m_2 v_2)$ shows. A statement, on the other hand, is a sequence of horizontally aligned expressions related by one or more relational processes, such as the equations (Doran, 2010: 35):

$$\gamma = 4\pi\varepsilon_0 \frac{n^2 h^2}{mZe^2} = \frac{n^2}{Z} a_0$$

Graphology and typography make up of its display plane in mathematical symbolism, being more functional than in written language. For example, the symbol $\bar{a}$ means that it is a vector (it has both a magnitude and direction), and a lack of arrow above it a scalar (purely a magnitude).

3.3.2 SF Framework for Visual Images

Visual images, including both mathematical ones and non-mathematical ones such as photos and realistic drawings, are abundant in physics textbooks, especially those for lower levels. They play an indispensable role in constructing knowledge for students and it is necessary to take the analysis of them into account. In the aim of elucidating the multimodal analysis in this research, this

90

section will outline the models for SF-MDA: O'Halloran's (2005) model to explore mathematical visual images, Martin and Rose's (2008) model to investigate non-mathematical visual images, and the adapted model from Unsworth's (2006a, 2006b) to analyze the ideational interaction between language and images.

3.3.2.1 O'Halloran's SF Model for Mathematical Visual Images

Mathematical visual images, including "abstract and statistical graphs, a range of genres of diagrams and computer-generated graphics", are an important component of meaning-making resources in mathematics (O'Halloran, 2005: 133). They can "give an intuitive understanding of the reality constructed through the symbolism and language", and may "mirror our perceptual understanding of the world and thus connect and extend common-sense experience to the mathematical symbolic descriptions" (O'Halloran, 2005: 129).

In order to make sense of what can be achieved visually, O'Halloran presents a systemic model for mathematical visual images, as shows in Table 3.14.

Table 3.14   SF Model for Mathematical Visual Images

(from O'Halloran, 2005: 133)

	MATHEMATICAL VISUAL IMANGES
CONTENT	**Discourse Semantics**
	Inter-Visual Relations
	Work/Genre
	Grammar
	Episode
	Figure
	Parts
DISPLAY	**Graphics**

The framework of mathematical visual images here contains two planes: content plane and display plane. The content plane includes both a discourse semantic stratum and a grammar stratum, while the display plane contains an image's graphics.

The discourse semantic stratum contains the rank of work/genre which refers to the entire visual image and inter-visual relations established between multiple

91

works. The grammar strata of mathematical visual images have three ranks from higher to lower in order: episode (the configurations of process/participant and circumstance in the visual image, figure (individual participant in the episodes) and parts (the features which make up the figure).

3.3.2.2 Martin's Model

Like language, visual images also construe three kinds of meanings, ideational, interpersonal and textual meanings, among which ideational meanings are mainly concerned with knowledge. Therefore, in exploring ways of knowledge building in physics textbooks in this study, the ideational meanings construed by visual images will be examined. According to Martin and Rose (2008), ideational meanings construed by visual images in scientific discourses can be described in terms of three sets of features, that is, their phenomenon focus, categories and representation, which give the options shown in Figure 3. 11.

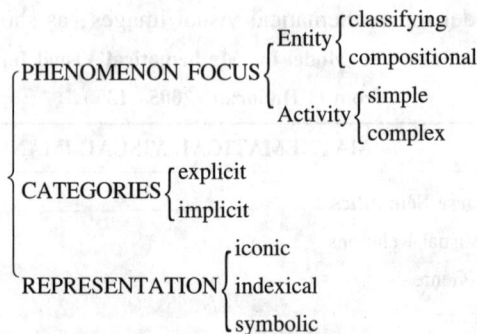

PHENOMENON FOCUS
- Entity
  - classifying
  - compositional
- Activity
  - simple
  - complex

CATEGORIES
- explicit
- implicit

REPRESENTATION
- iconic
- indexical
- symbolic

Figure 3.11　General Options in Technical Images for Ideational Meanings
(from Martin & Rose, 2008: 168)

As Figure 3. 11 shows, the focus of visual images in scientific texts may be either on entities or activities. The entities may classify or de/compose the images, while the activities may be simple (a single activity) or complex (a sequence). Categories within an image may be either explicit or implicit. An explicit image is labeled clearly, and an implict one needs readers to infer the meaning from the accompanying verbal text or assumed knowledge of the field. A photograph or realistic drawing is an iconic representation of an entity or activity. Diagrams are symbolic representations. Indexical images, such as outline drawings, are neither realistic icons, nor purely symbolic, but indicate some recognisable features of the represented entity or activity.

The knowledge, that is, the ideational meanings construed by visual images will be investigated in terms of phenomenon, categories and representation in this research.

3.3.2.3 The Adapted Model from Unsworth's

Images and language play their own special functions in building knowledge. However, knowledge constructed in a text is not only the sum of meanings by images and language; it also includes the interactive meanings between images and language. In this study, a system of ideational meanings at the intersection of language and image in scientific discource is needed.

Through analazing different types of texts, especially children stories, Unsworth (2006a, 2006b) presents types of ideational meanings at the intersection of language and images (see Figure 2.3 & Figure 2.4 in Chapter 2), concurrence, complementarity and connection. However, only three subtypes in concurrence are found relevant to this study: redundancy, exposition, instantiation. This system is adapted as a tool for analyzing the knowledge construed at the intersection of language and images, as is shown by Figure 3.12.

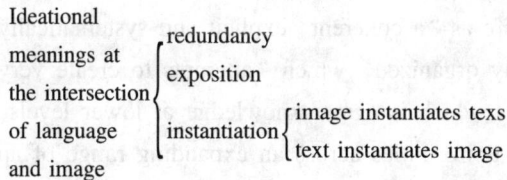

Ideational
meanings at the intersection of language and image
— redundancy
— exposition
— instantiation — image instantiates texs
     — text instantiates image

Figure 3.12   Ideational Meanings at the Intersection of Language and Image

3.4 Bernstein's Knowledge Structure and LCT's Semantics

SFL, SF-MDA and SE are important theories which are underlying the analysis framework in this study to profile ways of knowledge building in physics textbooks. The above sections have explored the relevant theories of SFL and SF-MDA. In the following section some broader theories within SE (Bernstein, 1999, 2000; Maton, 2007), which includes Bernstein's theory of knowledge structure and LCT's semantics, will be elaborated with an aim to form another part of the analysis framework in this project. Bernstein's theory of knowledge structure provides us with an important lens to see the nature of physical knowledge structure. LCT's semantics helps us to understand the physical literacy development from primary to secondary schools.

3.4.1 Bernstein's Knowledge Structure

Bernstein (1996, 2000) makes knowledge itself as the object of study, distinguishing "horizontal discourse" from "vertical discourse", the former producing everyday knowledge and the latter formal knowledge. According to Bernstein (1999a: 159), a horizontal discourse refers to everyday or "common-sense" knowledge and "entails a set of strategies which are local, segmentally organized, context specific and dependent". In contrast, a vertical discourse "takes the form of a coherent, explicit, and systematically principled structure" (Bernstein, 1999a: 159).

To account for the different forms taken by vertical discourses, Bernstein makes a further distinction between hierarchical knowledge structures and horizontal knowledge structures. He (1999a: 161-162) defines the hierarchical knowledge structure as "a coherent, explicit and systematically principled structure, hierarchically organized" which "attempts to create very general propositions and theories, which integrate knowledge at lower levels, and in this way shows underlying uniformities across an expanding range of apparently different phenomena". This kind of knowledge structures can be visually represented as a triangle, one motivated towards building an apex of greater integrating propositions, as Figure 3.13 shows.

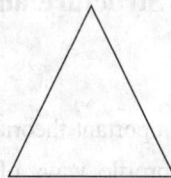

Figure 3.13 Hierarchical Knowledge Structure

Hierarchical knowledge structrures are exemplified by disciplines in natural

94

sciences a prime example of which is physics. In the image of the triangle, the pointy top represents the very general propositions and theories that subsume the wider range of more specific theories lower down.

On the other hand, a horizontal knowledge structure is defined as "a series of specialized languages with specialized modes of interrogation and criteria for the construction and circulation of texts" (Bernstein, 1999a: 162). This type of knowledge structure describes the disciplines of the humanities and social sciences, which are characterized by weak semantic development and weak internal coherence.

As opposed to integration in hierarchical knowledge structures, horizontal knowledge structures build their own field via an accumulation of languages. Theories in the horizontal knowledge structures develop in opposition to existing ones, each develops as a discrete entity, which can be represented by Figure 3. 14.

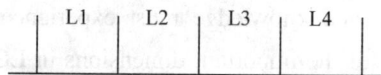

Figure 3. 14   Horizontal Knowledge Structure

The main difference between the hierarchical knowledge structure and the horizontal knowledge structure lies in the form taken by their development. According to Bernstein, a hierarchical knowledge structure develops by means of intergration of language, that is, seeking theories that embrace more empirical phenomena and comprise fewer axioms than existing theories. Intellectual progress is thus defined as the integration and subsumption of existing ideas within more overarching and generalising propositions. In contrast, a horizontal knowledge structure develops through accumulation of languages.

The classification of knowledge structures has provided us insights into the nature of disourses, but offered no tools for doing specific analyses. As such, Muller (2007, 2006) has highlighted the two dimentions introduced by Bernstein, verticality and grammaticality, which are used as tools of describing different fields' knowledge structures. These two attributes play a role in determining the capacity of a particular knowledge structure to progress. Verticality, namely, the degree of integratedness and subsume-ability of theory in Bernstein's definition, has to do with how a theory develops internally. Progress in hierarchical knowledge structures occurs through integration, while a theory in horizontal knowledge structures develops not through integration but rather through the introduction of a new language. According to Bernstein (2000), grammaticality, the external language of description, is about the capacity of a theory to generate empirical correlates and to be unambiguous. The stronger the grammaticality of language, the stronger is its capacity.

Considered as a typical hierarchical knowledge structure, the discipline of physics is expected to accumulate its knowledge in an integrated fashion across schooling. Bernstein's theory of knowledge structure may throw light on its explanation.

3.4.2 SD and SG in LCT

The concepts of SD and SG are closely related to ways of knowledge building, that is, any constructed knowledge must experience a waving of SD and SG. SD and SG are one of the important dimensions in LCT, the general picture of which is shown in Table 3.15.

Table 3.15   A General Map of LCT (from Martin & Matruglio, 2011: 8)

Principal	Referent relations	Concepts
Autonomy	external	positional autonomy, relational autonomy
Density	internal	material density, moral density
Specialisation	social-symbolic	epistemic relation, social relation
Semantics	meaning	SG, SD
Temporality	temporal	temporal C, temporal F

As the above table shows, semantics is only part of LCT — bits at differing stage of development, but it is concerned with meaning which is also the main focus of SFL. Semantics can be taken as an interface between LCT and SFL, and learning what semantics in LCT means may provide systemic linguists a good starting point to investigate language from a new perspective. Therefore, the notion of semantics is needed to be clarified in this section for providing a good understanding of the theoretical framework in this study.

SG and SD are two important dimentions of verticality concerned with the nature of knowledge structures. SG refers to the degree of abstraction from concrete particulars of specific contexts, that is, to the degree to which meaning is dependent on its context. SG may go in two directions, that is, strengthening SG and weakening SG, as Figure 3.15 shows.

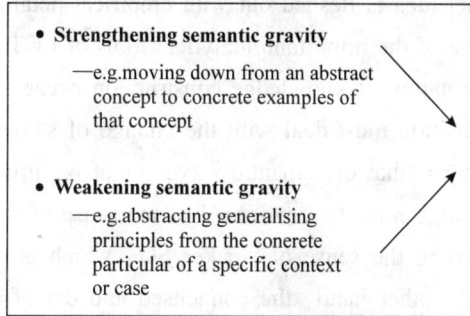

Figure 3.15   Processes of Weakening/Strengthening SG (from Maton, 2011: 3)

As the above Figure 3.15 shows, SG may be relatively stronger (+) or weaker (–). When SG is stronger (SG +) , meaning is more closely related to its context; when weaker (SG-) , meaning is less dependent on its context. One may also talk of *processes* of weakening SG, as one's understanding is lifted above the concrete particulars of a specific context or case, and strengthening SG, as abstract or generalized ideas are made more concrete.

SD refers to the degree of meaning condensation, that is, to the degree to which meaning is condensed within symbols (a term, concept, phrase, expression, gesture, etc.). SD may also go in two opposite directions, that is, strengthening SD and weakening SD, as Figure 3.16 shows.

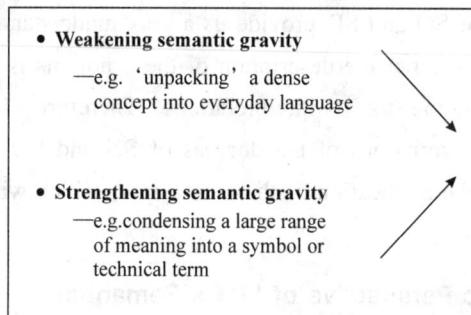

Figure 3.16   Processes of Weakening/Strengthening SD (from Maton, 2011: 4)

When SD is stronger (SD +), the symbol has more meaning condensed within it; when it is weaker (SD-), the symbol condenses less meaning. One may also talk of *processes* of strengthening SD, such as when a lengthy description is packaged up or condensed into a term or brief expression, and weakening SD, when an abstract idea is fleshed out with empirical detail.

SD and SG, one of the important analytical tools of LCT, may provide us a deep insight into the nature of knowledge construction because it is assumed that any knowledge acquisition must deal with the change of semantics. The process of knowledge learning is that of semantic waves, that is, ups and downs of SD and SG. The knowledge must be condensed in the sense of stronger SD and lifted out of the context in the sense of weaker SG, which is the ups of SD and downs of SG. On the other hand, the condensed and out-of-context knowledge need to be unwrapped in the sense of weaker SD and put in the context in the sense of SG for making it more accessible and more easy to understand, which is the downs of SD and ups of SG.

Waving of semantics is necessary for knowledge building. According to Maton (2009), weaker SG is one of the conditions for building knowledge or understanding over time. Shalem and Slonimsky (2010: 45) also emphasize that academic practices are constituted through de-contextualised knowledge and dis-embedded language. In Maton's (2009: 45) argument, *hierarchical* and *horizontal curriculum structures* can be distinguished according to whether a unit of study (lesson, module, year, etc.) builds upon the knowledge imparted in previous units through integration and subsumption or through segmental aggregation.

The concepts of SG and SD provide us a good understanding of the process of knowledge building, but the description of these notions is intuitive for lacking of manageable tools for its interpretations. Therefore, linguistic resources corresponding to the variations of the degrees of SG and SD may offer us substantial supports in the application of these concepts, which will be interpreted in the following section.

3.4.3 A linguistic Perspective of LCT's Semantics

In LCT's perspective, it is these ups and downs of SD and SG that necessitate knowledge construction; while in SFL's point of view, it is language that makes knowledge building possible. That is to say, LCT presents us an insight into the general features of knowledge building, and SFL offers us a view of the specific realization of knowledge building through language. Therefore, knowledge building may be studied from both these two points of view: exploring SD and SG from the perspective of SFL. Martin and Matruglio (2011) explore SD and SG in social science history from the perspective of SFL. The following section will first outline their model for interpreting LCT's SD and SG from a linguistic perspective, and then expand the model to the level of discourse semantics, which is the basis of analyzing the development of knowledge building in physics textbooks.

3.4.3.1 A Linguistic Perspective of SG

SG, interpreted as akin to mode, may be analyzed by means of the following three aspects of linguistic resources: deixis (specific/generic participants; particular/recurrent processes), arguability (finite/non-finite processes) and iconicity (nominalisation (processes) verbalisation (time/cause)) (Martin and Matruglio, 2011).

Deixis can be studied in terms of generity of participants and habituality of processes. The degree of genericity of participants, that is, generic or specific, decides the strength of SG. The more generic the participants, the weaker gravity they give; the more specific the participants, the stronger gravity they have. For example, "Mary is pulling *a brush* through her hair/*a book* from her bag" has a stronger gravity than "You use a force every time you move *something*, change its direction or change its shape". At the same time, the degree of habituality of processes, that is, particular or recurrent, influences the strength of SG. Recurrent processes will cause weaker SG than particular processes. For example, "You *use* a force every time you *move* something, *change* its direction or *change* its shape" has a weaker SG than "Mary *is pulling* a brush through her hair/a book from her bag".

Arguability means the finite or non-finite attribute of the process. A finite process (e.g. the volcano *erupted* (didn't it?)) results in a stronger SG, while a non-finite process (Mount Vesuvius erupting) leads to a weaker SG.

The iconicity refers to the iconic relationship between the construal of experience as ideational meaning and the expression of the meaning by means of language. The congruent expressions construe the experience more iconically than metaphorical forms. The degree of iconicity has an effect on SG. The more iconic an expression is to the experience it construes, the stronger SG it shows. On the other hand, the less iconic an expression is to the experience it construes, the weaker SG it has. Therefore, metaphorical forms mean weaker SG and congruent forms bring stronger SG.

Experiential grammatical metaphor and logical grammatical metaphor, the two important metaphorical forms to construe ideational meanings, are definitely connected with weaker SG. For example, the metaphorical expression "the *eruption* of Mt Vesuvius", which is involved in an experiential grammatical metaphor, has a weaker SG than the congruent expression "Mt Vesuvius *erupting*". Other kinds of grammatical metaphor have the same function of weakening SG, as the following examples (from Martin & Matruglio, 2011) show.

> (9) He practised as a lawyer... became a senator... became a consul... was sent as a governor of Bithynia
>
> (10) ... a career that *culminates* in his governorship (temporal metaphor)
>
> (11) Okay. You went to Melbourne, and you saw, or some of you went to Melbourne and saw, the plaster casts. Alright, did you feel, that you were looking at a, like a mummy? Nah, you felt you were looking at a plaster cast, didn't you?
>
> (12) The question of the treatment of skeletal remains *has evoked* impassioned debate in other parts of the world - (causal metaphor)

Example 9 and Example 11 are more related to context and they show stronger SG, while the other two examples are lifted from the context by grammatical metaphors and show weaker SG.

3.4.3.2 A Linguistic Perspective of SD

SD may be interpreted as akin to technicality: distillation (technicality) and iconization (axiology) (Martin & Matruglio, 2011). Iconization (axiology) is referred to in social science and has the similar function to distillation (technicality) in terms of SD, which is not the focus of this study and will not be explained here. Distillation is referred to in natural science and important for this research, which can be illustrated by the following examples:

100

(13) You push a pram. You push a swing.

(14) A push is a force.

The two pieces of experience construed in *You push a pram* and *You push a swing* are expressed in undistilled everyday language, so they contain lower SD. On the other hand, the experience construed in *A push is a force* is expressed in a distilled technicality which condenses the meanings of the above two sentences, so higher SD is created.

3.4.3.3 Specializaiton and Commitment

Besides these, Martin and Matruglio (2011) mention two other caveats influencing SD and SG, that is, *specialization* and *commitment*. Specialization, referring to unfamiliar concrete things, is often with weak SG and a little strong SD. Matin and Matruglio (2011) take *garum* and *inn/travern* as examples to illustuate this. For example, *garum* is the specialized form of *fish sause*, and *inn/travern* is the specialized expression to show the following meaning: in *a tavern* you can buy a bed for the night so you can sleep there, whereas *the inn* is mainly just for drinking. Therefore, *garum* and *inn/travern* is with weak SG and strong SD.

Commitment is about specificity of meaning and level of detail. The increasing of commitment may cause stronger SG and weaker SD. Commitment may be increased along the following three aspects: lexical delicacy, attribution of people or things, circumstantiation for processes. First, the commitment is increasing as the meaning of lexical items is going from generic to specific in lexical delicacy. For example, *something* in "moving *something*" is more generic than *a pram/swing* in "pushing a *pram/swing*", so the former is with less commitment than the latter. Second, the increasing of commitment comes from the attribution given to people or things. For example, there is an increasing in commitment from "A toy car needs *a push* to make it go" to "Emmar gives *a weak/strong push* to her car", with the attribution "weak/strong" modifying "push". Third, the increasing of the commitment occurs when circumstantiation is added to processes. As Martin and Matruglio (2011) illustrate, in the sentence "So there would be massive amounts of trade going on, and umm, you know people visiting their diplomats you know or their, their, ambassa/like their envoys and things like that all going back and forth across the countries", the commitment is

101

increased from the process *people visiting* to the addition of circumstantiation *their envoys and things like that going back and forth across the country.*

3.4.3.4 A Linguistic Perspective of SG & SD at the Level of Discourse Semantics

Martin and Matruglio's (2011) linguistic interpretation of SG and SD provides a good starting point in analyzing LCT's semantics, but his explanation focuses on the clause level. Aiming to find out the semantic development across different levels of physics textbooks, this study finds that the linguistic interpretation of SG and SD at the clause level is not enough, which cannot describe a whole picture in the text. Therefore, in this research the author expands its interpretation to the level of discourse semantics. The linguistic variables concerned with SG (deixis, arguability, iconicity) and SD (distillation) will be given a quantitative analysis. The more variables of SG and SD in a certain text means the higher occurrence of SG and SD in this text, which implies the stronger SG and SD of the text. On the contrary, the fewer variables of SG and SD in a certain text means the lower occurrence of SG and SD in this text, which implies the weaker SG and SD of the text.

3.5 Summary

Chapter 3 has developed a theoretical framework for the following analysis of knowledge building in physics textbooks. This framework mainly comes from three theories relevant to this study: SFL, SF-MDA and Bernstein's SE.

SFL is first presented in terms of strata, metafunction and ideational meaning system. Two new points are provided by the author. First, entity classifying model is adapted in new categories to meet the need of this research, and the procedures and methods for its application are explained. Second, the lexical taxonomic relation system is adapted as one suitable for scientific discourses, with a new category of causation-effect added to mainly explain the relations among technicalities.

Considering that science is hardly ever communicated through language alone (Lemke, 1998b), this research takes multimodality as a complementary perspective on knowledge building in school physics discourses, adopting a SF-MDA approach including O'Halloran's framework for mathematical symbols,

102

Martin's system for ideational meaning construed by visual images and the adapted model from Unsworth for the ideational meaning at the intersection between language and image.

In order to gain some deep insights into the knowledge itself, SE is explored in terms of Berstein's knowledge structure, LCT's SD and SG, and a linguistic model for analyzing SD and SG adapted from Martin.

In the following Chapters 4 and 5, the theoretical framework for analyzing knowledge building in physics textbooks will be given a more systematic and detailed exploration. Chapter 4 centers on its examination from the perspective of SFL and SF-MDA, and Chapter 5 focuses on its investigation from the linguistic point of view of semantics in LCT. In addition, the nature and structure of physical knowledge is discussed in these two chapters.

Chapter 4   Ways of Knowledge Building in Physics Textbooks

Chapter 3 has presented the theoretical and analytical framework of this study. This chapter is devoted to ways of knowledge building in physics textbooks in terms of field as a generalization of "what is going on", across genres and modalities. Textbooks are divided into three levels for the research purpose: textbooks of Level 1, textbooks of Level 2 and textbooks of Level 3.

In the following sections, genre development and characterization in physics textbooks will be explored first. Then field development across these textbooks will be investigated in terms of entities and activities. Finally, a multimodal analysis of visual images and its interactive relations with language will be presented.

4.1 Building Knowledge Through Genre

An important starting point for the analysis of physics textbooks is a characterisation of the texts in terms of genre. Martin and Rose's (2008) genre theory has made it possible to draw the separate register variables together and to make predictable text structures, which is helpful for pedagogical practices. Some researches (Veel, 1997; Christie & Derewianka, 2008) find genre development across schooling years in science which shifts from the congruent to the non-congruent and from the immediate to the abstract.

Many researches (Shea, 1988; Martin, 1993c; Veel, 1997; Martin & Rose, 2008) describe reports and explanations as the dominated genres in science textbooks. This study shows that, besides reports, explanations, procedures and procedural recounts which are regarded by Martin and Rose (2008) as four families of genres that characterise science, there are other kinds of texts which own features distinguished from those familiar ones and may be classified into new types, such as experimental procedures, picture commentaries, and stories. In the following section, these types of genres will be explored to see how physical knowledge is built through them.

4.1.1 Experimental Procedure: A Macro-genre Doing Science

Macro-genres characterize curriculum discourses and play a very important part in completing pedagogic tasks, as Christie (1997: 147) comments that, "a curriculum macrogenre constitutes a sequence of curriculum genres in which new understandings and new forms of consciousness are taught and learned".

The genre of procedure, the function of which is to offer students a sense of science by doing it, is very important in school physics texts. Sydney school genre theorists (e. g. , Martin & Rose, 2008) have identifies some stages (Objective, Materials, Steps, Results) as central to procedures, but this research suggests that in physics textbooks procedures should be expanded into experimental procedures with more stages: **Theoretical warming-up**, **Theoretical summary or Theoretical exploration**. **Theoretical warming-up** occurs at the beginning of all textbooks, **Theoretical summary** at the end of some textbooks of Level 1 and all of textbooks of Level 2 and **Theoretical exploration** at the end of textbooks of Level 3.

By analyzing all the texts with experiments, 28 in textbooks of Level 1, 52 in textbooks of Level 2 and 34 in textbooks of Level 3, these three stages are identified by their different goals in doing science. In a word, the necessity of these three stages lies in the final aim of doing science which is to deepen student's understanding of scientific knowledge. Theoretical warming-up can provide students a good orientation for the following experiment. Theoretical summary or theoretical exploration can help students consolidate the learnt knowledge. Hence, experimental procedures can be identified by three stages: stage of Theoretical warming-up before the experiment, stage of Experiment, and stage of Theoretical summary or Theoretical exploration after the experiment, which may be seen from Table 4. 1.

**Table 4.1　Stage Variations in Experimental Procedures
at Three Levels of Physics Textbooks**

Level 1 Physics Textbooks	Level 2 Physics Textbooks	Level 3 Physics Textbooks
Experimental procedure ● Theoretical warming-up ● Experiment 　—Objective 　—Materials 　—Steps（doing） 　—Results ● （Theoretical summary）	Experimental procedure ● Theoretical warming-up ● Experiment 　—Objective 　—Materials 　—Steps（"doing" or "doing & thinking"） 　—Results ● Theoretical summary	Experimental procedure ● Theoretical warming-up ● Experiment 　—Objective 　—Materials 　—Steps（doing & thinking） 　—Results processing ● Theoretical exploration

Although experimental procedures have the shared purpose of contextualising the particular scientific activity to be undertaken and establishing shared knowledge of the physical paradigm underpinning the activity, they can be seen as developing very differently at different levels of textbooks. This difference, which is mainly realized at the third stage of experimental procedure, is in response to different expectations of doing science in classroom which is moving from helping students sensing the scientific knowledge to enable them to understand and challenge the scientific knowledge.

Various purposes of experimental procedures at different levels of textbooks necessitate more delicate naming of its stages. First, there is a different naming at the third stage of experimental procedures. For experimental procedures at the first two levels of textbooks, *Theoretical summary* is adopted as the name of this stage to capture its aim of theoretical investigation. While, the third stage of experimental procedures at the third level of textbooks can be identified as *Theoretical exploration* to capture its purpose of challenging science. That is to say, the third stage of experimental procedures across three levels of textbooks develops from *Theoretical summary* to *Theoretical exploration*. Second, there a change of naming in the last phase of the second stage *Experiment*. For experimental procedures at the first two levels of textbooks, *Results* is adopted as the name of this phase to capture its aim of offering a theoretical summary. While, for those at

106

the third level of textbooks, *Result processing* can be identified as the name of this phase to capture its purpose of doing science.

In a word, the difference is reflected in the ordering and choice of their broad stages and the substages in experiments, which can be seen from Table 4. 2 and Table 4. 3.

Table 4. 2　Variations in Stages of Experimental Procedures in Physics Textbooks

Textbooks	Sum of experimental procedures	Occurrence-frequency							
		Theoretical warming-up		Experiment		Theoretical summay		Theoretical exploration	
Level 1	28	28	100%	28	100%	3	10. 70%	0	0
Level 2	52	52	100%	52	100%	52	100%	0	0
Level 3	34	34	100%	34	100%	0	0	34	100%

As Table 4. 2 shows, the three stages for experimental procedures at the first two levels of physics textbooks are *Theoretical warming-up*, *Experiment* and *Theoretical summary*. All the three stages are obligatory for experimental procedures in textbooks of Level 2, while *Theoretical warming-up* and *Experiment* are obligatory and *Theoretical summary* is optional for experimental procedures in textbooks of Level 1. The lacking of a *Theoretical summary* stage for experimental procedures in textbooks of Level 1 reflects the less theory-oriented knowledge building. For experimental procedures in textbooks of Level 3, they take *Theoretical warming-up*, *Experiment* and *Theoretical exploration* as obligatory. The replacement of *Theoretical summary* as *Theoretical exploration* in textbooks of Level 3 shows the emphasis on motivating students to think theoretically and to do science agressively.

The variations in experimental procedures in physics textbooks can also be characterised by a distinct change of stage choice in its experiment step, as Table 4. 3 shows.

Table 4.3   Variations in Substages of Experiment in Physics Textbooks

textbooks	Sum of experimental procedures	Sub-stages in genre of Experiment									
		Occurrence-frequency（%）									
		Objective		Materials		Steps				Results		Result processing	
						doing		Doing & thinking					
Level 1	28	28	100%	28	100%	28	100%	0	0	28	100%	0	0
Level 2	52	52	100%	52	100%	34	65.4%	18	34.6%	29	55.8%	23	44.2%
Level 3	34	34	100%	34	100%	0	0	34	100%	0	0	34	100%

As Table 4.3 shows, the sub-stages in experiments vary in terms of *Steps* and *Results*.

First, the purposes for steps in experiments are changing from instructing students to do experiments to asking them to have a reflection. In physics textbooks of Level 1, the purpose of *Steps* is just to give students instruction about how to complete the experiment or activity. In physics textbooks of Level 2, 34.6% of experiments require students to think when they are instructed to do experiments. In physics textbooks of Level 3, all the steps are instructing students both to do the experiment and to think out the reason for the phenomenon simultaneously. This implies that the knowledge constructed in higer-level physics textbooks are getting more complex.

Second, there is a variation in the substage of *Results*. In physics textbooks of Level 1, the substage of *Results* is just to present the results of experiment. In physics textbooks of Level 2, 55.8% of experiments present their results simply and other 44.2% of experiments not only provide the results but require students to process them. In physics textbooks of Level 3, all the experiments offer the results with a demanding for processing them. This shows that students are required to grasp the knowledge by doing and exploring the science, that is, physical knowledge in physics textbooks of Level 3 is built through students' doing and exploration.

On the whole, the above analysis of the variatiation in stages and substages in experimental procedures suggests that there is a steady development in terms of experimental procedures in physics textbooks from lower primary school years to upper primary school years then to junior school years. The examination of the recurrent local patterns of the stages in experimental procedures indicates that there are in fact different purposes realised in physics texts at different school levels.

The experimental procedure focused on in this study is really a macro-genre. Its three stages, that is, *Theoretical warming-up*, *Experiment* and *Theoretical summary* or *Theoretical exploration*, are in fact three independent genres. Among the three stages, *Theoretical warming-up*, *Experiment* and *Theoretical summary*, only *Theoretical summary* at the third stage is optional for experimental procedure in textbooks of Level 1. While for experimental procedure in textbooks of Level 2 and textbooks of Level 3, all the stages are obligatory.

All the genres occurring at the first stage *Theoretical warming-up* of experimental procedures include both reports and explanations, and those occurring at the second stage *Experiment* are procedures. For the genres occurring at the third stage *Teoretical summary* or *Theoretical exploration*, their types vary with different levels of textbooks: explanation for Level 1, explanation or report for Level 2 and question discussion for Level 3.

As for textbooks of Level 1, the total 28 genres occurring at the first stage *Theoretical warming-up* of experimental procedures include 8 reports and 20 explanations, thoses occurring at the second stage *Experiment* are procedures and those occurring at the third stage *Theoretical summary* belong to explanations.

Genre types occurring at each stage of experimental procedures and their logic-semantic relations can be shown in Table 4.4.

Table 4.4　Genre Types at Each Stage of Experimental Procedures and Their Logic-semantic Relations at the Three Levels of Physics Textbooks

Physics textbooks of Level one	Physics texbooks of Level two	Physics textbooks of Level three
Experimental procedure ● Theoretical warming-up = 　– realized by explanations or reports ● Experiment + 　– Realized by procedures ● (Theoretical summary) 　– Realized by explanations	Experimental procedure ● Theoretical warming-up = 　– realized by explanations or reports ● Experiment + 　– Realized by procedures ● Theoretical summary – 　realized by explanations or reports	Experimental procedure ● Theoretical warming-up = 　– Realized by explanations or reports ● Experiment + 　– Realized by procedures ● Theoretical exploration 　– realized by question discussion

The three stages in experimental procedures, that is, *Theoretical warming-up*, *Experiment* and *Theoretical summary*, have the same logic-semantic relations at all three levels of textbooks: the first stage is elaborated by the second stage which is in an extending relation with the third stage in turn.

Three examples are chosen respectively from the three levels of physics textbooks to illustrate the experimental procedure analysis, as is shown in Tables 4.5, 4.6 and 4.7.

Table 4.5　Example of Experimental Procedure from Textbooks of Level 1
(from Nunn, 2003: 7)

Stages	Text
Stage 1: Theoretical Warming-up	
Classification Description	All kinds of forces Forces are at work everywhere you look, pushing and pulling to make things move. Nothing can move on its own. Without forces everything would be quite still.

续表

Stages	Text
Stage 2: Experiment	
Objective	Elastic force
Materials	(Pop socks, a length of sewing elastic shown in images)
Steps	Roll some old pop socks into a ball.
	Then ask an adult to help you tie on a length of sewing elastic.
	Hold the end of the elastic and bounce the ball.
Stage 3: Theoretical summary	
Phenomenon	(the bouncing of the ball)
Explanation	The force of the ball falling pulls against the elastic and stretches it. The elastic then pulls the ball up as it springs back into shape.

Table 4.5 is an experimental procedure from one of physics textbooks of Level 1, aiming to make student understand elastic force. The first stage *Theoretical warming-up* offers students a sense of force in general by a *report*, then the second stage *Experiment* which is realized by a *procedure* motivates student to test elastic force by means of making a pock sock ball, and the final stage *Theoretical summary* which is realized by an *explanation* explaining to students why the sock ball is bouncing.

Table 4.6　Example of Experimental Procedure from Textbooks of Level 2
(from Wilson, 2001: 8)

Stages	Text
Stage1: Theoretical Warming-up	
Phenomenon	Squeezing and twisting
	Forces can make things change shape.

续表

Stages	Text
Stage1: Theoretical Warming-up	
Explanation	Whenever something is bent, twisted, squashed or stretched a force is acting on it. Springy or elastic materials try to go back to their original shape when the force that made them change shape is taken away. This means they can store up energy and then release it to make things move. Wind-up toys and some watches work like this.
Stage2: Experiment	
Objective	Wind-up toy This intriguing toy shows how the energy stored in a twisted elastic band can cause movement.
Materials	Ask an adult to find and break off the heads of a couple of safety matches for you. YOU WILL NEED A cotton reel A small elastic band Headless safety matches Sticky Tape A candle A knife A skewer
Steps	1. Cut a thin slice from the wick end of the candle. Make the hole In the middle of the slice big enough for the elastic band to fit through. Cut a groove in one side. 2. Poke the elastic band through the hole. Ask an adult for a headless matchstick, then put this through the loop and pull on the other end of the elastic band so the matchstick fits into the groove. Thread the long end of the elastic band through the reel.

续表

Stages	Text
Stage2：Experiment	
Steps	3. Push half a matchstick through the loop of elastic band you have just pulled through. Stop it from turning, either with sticky tape or by wedging it with another half matchstick pushed into one of the holes in the reel. 4. Wind up your toy by holding the reel and turning the long matchstick round and round.
Result	Put it down and watch it crawl!
Stage3：Theoretical summary	
Phenomenon **Explanation**	What's going on? As you use a turning force to twist the elastic band, you are storing up energy. Scientists call this potential energy. When you let go, the elastic band unwinds. This turns the matchstick leg and pushes the toy along. The potential energy in the twisted elastic band is turned back into movement energy.

　　Table 4.6 is an experimental procedure from one of physics textbooks of Level 2, aiming to make student understand elastic force, too. The first stage *Theoretical warming-up* explains to students the phenomenon of squeezing and twisting by a *explanation*, then the second stage *Experiment* which is realized by a *procedure* motivates student to test it by means of making wind-up toy, and the final stage *Theoretical summary* which is realized by an *explanation* explaining to students why the toy is moving.

Table 4.7　Example of Experimental Procedure from Textbooks of Level 3

(from Spiders, 1991: 10-11)

Stages	Text
Stage1: Theoretical warming-up	
Classification	Making things move
Description	
The cause of movement	What makes something that is stationary start to move? Often, movement is brought about by direct contact. For example, to make a supermarket trolley move, you push it, and to remove a stopper from a bottle, you pull it. In other cases, we use motors or engines to generate the force needed to start something moving. If you were asked, "What do you think is the most common cause of movement?", what would you say? There IS really only one answer: gravity.
The cause of stopping	If an object has been made to move by a force, what happens when the force stops? The pushing force used to launch a simple paper gilder stops immediately the glider is released, but the glider does not stop. It carries on going until air friction (see page 26) and gravity eventually bring it to a standstill.
Newton's laws of motion	The question that we started with is a difficult one to think about. This is because on Earth, whenever anything moves, gravity and friction always act upon it. We have to use our imagination and think of a place where these two forces do not exist. Think about a spaceship out in deep space, where there is absolutely nothing: no planets to cause gravity, and no matter to cause friction. Once the spaceship got there, it could switch off its engines and carry on in the same direction at exactly the same speed. This is because there is nothing to slow it down or stop it. These are the sorts of question that Sir Isaac Newton asked himself. He made his answers into scientific laws that say: "An object that is stationary will start to move only when forces are applied to it." and "Once an object has been made to move, it will carry on at the same speed and in the same direction unless other forces cause it to change speed, stop or alter its direction."

续表

Stages	Text
Stage1: Theoretical warming-up	
An example	The launch of the space shuttle. A huge pushing force must be created in order that the spacecraft escapes the Earth's gravitational pull. In space, the engines can be switched off and the craft will carry on moving.
Stage2: Experiment	
Objective	ACTIVITY
	TESTING NEWTON'S LAWS OF MOTION
Materials	YOU NEED
	● a toy car
	● a ramp
	● elastic bands
Steps	1 Use different methods (pushing, catapulting, rolling down the ramp) to start the toy car moving. Can you say what forces made it move in each case?
	2 Repeat each method. This time describe the forces that make the vehicle slow down or stop.
	3 Can you think of a way of making the vehicle change direction?
Result processing	4 Look at your answers. Do you agree with Sir Isaac Newton?
Stage3: Theoretical exploration	
Question discussion	TEST YOURSELF
Question1	1. What is the most common cause of movement?
Question2	2. Which two forces always act when objects move on Earth?
Question3	3. Why would a spaceship carry on moving in deep space even if its engines had been turned off?

Table 4.7 is an experimental procedure from one of physics textbooks of Level 3, aiming to make student understand Newton's laws of motion. The first

stage Theoretical warming-up describes this law by a *report*, the second stage *Experiment* which is realized by a *procedure* motivates student to test it, and the final stage *Theoretical exploration* which is realized by *question discussions* presses students to think further on the use of Newton's law.

4.1.2 Picture Commentary: A Macro-proto-genre

For physics textbooks of Level 1, a new genre type needs to be paid attention to in that it shows some global linguistic patterns which are distinct from those in higher-level physics textbooks. In this study, it is identified as a picture commentary because its meaning development centres on the image accompanying the text. Although texts of picture commentaries are short and containing only several sentences, each sentence is just like one type of the condensed full genres of report, explanation and discussion, realizing different functions respectively: organizing science, explaining science and challenge science. Therefore, the stages of picture commentaries seem different proto-genres of report, explanation and discussion. They together combine into a macro-proto-genre to construct for students the scientific knowledge. In other words, a picture commentary is the recontextualisation of a full macro-genre in school science into a macro-proto-one to meet students' cognitive and understanding ability, which enables them to sense the physical phenomena of the world in a conscious and scientific way.

The purpose of a picture commentary is to help students sense the scientific knowledge in a vivid common-sense way, and so the meaning of all its stages is related to the image. This research finds out that a full picture commentary is composed of three stages, *Picture explanation*, *Picture question* and *Picture description*. *Picture explanation* and *Picture question* are optional stages and *Picture description* an obligatory stage. In a picture commentary, the description of a physical phenomenon is usually expanded to other similar phenomena for motivating students to think, which can be illustrated by the text in Figure 4.1.

As Figure 4.1 shows, the text above functions as a picture commentary, which describes the relation between force and motion. This picture commentary provides students a familiar daily life phenomenon which in fact reflects

116

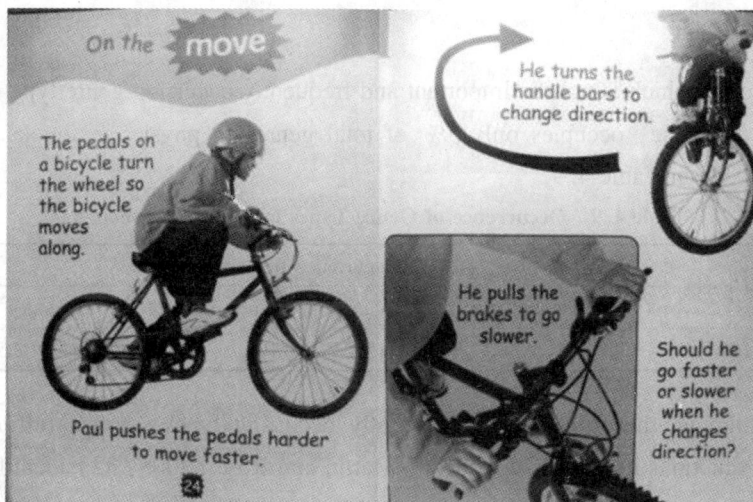

Figure 4.1   Example of a Picture Commentary (from Riley, 2001: 24-25)

Newton's second law of motion. The generic structure of this picture commentary is set out as follows in Table 4.8, with stages labeled and in bold.

Table 4.8   Picture Commentary in Physics Textbooks of Level 1 (from Riley, 2001: 24-25)

Stages & phases	Text
Picture explanation	
Phenomenon	On the move
Explanation	The pedals on a bicycle turn the wheel so the bicycle moves along.
Picture description	Paul pushes the pedals harder to move faster.
	He turns the handle bars to change direction.
	He pulls the brakes to go slower.
Picture question	Should he go faster or slower when he changes direction?

As Table 4.8 displays, this picture commentary is characterized by three stages: *Picture explanation*, *Picture description* and *Picture question*. The the first stage explains why the bicycle shown in the image is moving, and the second stage describes the change of bicycle's motion state — move faster, go slower, or direction changing. The three kinds of motion state constitute the three phases of the *Picture description* which is yet not elaborated fully. Finally, in the third stage, a question is put forward to students for further exploration.

117

4.1.3 Story

Story, which is not the important and frequently occurring genre type in scientific discourse, occupies only 5% of total genres in physics textbooks. This can be seen in Table 4.9.

Table 4.9　Occurrence of Genre Types in Physics Textbooks

Sum of genes	Occurrence-frequency							
	(proto-) report		(proto-) explanation		procedure		story	
219	69	31.5%	34	15.5%	105	47.9%	11	5%

Although they are not the frequently occurring types, stories fulfill their unique functions in physics textbooks. Martin and Rose (2008: 32) identify five types of story genres, which are shown in Table 4.10.

Table 4.10　Family of Story Genres

Staging: attitude	experience	response	experience
recount: variable	Record	[prosodic]	—
anecdote: affect	Remarkable	Event	Reaction
Exemplum: judgement	Incident	Interpretation	—
Observation: appreciation	Event	Description	Comment
narrative: variable	Complication	Evaluation	Resolution

Among the five types of story genres, only recounts and observations are found in physics textbooks. Recounts are all biographical ones describing the life of some famous person in the field of science. The occurrence of these stories across three levels of physics textbooks is shown in Table 4.11.

Table 4.11　Variations of Story Types Across Three Levels of Physics Textbooks

Textbooks	Sum of stories	Number-Frequency			
		Observation		Biographical recount	
Level 1: (3 books)	0	0	0	0	0
Level 2: (3 books)	7	7	63.6 %	0	0
Level 3: (3 books)	4	2	18.2 %	2	18.2 %
Three levels: (9 books)	11	9	81.8 %	2	18.2 %

As is shown in the above table, there are 11 stories in total at last two levels of physics textbooks, 9 (81.8%) of which are observations and 2 (18.2%) of which are biographical recounts about some famous scientists. In other words, in terms of story types found in physics textbooks at different school levels, observations with the frequency of 81.8% is more often used than biographical recounts whose frequency is 18.2%. There is a declining tendency to the occurrence of observations from 63.6% in textbooks of Level 2 to 18.2% in Level 3 textbooks, and no observations occur in textbooks of Level 1. As to the biographical recount, it doesn't show itself at the first two levels of physics textbooks, but shows itself only in textbooks of Level 3 with 18.2%.

The reason for taking observations as the favorite story type in textbooks at the lower school level is that the explicit appreciation of the story needs to be illuminated for younger students in view of their cognition. On the other hand, biographical recounts occur only in textbooks of Level 3, which reflects the less important function of the story in building scientific knowledge, as the following example shows in Table 4.12.

Table 4.12   Biographical Recount

[*About Science*] (**from Shadwick & Barlow, 2003: 208**)

Orientation

An English scientist, Sir Isaac Newton, was one of the first people to examine forces.

Record

He was born in 1642, and at the age of 27 became a professor of mathematics (a sub-branch of science). Newton is best known for the work he did on forces and their effect on the motion of an object.

Reorientation

In fact, the unit we use to measure force, the *newton*, with the symbol N, is named in his honour. He developed three laws of motion (you will learn more about these in a few years' time)

The above story is about Sir Isaac Newton in the form of a biographical recount, which mainly focuses on his contributions to force after the introduction of

119

his life span. The concluding sentence *He developed three laws of motion* summarizes his contributions in physics and provides a context for the following detailed explanation of the three laws of motion. Although this recount emphasizes his contribution to the main physical concept *force and motion*, it mainly displays an interpersonal function which enables students to have a general idea about who is this great person that makes such an important contribution to these notions. In this way, the inhuman knowledge about *force and motion* may be humanized by relating it to a real scientist who discovers it.

Although such kind of biographical recount can somehow bridge the distance between students and the objective truth, it is unable to help building knowledge in physics which need other forms of genres.

The main function of a story in physics textbooks is to interact with students. According to Martin and Rose (2008: 49), a story can draw a child's attention instantly and ignite and hold their imagination. However, it also realizes other functions in physics textbooks, especially at the lower school level, providing a context for the built knowledge or expanding the knowledge, which can be shown by the following story examples in Table 4.13, one observation from physics textbooks of Level 2.

Table 4.13   Observation

[*Science: Forces and motion*] (**from Wilson, 2001: 7**)
Newton's apple
Orientation
Big discoveries are sometimes made by chance.
Event
Sir Isaac Newton was a scientist who lived in England 300 years ago. The story goes that he was sitting in his garden when he saw an apple fall from a tree. He realized that there must be an invisible force pulling the apple down towards the Earth. He wondered if this force, called gravity, might affect the Moon, the stars and the planets as well.
Commment
His ideas about gravity completely changed our understanding of the Universe.

The text preceding the above observation introduces *weight*, the force of gravity pulling things down, which is measured in newtons (N) named after Sir Isaac Newton. Therefore, it will be natural for students to be interested in this great scientist and wonder why weight is named after him. An observation about how gravity is discovered by him can provide a context for this. In addition, the brief explanation of the concept gravity and comment on this idea in the observation may expand students' understanding of this knowledge.

In a word, genre, which has been explored in the above section, throws some light on the general ways of knowledge building in physics textbooks. The experimental procecure functions as a macro-genre, which combines reports, explanations and procecures to pack the knowledge for students. A picture commentary helps to build the scientific knowledge in a vivid common-sense way for students at the lower school level, and the story, although it doesn't occur often, plays a role in providing a context for building or expanding the knowledge.

4.2 Building Knowledge Through Entities and Activities

The investigation of genre in the above section provides us a rough idea of how knowledge is wrapped up on the whole in physics textbooks. Genre, which is located at the highest level outside language, is realized by means of register in three variables, field, tenor and mode. In view of the research goal, which is to explore knowledge building in school science, field will be focused on in the following section because it is field that is the main basis of knowledge.

In a broad sense, all the three levels of physics textbooks together construe the same field of social activities: scientific field of physical force and motion. At the same time, based on the linguistic syndromes identified at each level of textbooks, three more specific subfields are set up within this broad physics field: lower primary school physics field, upper primary school physics field and junior school physics field.

Textbooks of Level 1 construe a less scientific field by describing what forces can do to catch the connection with reality, making young students familiar with the idea of "feeling a force" when something pushes or pulls them. Textbooks of Level 2 construe a more scientific field by building more abstract ideas on this foundation through experiments and careful thinking. Textbooks of

121

Level 3 construe a much more scientific field by defining what a force is and providing a careful explanation about the counter-intuitive relationship between forces and motion, leading to further concepts of speed, velocity, momentum and acceleration. It is proposed that ways of knowledge building vary in the three school physics sub-fields, that is, across three levels of physics textbooks.

At the discourse semantic level, field can be examined through the analysis of ideation, which is concerned with what is going on and with the lexical relations between people and things in a text. Seen from the perspective of field, these people and things in a text are entities, and what is going on are activities which are realized by processes. Therefore, the variation among the different sub-fields, which are construed by different levels of physics textbooks, can be shown by an analysis of entities and processes according to the framework proposed by the author (see Figure 3.9 & Table 3.11).

The following sections will show how the different patterns of entity types and characteristics of processes within these three sub-fields are associated with knowledge building in school physics. Through field exploration, specifically a close analysis of both entities and processes across the main genres, the author will investigate how knowledge is built in physics textbooks.

4.2.1 Building Knowledge Through Entitities in Physics Textbooks

In this section, patterns and frequency of entity types will be shown and discussed in aim to discover the similarities and differences of knowledge building in physics textbooks which correspond to three sub-fields.

4.2.1.1 Similiarities in Knowledge Building by Means of Entities

The analysis of entity types in physics textbooks shows that ways of knowledge building in each sub-field share some similarities of the whole field. The top five types of entities occurring across the three sub-fields in school physics are the same, which are in turn concrete everyday entities, generic entities, technical entities, pronouns and metaphoric process entities. This can be seen clearly from Table 4.14.

Among the five types of frequently occurring entitities, concrete everyday entities and generic entities are those belonging to the common-sense field, while technical entities and metaphoric process entities are those occurring in the uncommon-sense field. This shows that the field construed by physics textbooks is not totally common-sense or uncommon-sense, but a combined field of both common-sense and uncommon-sense. In other words, physical knowledge is constructed by means of both common-sense entities and uncommon-sense entities. There are some similarities in ways of knowledge building by means of entities across different levels of physics textbooks, which is explored further in the following section.

Table 4.14 The Frequency of Each Type of Entities

Kinds of Entities			Number-Frequency (× 1000)					
			Level one (4168 words)		Level two (19658 words)		Level three (21332 words)	
pronouns			81	19.434	397	20.195	511	23.955
common sense	concrete everyday	—	574	137.716	1956	99.959	1679	78.708
	generic	—	139	33.349	920	46.800	1109	51.99
	semiotic	—	2	0.480	52	2.645	89	4.17
uncommon sense	technical	technical terms	92	22.073	662	33.676	1020	47.82
		Physical and mathematical symbols	0	0.000	38	1.933	41	1.92
	specialized	—	11	2.639	102	5.189	43	2.02
	metaphoric process	—	30	7.198	158	8.037	296	13.88
	metaphoric quality	—	2	0.480	30	1.526	35	1.64

4.2.1.1.1 Common-sense Entities

The first part of this section focuses on the function of common-sense entities in building physical knowledge. Not all things and people, which are talked about in constructing school physics knowledge, are far away from students' daily life. Some are common-sense entities which can make the abstract concepts more accessible to them. Concrete everyday entities and generic entities, the two types of often-ocurring common-sense entities, play a very important role in construing their field to help building scientific knowledge.

(1) *Concrete everyday entities*

Concrete everyday entities are the most often occurring ones throughout the three school physics sub-fields, most of which are realized by common nouns and some of which are realized by proper nouns.

(a) *Concrete everyday entities realized by common nouns*

This type of entities includes both human ones and inhuman ones. They can help construing a more common-sense field to recontextualize the scientific knowledge in a way familiar and relevant to students' daily life, which is shown in the following two aspects: doing experiments or explaining a concept/theory.

First, it is found that in doing experiments to test a theory, the materials needed are usually those familiar to students and easy for them to find. For example, in the experiment for understanding acceleration, the materials requested belong to concrete everyday and are common in students' life, as Table 4.15 shows:

Table 4.15 Some Materials Requested in the Experiment of Understanding Acceleration in Physics Textbooks of Level 2 (from Farndon, 2003: 12)

You will need
Several sheets of plain white paper
A compass
Food coloring or ink
A small toy truck or car
Scissors
A stopwatch
An empty soda bottle
A plank of wood
A tape measure

It can be seen that the aim of this test is to deepen students' understanding of accelaration, but the easily accessed and familiar experiment materials (*paper, compass, ink, toy car and ect.*) construe students a common-sense field.

Second, in explaining scientific knowledge in terms of a concept or theory, concrete everyday entities are also found, which may be illustrated by the excerpts in Table 4.16. Examples of these entities in school physics context are bold in the following excerpts.

124

Table 4.16　Examples of Concrete Everyday Entities in School Physics Context

1)[*Start Science: Forces and Motion*] (**from Nunn, 2003: 22**)

Slowing down

A **book** won't keep moving when you give **it** a push. The **book** rubs against the **table** and makes friction. Friction slows the **book** down and stops **it**.

Smooth surfaces

Ice skates and ice both have smooth surfaces. **Ice skates** slide easily over **ice** because they make very little friction.

2)[*Force and Motion*] (**from Royston, 2002: 14-15**)

Changing shape

Forces can be used to make some things change shape. **Soft clay** is easy to push and pull into many (different) shapes.

This **boy** is squeezing the empty **carton** to push the **air** out. He is making the **carton** flatter and smaller. Now it will take up less space in the **trash can**.

Getting Faster (**from Royston, 2002: 18-19**)

The harder you push something, the faster it moves. **This girl** is pushing a **toy train** across the **floor**. If **she** gives **it** a bigger push, it will move faster.

These runners are working hard to run as fast as **they** can. Their **feet** push down and backward on the **ground**. This pushes **them** up and forward.

In building the knowledge of "force and motion", the human concrete everyday entities realized by common nouns extend from the common people (such as girl, boy, person) students encounter in daily activities, to all kinds of athletes (such as tightrope walker, oarsman, skaters) in concrete activities to give students some easy-understanding illustrations of this knowledge. The inhuman concrete everyday entities include those things and animals which often occur in students' surroundings. In the first example in Table 4.16, four concrete entities (**book, table, ice skates** and ice), which are also familiar to students, are used to construe a common-sense field to help the knowledge introduction of *friction*. In the second example explaining *the effects of force*, **soft clay, boy, cartoon, air, trash can, girl, toy train, floor, runners, feet** and **ground**, these concrete everyday entities which are realized by common nouns again help recontextualizing scientific knowledge in a more common-sense field for students to easily grasp.

　　(*b*) *Concrete everyday entities realized by proper nouns*

The proper noun entities belong to the category of concrete everyday ones. Some of them are human ones representing people such as "Jessica, Paul, Michael and Sir Isaac Newton", and others are inhuman ones naming things or places such as "leaning Tower of Pisa, France and Paris".

Human proper noun entities can be classified into two types in school physics field. The first type is the typical and most often occurring one and they are familiar to students. The second type presents to students some famous physicists or some memorable participants who are unfamiliar ones in students' daily life in explaining some physical knowledge. Examples of these two types of human proper noun entities in school physics field are shown in Table 4. 17.

Table 4. 17   Entities Realized by Human Proper Nouns in School Physics Field

Type1: entities familiar to students

[*Push and Pull*] (**from Riley, 2001: 14-15**)

Aisha pulls **Trevor** into the pool. *Trevor* gets wet! **Aisha** has a stronger pull than **Trevor**. **Trevor** and **Aisha** play again. This time **Trevor** pulls as hard as **Aisha**. What do you think will happen?

Type2: unfamiliar entities in students' daily life

[*Science-Forces and Motion*] (**from Wilson, 2001: 7**)

1) On Earth, everything has weight. This is the force of gravity pulling things downward

Newton's apple

Big discoveries are sometimes made by chance. **Sir Isaac Newton** was a scientist who lived in England 300 years ago. The story goes that **he**(= **Sir Isaac Newton**) was sitting in his garden when **he** (= **Sir Isaac Newton**) saw an apple fall from a tree. **He** (= **Sir Isaac Newton**) realized that there must be an invisible force pulling the apple down towards the Earth. **He** (= **Sir Isaac Newton**) wondered if this force, called gravity, might affect the Moon, the stars and the planets as well. His ideas about gravity completely changed our understanding of the Universe.

2)[*Motion*] (**from Farndon, 2003: 9**)

The gun works out the speed from how much the returning waves are stretched or squeezed by the movement of the ball. This stretching or squeezing is called the Doppler effect, so the guns are sometimes called Doppler radar guns. Guns like these have shown that top male tennis stars like **Mark Philipousis** serve at over 140 mph (230 km/h).

This short text of Type 1 in Table 4. 17 is chosen from one of physics textbooks of Level 1, and it is aimed to transmit to students the scientific knowledge about the strength of *force*. At the lower primary school physics field, the knowledge is recontextualized into a common-sense form to be accessible to students. This is achieved by construing a common-sense field to which proper noun entities Aisha and Trevor contribute a lot. They are just like students' playing partners creating them a familiar daily-life picture.

Unlike the first type of proper noun entities, the second type of human proper noun entities names some people unfamiliar to students' daily life. However, they still help construing a common-sense field because they are concrete and introduced to interest students by letting them know something about these famous persons, which mainly provides interpersonal meaning. In the first example of Type 2, after saying something about gravity, **Sir Isaac Newton**, a greatest physicist, is introduced by a story about how he discovers gravity by chance. The main aim is not to further build the knowledge of gravity but to get rid of students' alienation from this great scientist and science. The second example of Type 2 explains the scientific knowledge *the Doppler effect*. **Mark Philipousis** as a tennis star is mentioned to transform the scientific knowledge into the common-sense knowledge by means of offering students a common-sense example of Doppler radar guns to construe a common-sense field.

Like human proper noun entities, inhuman proper noun entities play their unique roles in construing physical knowledge. Examples of these inhuman proper noun entities in school physics field are diplayed in Table 4. 18.

Table 4. 18　Entities Realized by Inhuman Proper Nouns in School Physics Field

1. [*Science-Forces and Motion*] (from Wilson, 2001: 7)

On Earth, everything has weight. This is the force of gravity pulling things downward....

Newton's apple

Big discoveries are sometimes made by chance. Sir Isaac Newton was a scientist who lived in England 300 years ago. The story goes that he was sitting in his garden when he saw an apple fall from a tree. He realized that there must be an invisible force pulling the apple down towards the **Earth**. He wondered if this force, called gravity, might affect the **Moon**, the stars and the planets as well. His ideas about gravity completely changed our understanding of the **Universe**.

2. [*What are forces and motion*?] (from Sarah, 2002: 27)

When it (= the Golden Gate Bridge) was completed in 1937, the **Golden Gate Bridge** in **San Francisco** was the largest suspension bridge in the world.

Since proper nouns name a specific (usually a one-of-a-kind) item, all the inhuman proper noun entities in physics textbooks will be unique by themselves. They help to construe a common-sense field familiar to students in order to make scientific knowledge constructed easier to be understood. The **Earth**, **Moon** and Universe in the first example illustrate gravity and the **Golden Gate Bridge** in **San Francisco** in the second example explains how bridge building takes forces into consideration.

(2) *Generic entities*

Generic entities are the second most often used common-sense entities across three school physics sub-fields. Although they refer to either a class of some things or an abstract thing, this type of entities still tend to construe a common-sense field for the recontextualization of scientific knowledge. Examples of these entities in school physics context are illustrated in Table 4.19.

Table 4.19   Examples of Generic Entities in School Physics Context

[*Science-Forces and Motion*] (**from Wilson, 2001: 22**)

What's going on?

Some **things** slide along the wooden board more easily than **others** (= other things) because there is less friction between their bottom **surface** and the board. **They** (= some things) will probably be the objects that feel smoother to the touch. **Things** slide much more easily along a smooth **surface** like the plastic tray for the same reason. ...

[*Motion*] (**from Farndon, 2003: 13**)

Gravity acceleration

As something accelerates and travels faster, it covers a greater **distance** in each **time period**. Here, the drops of ink fall from the truck at a steady rate. Yet as the truck rolls down the **slope**, the ink drops get farther and farther apart, showing it is traveling farther and farther in the same **time**. This means it must be accelerating. This experiment is simple in **theory**, but it can be hard to make-work well. The longer and more gentle the **slope**, the better it(= the slope) will work. Check that the cap drips ink evenly. Start with the **hole** too small, and then enlarge **it**(= the hole).

In the first example, the entities **things**, **objects** and **surface**, which classify some things, are adopted to construe a more common-sense field helping students understand the scientific concept *friction*. In the second example the generic entities **distance**, **time period**, **rate** and **theory**, which are more abstract, serve to explain the concept *gravity acceleration*.

4. 2. 1. 1. 2 Uncommon-sense Entities

As a science, school physics must build its knowledge in an uncommon-sense field. Although common-sense entities can make the abstract concepts more accessible to students, knowledge buiding need the power of uncommon-sense entities. Technical entities and metaphoric process entities, the two types of often-occurring uncommon-sense entities, play very important roles in construing the uncommon-sense field to help building scientific knowledge.

1) *Technical entities*

Technical entities include two subtypes: technical terms, and physical and mathematical symbols.

a) Technical terms

A technical term has a specific meaning within a specific field of expertise. Technical terms play a very important role in construing an uncommon sense field where the scientific knowledge is built. Examples of these entities in school physics context may be illustrated by the excerpts in Table 4. 20 in bold.

Table 4. 20   Technical Entities in School Physics Context

[*Start Science -Force and Motion*] (from Nunn, 2003: 20-22)
Friction
When two surfaces rub together, they make a force called friction. Smooth surfaces rubbing together make less friction than rough surfaces.
Picture search
Look for rough surfaces
Look for smooth surfaces
Slowing down
A book won't keep moving when you give it a push. The book rubs against the table and makes **friction.** **Friction** slows the book down and stops it.
Smooth surfaces
Ice skates and ice both have smooth surfaces. Ice skates slide easily over ice because they make very little **friction.**
Heat
When you have cold hands, rub them together. **Friction** makes heat so rubbing your hands together warms them up.
Rough surfaces
The sole of a snow boot has a rough surface. It makes **friction** as it rubs against the snow and stops you from slipping.

Technical entities realized by technical terms help us construe an uncommon sense field to construct scientific knowledge. Something needs to experience two processes to become technicality: distillation and transcendence of the text. That is to say, only experiencing distillation and transcendence, can technical terms become real scientific entities and help construing an uncommon-sense field for building scientific knowledge.

In the above excerpt, the scientific concept of **friction** develops as a technicality by experiencing the two processes of distillation and transcendence through which the uncommon-sense field is construed at the same time. **Friction** is not the renaming of force but refers to a different type of force which occurs when two things rub together. Whenever friction is mentioned in the following text, such as "less **friction**", "**Friction** slows the book down and stops it", "little **friction**", it is the distillation of its uncommon-sense meaning that needs to be understood. Every time it is understood as its distilled meaning, this term **friction** is getting a little nearer to become a permanent technicality. The reoccurring of the technical term **friction** shows us a scientific field, in other wors, whenever this term **friction** is talked in terms of its scientific meaning it construes students a field of physics.

(*b*) *Physical and mathematical symbols*

Besides technical terms, physical and mathematical symbols are indispensable to express scientific concepts. Mathematics is very important in science. Karl Marx has emphasized that, a subject can only become a science after it takes uses of mathematics successfully. Just like technical terms, the physical and mathematical symbols in primary school textbooks are also helping construing students a scientific field, which also experience two processes of distillation and transcendence.

As systemic and concise ways to express physical concepts, these symbols and formulas are highly condensed. They may contain a huge amount of information in short expressions, that is, the distillation of meanings. As the following example in Table 4.21 shows, force equation $\mathbf{F} = \mathbf{ma}$ makes Newton's second law of motion expressed so simply and accurately.

Table 4.21　Example of Mathematical Equation

> [*Motion*] (**from Farndon, 2003: 19**)
>
> Force equation
>
> The relationship between force (F), mass (m) and acceleration (a) is summed up in the equation: $F = ma$.
>
> This shows the force of an object depends on the combination of its mass and acceleration. This is why the impact of a slow moving truck and a fast moving bullet are equally devastating. Both have tremendous force-the truck because of its large mass, the bullet because of its huge acceleration. The equation can also be swapped: $a = F/m$

This equation $F = ma$ should be understood from three levels of its meaning. First, students should understand the three scientific concepts referred by (F) (force), m (mass) and a (acceleration). Second, students should know the quantity relationship among the symbols, which shows that the force of an object depends on the combination of its mass and acceleration. Third, the causative relationship implied by this equation $F = ma$ should be elucidated. In fact, Newton's second law of motion expressed by $F = ma$ emphasizes that it is force which causes the change of an object's state of motion, that is, it is force that causes acceleration. The mathematical equations with physical symbols mean more than these quantity relationships, so students should be taught something more beyond the quantity relationship expressed by the mathematical form of this equation and should grasp the deep meaning behind it.

The simple and concise equation can make the complex knowledge it conveys transcended easily and accurately late in the following texts. Therefore, only after fully understanding what the concise physical and mathematical symbols mean, can students grasp the complex and huge knowlege expressed in them fully. As condensation and abbreviation of physical concepts, they are indispensable to build the knowledge of physics.

In a word, there is a bidirectional relationship between technical entities and the scientific field. It is just these technical entities which construe a scientific field to construct physical knowledge.

(2) Metaphoric Entities

Technical entities help to pack the physical knowledge, while metaphoric entities are useful in achieving the process of knowledge packing. Metaphoric entities include two types: metaphoric process and metaphoric quality.

The large use of grammatical metaphors, particularly experiential metaphors, is an obvious characteristic within the scientific field (Martin, 1993e; Halliday & Martin 1993; Martin & Rose, 2007). The use of metaphoric processes move students from their common-sense field in which processes are construed congruently into a verb to an uncommon-sense field where processes are construed metaphorically into a noun. By means of grammatical metaphor the daily-life processes are transformed into abstract entities. Dead grammatical metaphors are excluded from metaphoric entities because they help construe technical entities. Examples of metaphoric process entities are shown in Table 4.22.

Table 4.22   Examples of Metaphoric Process Entities in School Physics Context

> **[*Motion*] (from Farndon, 2003)**
>
> Everything in the universe is moving. **Some movement** is really obvious, like a car speeding along a highway, or a ball bouncing on the pavement. **Other movement** is less noticeable, like the **whirling** of the earth beneath our feet or **the vibration** of tiny atoms.
>
> Without **movement** nothing would ever happen. Over the centuries scientists have given a great deal of **attention** and **effort** to how and why things move. In fact, there is a whole branch of science devoted to **the study** of **movement**, called dynamics. Scientists have discovered that nearly all **movement** obeys the same basic laws. Only things smaller than atoms behave differently.
>
> Scientists who study **movement** use the word "motion" because it has a particular meaning. Motion is the **change** in position and **orientation** of an object.

As the above example shows, the process *moving* is construed metaphorically as an abstract entity which is further classified into two types of *some movement* and *other movement* with its subtypes of *whirling* and *vibration*. When the *movement* is studied by scientists, it is replaced by a technical term *motion* which is further defined as *Motion is the change in position and orientation of an object* by means of using other metaphoric process entities. Without metaphoric process entities *movement*, ***change*** and ***orientation*** is no technical entity *motion* introduced, and hence is no scientific field construed to build scientific knowledge.

The entities of metaphoric quality (e. g. , *a quarter full*, *fit*, *length*, *good*, *depth*, *height*, *patience*, *strength*, *standstill*, *difference*) in school physics context occur only 14 times and can be ignored.

4.2.1.1.3 Pronouns

Entities realized by pronouns, common-sense and uncommon-sense entities are three main categories of entities in scientific discourses. Entities realized by pronouns include both indefinite pronouns and personal pronouns, playing a unique role in building the school physics field. Entities realized by indefinite pronouns include ten types, five of which are human ones "anyone, nobody, someone, anybody and each other" and the other five of which are inhuman ones "something, everything, anything, nothing and each".

(1) *Entities realized by indefinite pronouns*

All the entities realized by inhuman indefinite pronouns help to construe a scientific field. They function as generalization of a principle in explaining some physical phenomenon, which is expressed by means of deduction and induction. Examples of these entities used in a deductive way in school physics context are shown in Table 4.23.

(*a*) *Inhuman indefinite pronouns*

Table 4.23   Entities realized by indefinite inhuman pronouns in school physics context(1)

Inhuman indefinite pronouns:
Type 1 Deduction
Text 1 [*Forces and Moiton*] (**from Royston, 2002: 12-13**)
Forces can also be used to make something stop moving. This dog wants to move forward. Its owner is pulling it backward.
Pushing or pulling **something** that is moving can slow it down or stop it. The players in yellow are pulling the player in white. They are trying to stop him.
Text 2 [*What are forces and motion?*](**from Sarah, 2002: 5**)
Gravity pulls **everything** towards Earth. To fly, a plane must create enough lift to overcome gravity.

In the above two excerpts, **something** and **everything** are used in a deductive way to generalize the effects of "force". One of the force effects is to change the motion state of something, that is, to make it stop moving or slow down, which is construed as an accepted truth in physics mainly through indefinite pronoun **something** in the first excerpt at the primary school level. However, **something** is too generic a phenomenon for elementary students to understand. It is then exemplified by *this dog* and *the player in white* to construe a more concrete and common-sense field, and thus make the difficult physical knowledge easier for students to grasp in a familiar way to them. In the second excerpt, the element **everything** also plays a very important role in helping the figure "Gravity pulls **everything** towards the Earth" to construe students a scientific field. The abstraction caused by **everything** is lessened by the following example of *a plane*.

Besides the deductive way of constructing knowledge, entities realized by indefinite pronouns can also be used in an inductive manner, which can be illustrated by the following two excerpts, as Table 4. 24 shows.

Table 4. 24   Entities Realized by Indefinite Inhuman

Pronouns in School Physics Context (2)

Type 2 Induction
Text 1 [*Science-Forces and Moiton*] (**from Wilson, 2001: 4**)
Every time you ride a bike, turn the door handle or even just move your arm, you are using forces. They are the invisible pushes and pulls that make **everything** happen.
Text 2 [*Motion*] (**from Farndon, 2003: 24-25**)
Action and reaction
Every time two objects come in contact, they interact. As they touch, they exert forces on each other. When someone walks, their feet push down on the ground and the ground pushes back up with exactly the same force. If the ground reacted with any less force, the feet would sink into the ground. If the ground pushed harder, it would push the feet up.
When the oars of a boat push on the water, the water pushes back with equal force. If it did not react like this, only the water would move, and the boat would stay still. In fact, whenever **anything** moves or interacts, there is always this balance of opposing forces-an "action" force that pushes, and a "reaction" force that pushes back with exactly the same force in the opposite direction.

The first excerpt, which includes two sentences, is explaining one of the force effect, that is, to make something moving. In the first sentence, some concrete entities such as *a bike*, *the door handle* and *your arm* are offered to help construe a concrete and common-sense field, which familiarizes students with their everyday knowledge. In the following sentence, **everything** is used to help packing their everyday knowledge into a scientific principle, that is, "[T]hey

(= forces) are the invisible pushes and pulls that make **everything** happen". In the second excerpt, which explains *Action and reaction*, two examples of someone's walking and the oars of a boat pushing on the water are first described, then **anything** occurs to generalize these two specific phenomena into scientific knowledge "whenever **anything** moves or interacts, there is always this balance of opposing forces-an 'action' force that pushes, and a 'reaction' force that pushes back with exactly the same force in the opposite direction".

(*b*) *Human indefinite pronouns*

Unlike entities realized by inhuman pronouns, those realized by human indefinite pronouns do not contribute to construe the uncommon-sense field to construct scientific knowledge. Entities realized by human indefinite pronouns tend to construe a common-sense field, not helping building scientific knowledge by generalizing a common phenomenon but showing that it is not necessary or difficult to mention definite participants. They refer to participants who cannot or are not necessary to be pointed to exactly in doing experiments, which can be illustrated by the three excerpts in Table 4. 25.

Table 4. 25　Entities Realized by Human Idefinite Pronouns in School Physics Context

Text 1 [*Science-Forces and Moiton*] (**from Wilson, 2001**)
Nobody is quite sure what causes gravity, but without it we would all go flying off into space!
This experiment shows how centripetal force increases the faster something spins round. Find a space away from **anyone** else to do this!
Text 2 [*What are forces and motion*?] (**from Sarah, 2002: 13**)
Ask **someone** else to measure how long the elastic is when the canister is at the same height as the top of the books.
Text 3 [*Motion*] (**from Fardnon, 2003: 24, 29**)
Action and reaction
Every time two objects come in contact, they interact. As they touch, they exert forces on each other. When **someone** walks, their feet push down on the ground and the ground pushes back up with exactly the same force. If the ground reacted with any less force, the feet would sink into the ground. If the ground pushed harder, it would push the feet up.
Less than two centuries age, the fastest things **anybody** really knew about were birds.
Nobody had ever travelled faster than on a galloping horse

"Nobody", "anyone", "someone" and "anybody", the four entities realized by human indefinite pronouns in the above three excerpts, mean what they mean literally. They are a generic classification of human, referring to some person who need act as a participant in the processes but whom we cannot and need not exactly know he is. Therefore, they perform no generalizing role of packing concrete entities into a generic one to construct some scientific truth in the scientific field.

(2) *Entities Realized by Personal Pronouns*

Entities realized by personal pronouns include four types shown respectively by "we", "you", "yourself" and "us", which help to construe a common-sense field familiar to students in the following two ways. First, some participants realized by personal pronouns refer to students directly. Second, others may involve students into participating in the activities indirectly, that is to say, these entities realized by personal pronouns express a generic meaning referring to any human. Examples of the two functions performed by these entities in the school physics context are shown in Tables 4. 26 & 4. 27.

Table 4. 26 Entities Realized by Personal Pronouns in School Physics Context (1)

Type 1: entities referring to students directly
Text 1 [*Push and Pull*] (**from Riley, 2001: 10-11**)
An engine pulls a train. A tractor pulls a trailer. A dog pulls on its lead. Tim pulls on a jumper. Can you think of three more pulls?
Text 2 [*Science—Forces and Motion*] (**from Wilson, 2001: 4**)
Have **you** ever wondered why things move the way they do? What makes them start moving? Why do things fall when you drop them? Why is swimming so much harder than walking? **You** will discover answers to these questions, and many others, in this book.
Text 3 [*Start Science — Forces and Motion*] (**from Nunn, 2003: 7**)
Roll some old pop socks into a ball. Then ask an adult to help you tie on a length of sewing elastic.
Try things out for **yourself** —but see warnings below.
Don't use sharp or hot things or make mixtures by **yourself.**
You need: A box of things for your experiments, plastic bottles, cardboard tubes, poster putty, sticky tape, ruler, scissors, magnetic strip.

In the above excerpts, the entities realized by personal pronouns **you** and **yourself** help construing a common-sense field by referring to students directly in two ways: motivating students to have a deep reflection on the relevant knowledge and arousing their learning interests; involving them into doing the experiments.

In Text 1, four examples about one participant pulling another are given first, and then students expressed by the personal pronoun **you** are motivated to think about more such kind of experience. In Text 2, **you** also means students, but here they are not only motivated to have a further thinking but also interested. While in Text 3, **you** and **yourself** refer to students participating in the experiments to making a pop sockball. They seem to help construing a scientific field, but it exists more like a common-sense one since the materials used for the experiment are all daily concrete ones. The common-sense field provides a foundation for later scientific knowledge construction.

Table 4. 27   Entities Realized by Personal Pronouns in School Physics Context (2)

Type 2: entities expressing a generic meaning
Text 1 [*Science—Forces and Moiton*] (**from Wilson, 2001: 24**)
We say that ice is less dense than water, in other words a cube of ice weighs less than a cube of water the same size. So for so good, but how can a steel ship stay afloat?
Air and water resistance
It takes a lot of effort to swim. This is because **you** have to push the water out of your way as you move forwards. Then there's the friction of the water sliding against your skin, and the swirling water behind **you** trying to pull **you** back. Air has the same dragging effect, but **you** have to go faster before you really start to notice it. Drag isn't all-bad. However, if your arms and legs slid through the water without any resistance, **you** wouldn't be able to push **yourself** forwards in the first place!
Forces are all around **us**.
Text 2 [**Force and Motion**] (**from Royston, 2002: 11**)
You can move in many different ways. This woman is swimming. The muscles in her arms, legs, and feet make a force that moves her through the water.

As the above examples in Table 4. 27 show, the entities realized by personal pronouns (we, us, you, yourself) have a generic meaning, referring to all human beings. Their use helps construing a common-sense field by means of putting students into the imagined roles of participants in the processes and extending to other participants to build a kind of common-sense knowledge.

In Text 1, the generic **we** may refer to anyone or nobody and it just transmits to us a kind of supposed knowledge which will be offered in the following part of the sentence. Similarly, **you** appears in this text doesn't point to a certain person, the reader or the student, but implies anyone whoever swims in the water or goes in the air. It is just this sort of generic meaning conveyed by personal pronouns that provides a truthful sense for the built knowledge. **Us** in the sentence *Forces are all around us* fulfills the same generic function and can be replaced by **you** without changing too much meaning. In Text 2, the generic meaning implied by **you** is shown clearly by the illustration of *this woman*, who is just one of the examples of you in the above sentence.

4.2.1.2 Variations of Entities in Knowledge Building

As the sub-fields of the whole school physics field, the lower primary school physics field, the upper primary school physics field and the junior school physics field share some similarities in building knowledge by means of entities. At the same time, as an independent sub-field, each shows different entity patterns in knowledge building. The following section will show and discuss the variations of entities in knowledge building across the whole school physics field.

4.2.1.2.1 Variations of Common-sense Entities in Buiding Knowledge

In school physics field, common-sense entities play a very important role in the illustration of a theory or the description of experiments. Therefore, they are necessary to be used for building knowledge. However, with the school physics subfields getting more and more uncommon-sensed from the lower school level to the higher school level, the common-sensence entities are supposed to occur decreasingly, which is in fact proved so. The distribution of common-sense entities at the three school levels is shown in Table 4.28 numerically and in Figure 4.2 visually.

Table 4.28 The Frequency of Common-sense Entities Across Three School Physics Sub-fields

Kinds of Entities	Occurrence-Frequency(×1000)					
	Sub-field Level 1		Sub-field Level 2		Sub-field Level 3	
	4168 words		19658 words		21332 words	
Common sense	715	171.55	2928	148.95	2877	134.87

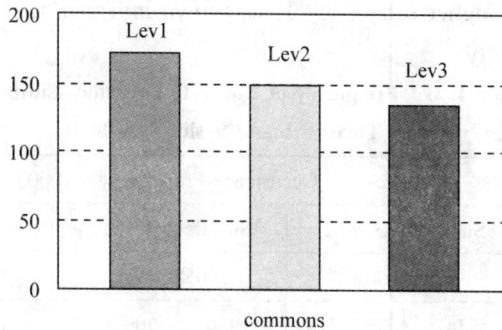

**Figure 4. 2　The Variation of Common-sense Entities
Across Three School Physics Sub-fields**

As shown in Table 4. 28 and Figure 4. 2, common-sense entities tend to distribute decreasingly across the textbooks from the lower school level to the higher school level, with 171. 55/1000 in the lower primary school physics context, 148. 95/1000 in the upper primary school physics context and 134. 87/1000 in the junior school physics context. The decreasing frequency of common-sense entities means that there is a less and less focus on daily-life participants and things with the rising of school physics field to a higher level. From the lower primary school physics field to the upper primary school physics field and then to the junior school physics field, the common-sense entities in these fields are becoming fewer and fewer.

However, as to the different subtypes of common-sense entities, their frequency is not changing along the same line across the three school physics sub-fields. The frequency of concrete everyday entities is rising across the three school physics sub-fields, while that of both generic and semiotic entities is decreasing up the three levels of physics, which reflects the variation of types of common-sense entities in building knowledge across different levels of physics textbooks. This will be examined in the following part.

(1) *Variations of Concrete Everyday Entities Across Three Levels of Textbooks*

One of the main sub-types of common-sense entities, concrete everyday entities realized by common nouns and proper nouns, are decreasing their number of occurrences with the school physics sub-fields developing from the lower school level to the higher school level, as shown in Table 4.29 numerically and in Figure 4.3 visually.

Table 4.29　Frequency of Concrete Everyday Entities

Across Three School Physics Sub-fields

Kinds of Entities	Occurrence-Frequency(×1000)					
	Sub-field Level 1		Sub-field Level 2		Sub-field Level 3	
	4168 words		19658 words		21332 words	
Concrete everyday	574	137.716	1956	99.959	1679	78.707

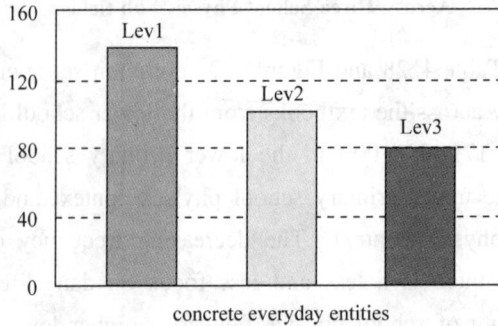

Figure 4.3　Variations of Concrete Everyday Entities

Across Three School Physics Sub-fields

As shown in Table 4.29 and Figure 4.3, there is a decreasing occurrence of concrete everyday entities across the three school phyisics sub-fields, with 137.716/1000 in the lower primary school physics context, 99.959/1000 in the upper primary school physics context and 78.708/1000 in the junior school physics context. This implies that fewer and fewer daily-life participants are talked about in textbooks of the higher school level. In other words, from the lower school physics context to the upper school physics context and then to the junior school physics context, concrete everyday entities are getting fewer and fewer. It means a shift of knowledge from the common-sense kind in the lower school level sub-field to the scientific type in the higher school level sub-field. The knowledge constructed in the higher school level sub-field is lifted above everyday contexts.

(2) *Variations of Generic Entities Across Three Levels of Textbooks*

Generic entities, another main sub-type of common-sense entities, are increasing their occurrence from the lower level of school physics sub-field to the upper level of school physics sub-field, as shown in Table 4. 30 numerically and in Figure 4. 4 visually.

Table 4. 30   Frequency of Generic Entities Across Three School Physics Sub-fields

Kinds of Entities	Occurrence-Frequency(×1000)					
	Sub-field Level 1		Sub-field Level 2		Sub-field Level 3	
	4168 words		19658 words		21332 words	
Genericc entities	139	33. 349	920	46. 8	1109	51. 99

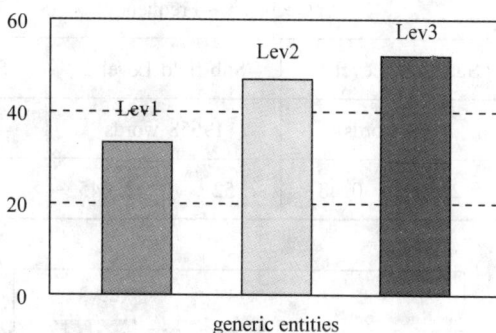

**Figure 4. 4   Variations of Generic Entities
Across Three School Physics Sub-fields**

As Table 4. 30 and Figure 4. 4 display, the frequency of generic entities rises from 33. 349/1000 in the lower primary school physics context to 46. 8/1000 in the upper primary school physics context and to 51. 99/1000 in the junior school physics context. This increasing occurrence of generic entities across the three school phyisics sub-fields suggests that more and more participants are construed either as a class of people or things or as an abstract phenomenon along the schooling. From the lower school physics context to the upper school physics context and then to the junior school physics context, generic entities occur more and more in these fields. It means that the way of knowledge building is shifting from a proper and concrete kind in the lower school level sub-field to a general and abstract type in the higher school level sub-field. The knowledge constructed in the higher school level sub-field is more general and abstract than that in the

141

lower school level sub-field.

· (3) *Variations of Semiotic Entities Across Three Levels of Physics Text-books*

Semiotic entities, a less important sub-type of common-sense entities, take a very small percentage on the whole. They are the least occurring entities at the lower and upper primary school physics fields, and the second least occurring ones at junior school physics field. Their distribution in the three school physics sub-fields can be shown in Table 4. 31 numerally and in Figure 4. 5 visually.

Table 4. 31   Frequency of Semiotic Entities Across Three School Physics Sub-fields

Kinds of Entities	Occurrence-Frequency(× 1000)					
	Sub-field Level 1		Sub-field Level 2		Sub-field Level 3	
	4168 words		19658 words		21332 words	
Semiotic entities	2	0. 48	52	2. 645	89	4. 17

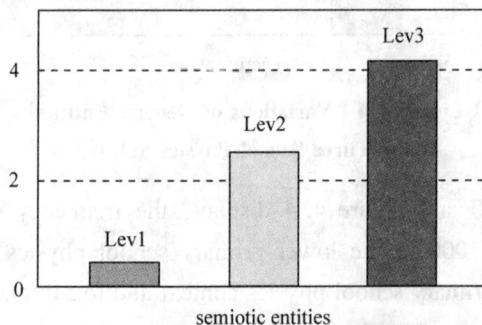

Figure 4. 5   Variations of Semiotic Entities Across Three School Physics Sub-fields

As Table 4. 31 and Figure 4. 5 illustrate, there is a frequency of 0. 48/1000 for semiotic entities in the lower primary school physics context, 2. 645/1000 in the upper primary school physics context and 4. 17/1000 in the junior school physics context. From the lower school physics context to the upper school physics context and then to the junior school physics context, semioic entities appear more and more in these fields.

Semiotic entities, such as *answers*, *story*, *idea* and *questions*, are the condensation of linguistic meanings, which is shown in Table 4.32.

Table 4.32　Semiotic Entities in School Physics Field

[*Push and Pull*] (**from Riley, 2001**: **16-17**)

Squash and stretch

A push can squash something. You push on clay to squash it flat. A pull can stretch something. You pull an elastic band to stretch it. Karen squashes a balloon. What will happen to the balloon? Jessica stretches a lump of clay. What will happen to the clay? Think about both **answers** before turning the page to find out what happens.

[*Science-Forces and Motion*] (**from Wilson, 2001**: **11**)

FLASHBACK

Galileo's story In the 1590s, an Italian Scientist called Galileo wondered if things would fall at the same speed regardless of how heavy they were,

He tested his **idea** by dropping cannon balls of different weights from the Leaning Tower of Pisa. They always took the same time to hit the ground. His experiment got him into trouble with the Pope, who did not approve of his scientific approach to answering **questions**!

This increasing occurrence of semiotic entities across the three school physics sub-fields also suggests that the knowledge constructed at the higher school level sub-field is more general and abstract.

4.2.1.2.2 The Variation of Uncommon-sense Entities in Building Knowledge

In school physics field, common-sense entities are used for eliminating students' alienation to scientific concepts by means of illustrating the theory or describing the experiments. However, uncommon-sense entities, which occupy a small proportion of the whole entities, are playing a more important role in building the scientific concept of **force** and **motion** because they lead to construe the uncommon-sense field. Therefore, with the school physics subfields getting more uncommon-sensed from the lower school level to the upper school level, the uncommon-sense entities is supposed to occur increasingly, which is in fact proved so. This can be shown in Table 4.33 numerically and in Figure 4.6 visually.

**Table 4.33   The Frequency of Uncommon-sense Entities
Across Three School Physics Sub-fields**

Kinds of Entities	Occurrence-Frequency(×1000)					
	Sub-field Level 1		Sub-field Level 2		Sub-field Level 3	
	(**4168** words)		(**19658** words)		(**21332** words)	
uncommon-sense	163	39.11	990	50.36	1435	60.27

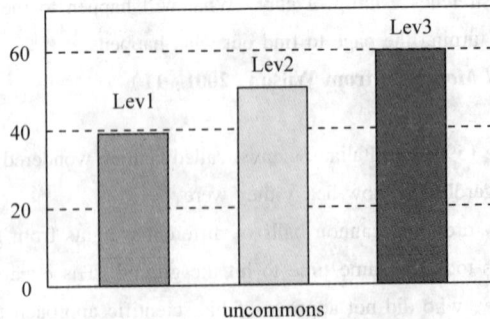

**Figure 4.6   Variation of Uncommon-sense Entities
Across Three School Physics Sub-fields**

As Table 4.33 and Figure 4.6 show, there is an increasing occurrence of uncommon-sense entities across three levels of physics textbooks, with 39.11/1000 in the lower primary school physics context, 50.36/1000 in the upper primary school physics context and 60.27/1000 in the junior school physics context. The increasing frequency of uncommon-sense entities means that there is a more and more focus on participants and things which occur in the scientific field with the the rising of physics to a higher level. From the lower school physics context to the upper school physics context and then to the junior school physics context, the uncommon-sense entities in these fields are used more and more.

Uncommon-sense entities occur with an increasing tendency from the lower primary school physics subfield to the junior school physics subfield. However, as to the different subtypes of uncommon-sense entities, which include technical ones, specialized ones and metaphoric ones, the changing tendency of their frequencies is not along the same line across the three school physics sub-fields. The occurring frequency of metaphoric entities and entities realized by technical terms is rising across the three school physics sub-fields, while that of entities realized by mathematical and physical symbos is declining. The occurring frequency of specialized entities has a rising tendency from the lower primary school physics sub-field to the upper primary school physics subfield, and then shows a decreasing tendency from the upper primary school physics subfield to the junior school physics subfield. The variation of subtypes of uncommon-sense entities reflects the various ways of knowledge building in physics textbooks at different school levels. The following section focuses on this aspect.

(1) *Variations of Metaphoric Entities in Building Knowledge*

Metaphoric entities include two types, metaphoric processes and metaphoric qualities, of which the former takes a larger percentage than the latter.

(a) *Variations of Metaphoric Process Entities in Building Knowledge*

As the school physics sub-fields develop from the lower school level to the higher school level, there is an increasing occurrence of metaphoric process entities, which can be seen clearly from Table 4.34 numerically and Figure 4.7 visually.

Table 4.34　The Frequency of Metaphoric Process Entities
Across Three School Physics Sub-fields

Kinds of Entities	Occurrence-Frequency ($\times 1000$)					
	Sub-field Level 1		Sub-field Level 2		Sub-field Level 3	
	(4168 words)		(19658 words)		(21332 words)	
Metahoric process	30	7.198	158	8.037	296	13.88

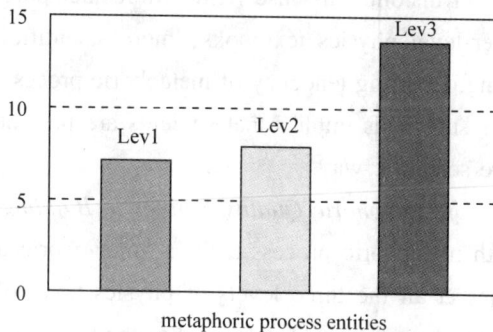

Figure 4.7　Variation of Metaphoric Process Entities
Across Three School Physics Sub-fields

As Table 4.34 and Figure 4.7 show, metaphoric process entities in these fields show themselves more and more, with 7.198/1000 at the lower primary school physics subfield, 8.037/1000 at the upper primary school physics subfield and 13.88/1000 at the junior school physics subfield.

The entities realized by metaphoric processes wrap up the meaning of verbs into nouns to make the introduction of technical concepts possible, as the text in Table 4.35 illustrates. The metaphoric process entities are in bold.

Table 4.35　Metaphoric Process Entities Helping the Introduction of Technical Concepts

[*Forces and Motion*] (**from Royston, 2002: 4-5**)

What Is a Force?

A force makes things move. These people are moving a piano. One man is pushing it. The other man is pulling it.

Pulls and **pushes** are forces. This girl is pushing down on the pedals to make the bicycle move forward.

In the above text which introduces the concept "force", metaphoric process entities "pulls" and "pushes" are acting as an intermediate. The processes "pushing" and "pulling" cannot be directly related to the concept "force". They must become as entities first through metaphoric processes and then have the opportunity to function as the attributes of the concept "force". The entities realized by metaphoric processes play an important role in introducing technicalities, helping to construe an uncommon-sense field. More metaphoric process entities are used at a higher-level physics textbooks, more scientific a field they construe. The increasing occurring tendency of metaphoric process entities across the three school physics sub-fields implies that students are presented the knowledge in a more and more scientific way.

(*b*) *Variations of Metaphoric Quality Entities in Building Knowledge*

Contrasted with metaphoric process entities, metaphoric quality entities occur only a few times at all the three levels of physics textbooks. As the school physics sub-fields develop from the lower level to the upper level, there is an increasing occurrence of metaphoric process entities, as shown in Table 4.36 numerically and in Figure 4.8 visually.

Table 4. 36　The Frequency of Metaphoric Quality Entities

Across Three School Physics Sub-fields

Kinds of Entities	Occurrence-Frequency (×1000)					
	Sub-field Level 1		Sub-field Level 2		Sub-field Level 3	
	4168 words		19658 words		21332 words	
metaphoric quality	2	0. 48	30	1. 526	35	1. 64

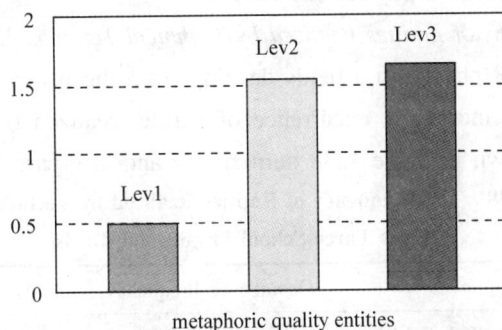

Figure 4. 8　Variation of Metaphoric Quality Entities

Across Three School Physics Sub-fields

As Table 4. 36 and Figure 4. 8 show, metaphoric quality entities in these fields show themselves in an increase tendency, with 0. 480/1000 at the lower primary school physics subfield, 1. 526/1000 at the upper primary school physics subfield and 1. 640/1000 at junior school physics subfield.

Metaphoric quality entities help to construe the school physics field in an un-common-sense way, but they do not contribute much to technicality introduction. There are a few of them occurring in school physics fields, as Table 4. 37 shows.

Table 4. 37　Metaphoric Quality Entities Occurring in School Physics Field

	Metaphoric Quality Entities
lower school physics sub-fiels	length
upper school physics sub-field	Depth, difference, fit, a quarter full, good, height, patience, strength, tendency
junior school physics sub-field	ability (of an object), accuracy, beauty, confidence, depth, difference, efficiency (of the lever), height, length, potential, pressure differences, stability (of an object), standstill, strength and flexibility, tension

147

(2) *Variations of Technical Entities in Building Knowledge*

Technical entities are very important in the scientific field in that scientific concepts are distilled by them. They include two subtypes: technical terms, and mathematical and physical symbols. For entities realized by technical terms, their occurrence is rising across the three school physics sub-fields, while for entities realized by mathematical and physical symbols, their occurrence is declining across these three school physics sub-fields.

(a) *Variations of Entities Realized by Technical Terms in Knowledge Building*

As the school physics sub-fields develop from the lower level to the upper level, there is an increasing occurrence of entities realized by technical terms, which can be shown in Table 4.38 numerically and in Figure 4.9 visually.

Table 4.38   The Frequency of Entities Realized by Technical Terms
Across Three School Physics Sub-fields

Kinds of Entities	Occurrence-Frequency (×1000)					
	Sub-field Level 1		Sub-field Level 2		Sub-field Level 3	
	4168 words		19658 words		21332 words	
Technical terms	92	22.073	662	33.676	1020	47.82

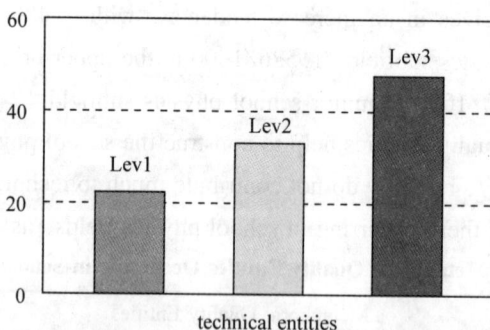

Figure 4.9   Variation of Entities Realized by Technical Terms
Across Three School Physics Sub-fields

As Table 4.38 and Figure 4.9 display, entities realized by technical terms in these fields show themselves in an increasing tendency, with 22.073/1000 at the lower primary school physics subfield, 33.676/1000 at the upper primary school physics subfield and 47.82/1000 at the junior school physics subfield.

Technical terms, which are the meaning condensation of scientific concepts, help construing a scientific field by means of organizing them into taxonomies. According to Halliday (1989), technical taxonomies are one of the main difficulties that are characteristic of scientific English. He points out that their complexity lies in that technical taxonomies "are not simply groups of related terms; they are highly ordered constructions in which every term has a definite functional value" (Halliday, 1989: 164). It is these technical taxonomies which make the field sound more scientific. The much more use of technical terms in higher-level physics textbooks suggests that a more uncommon-sense field is set up.

(b) *Variations of Entities Realized by Mathematical and Physical Symbols in Knowledge Building*

Entities realized by mathematical and physical symbols do not appear at the lower primary school sub-field. Their occurrence decreases a little from the upper primary school physics sub-field to the junior school physics sub-field, as is shown in Table 4.39 numerically and in Figure 4.10 visually.

Table 4.39 The Frequency of Entities Realized by Mathematical and Physical Symbols Across Three School Physics Sub-fields

Kinds of Entities	Occurrence-Frequency (× 1000)					
	Sub-field Level 1		Sub-field Level 2		Sub-field Level 3	
	4168 words		19658 words		21332 words	
Mathematicl and physical symbols	0	0	38	1.933	41	1.92

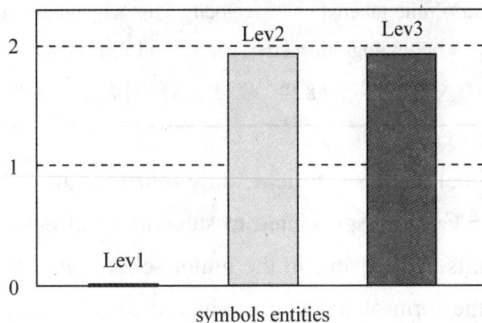

Figure 4.10 Variation of Entities Realized by Mathematical and Physical Symbols Across Three School Physics Sub-fields

149

As shown in Table 4. 39 and Figure 4. 10, entities realized by mathematical and physical symbols in these fields show themselves in an increasing tendency from the upper school physics context to the junior school physics context, with 1. 933/1000 for the former, 1. 92/1000 for the latter.

Although there is no big difference in the occurrence of entities realized by mathematical and physical symbols between the upper primary school physics sub-field and the junior school physics sub-field, these entities are expressed in a more complex form in the latter sub-field, that is, more formulas are used. This can be shown clearly by Table 4. 40.

Table 4. 40   Entities Realized by Mathematical and Physical

Symbols in School Physics Field

	Entities realized by mathematical and physical symbols
upper school physics sub-field	$a = (v - u)/t$, $v = u + at$, $F = ma$, $a = F/m$, poundals, $g = (9. 8m/s^2)$, 'kilograms, kg, 'pounds, GRAMS, newtons, Kilometer, 63km/h, kilometers per hour, (kph), miles per hour, (mph), meters per second, m/s
junior school physics sub-field	6 x 108 kg, weight on Earth = mass in kilograms × 10, weight on planet = weight on Earth × strength of gravity, kilograms, newtons (N), work = force x distance, joules (J), Work (joules) = Force(newtons) ∗ Distance (metres), the kilojoule (1 kJ = 1,000J), mega joule (1 MJ = 1,000,000J) mega, Force due to gravity = weight =9. 8 ∗ mass, kinetic energy = $1/2mv^2$, metres per second (m/s) : distance (m)/time taken (s) = velocity (m/s), momentum = mass x velocity = mv, kilogram-metres per second (kg m/s), momentum = mv = 5. 6 x 4 = 22. 4 kg m/s, $mv = (m1v1) + (m2v2)$

In the upper school physics sub-field, only four formulas $\mathbf{a} = (v - u)/t, \mathbf{v} = \mathbf{u} + \mathbf{at}$, $\mathbf{F} = \mathbf{ma}$, $\mathbf{a} = \mathbf{F/m}$ are presented to students, and other symbols are all about the physical units. However, in the junior school physics sub-field, most of the symbols are in the form of formulas, which means the knowledge constructed at this physics level is becoming more abstract and scientific.

(3) *Variations of Specialized Entities in Building Knowledge*

150

Specialized entities, referring to those instruments (such as pulley, gear or force magnifier) used in physical experiments, has a changing frequency of occurrence across the three school physics sub-fields, as is shown in Table 4. 41 numerically and in Figure 4. 11 visually.

Table 4. 41   The Frequency of Specialized Entities Across Three School Physics Sub-fields

Kinds of Entities	Occurrence-Frequency (×1000)					
	Sub-field Level 1		Sub-field Level 2		Sub-field Level 3	
	(4168 words)		(19658 words)		(21332 words)	
Specialized entities	11	2. 639	85	4. 324	43	2. 02

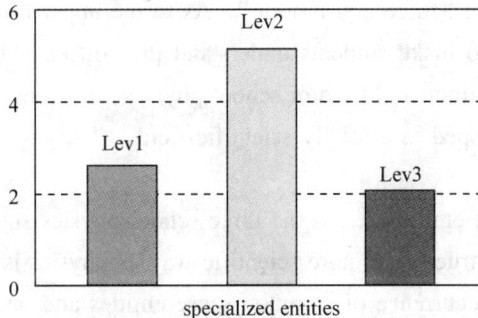

Figure 4. 11   Variation of Specialized Entities Across Three School Physics Sub-fields

As Table 4. 41 and Figure 4. 11 display, the occurrence frequency of specialized entities is 2. 639/1000 in the lower primary school physics sub-field, then rising to 4. 324/1000 in the upper primary school physics sub-field, and declining to 2. 02/1000 in the junior school physics sub-field.

The occurrence of specialized entities from rising to declining depends on the nature and purpose of each level of the school physics. Table 4. 42 summarizes specialized entities at the three levels of physics subfields.

Table 4. 42　Types of Specialized Entities at the Three Levels of Physics

	Specialized Entities
lower school physics sub-fiels	lever, pulley, experiments
upper school physics sub-field	bubble chamber, double pulley, experiment, force magnifiers, force meter, gears, laser lights, laser satellite trackers, lever, movement magnifiers, pulleys, radar waves
junior school physics sub-field	ailerons, elevators, experiment, flaps, force measurer, force meter, lever, newton meter, physics experiment, rudder

For the lower primary school physics, its aim is to offer students a sense of the scientific concept "force and motion". As to the upper primary school physics, its purpose is to make students understand the concept "force and motion" through doing experiments. In junior school physics, the concept "force and motion" should be grasped in a totally scientific field.

4. 2. 1. 3 Summary

The analysis of entities across the three school physics sub-fields shows that the sub-field is construed in a more scientific way as physics is taught at a higher school level. The occurrence of common-sense entities and uncommon-sense entities at three levels of textbooks is shown in Table 4. 43.

Table 4. 43　The Frequency of Common-sense Entities and Uncommon-sense Entities

Kinds of Entities	Occurrence-Frequency(×1000)					
	Level one		Level two		Level three	
	(4168 words)		(19658 words)		(21332 words)	
Common sense	715	171. 55	2928	148. 95	2877	134. 87
uncommon sense	163	39. 11	990	50. 36	1435	60. 27
Common sense/uncommon sense	4. 39	2. 96	2. 23			

As shown in Table 4. 43, the frequency of common-sense entities (171. 55/1000) is 4. 39 times more than that of uncommon-sense ones (39. 11/1000) in textbooks of the first school level. This suggests that, although students are oriented into a scientific discourse of physics, the knowledge of "force and motion" is built in a more common-sense way in the lower primary school physics sub-field. In the upper primary school physics subfield, few common-sense entities are used and their frequency (148. 95/1000) is only 2. 96 times more than that of uncommon-sense ones (50. 36/1000), which shows that the scientific knowledge of "force and motion" at this level of physics textbooks is constructed in a less common-sense way. In the junior school physics subfield, the use of common-sense entities is continuously dropping and their frequency (134. 87/1000) is only 2. 23 times more than that of uncommon-sense ones (60. 27/1000), which implies that the way to build scientific knowledge of "force and motion" is getting more and more uncommon-sense in textbooks of this school level.

The important physical concept "force and motion" tends to be constructed from a more common-sense way to a more uncommon-sense manner, which matches with the nature of this concept and with students' intelligence level.

"Force", a basic but difficult concept in physics, means an interaction between two objects. For students of the lower primary schools, it is difficult to understand the abstract concept "force" since it cannot be sensed directly and what we can sense about it is only the two objects and the effects of the force, so more common-sense entities need to be used for eliminating students' alienation to this concept. For students of higher school levels, their rough and intuitive understanding of the concept "force and motion" needs to be deepened by means of a more scientific way of instruction, that is, the knowledge should be constructed in an uncommon field with less occurrence of common-sense entities.

On the whole, both common-sense entities and uncommon-sense entities in physics textbooks play their important roles in presenting the concept of "force and motion". Common-sense entities help to construe students a common-sense field to recontextualize the scientific knowledge in a way familiar to their life, and uncommon-sense entities realize the construction of scientific knowledge.

Besides entities, activities realized by processes are another component of field, which will be studied in the following section.

4.2.2 Building Knowledge Through Activities

With an aim to explore ways of knowledge building, this section focuses on processes which realize another dimension of field—activities. Field, in SFL's perspective, is taken as a set of activity sequences, and each step in each of these activity sequences must be involved in configurations of processes. Halliday and Matthiessen (2004: 323) adopt the term "domain model" to refer to the ideational semantic correlate of a particular field, that is, a particular domain model specifies the ideational semantics of a particular field. Halliday and Matthiessen (2004: 323) continue to contend that "[E] ach field thus has its own semantic profile, which can be seen against the background of the overall semantic potential".

Therefore, the domain models of three different sub-fields of school physics must have their own semantic characterization respectively, which can be illustrated by means of an analysis of variations of process types. In the analysis, all the clauses in textbooks, including both ranked and unranked ones, are analyzed in terms of the six processes, which are respectively material, mental, relational, behavioral, verbal and existential ones. Then, the percentage of each process type in all the six ones is calculated. In the analysis of this study, several significant characteristics of processes are found obvious in building physical knowledge across the three levels of textbooks.

First, the top three often-occurring processes are material, relational and mental in order, among which the first type is predominating in physics textbooks, which can be shown by Table 4.44 numerically and Figure 4.12 visually.

Table 4.44　Processes Variations in Physics Textbooks

Textbooks	Sum of Processes	Occurrence-frequency										
		Material		Relational		Mental		Behavioural		Verbal		Existential	
Level1	523	403	0.77	89	0.17	14	0.03	8	0.02	6	0.01	3	0.01
Level2	2396	1622	0.68	609	0.25	93	0.04	12	0.01	38	0.02	22	0.01
Level3	2723	1613	0.59	814	0.30	164	0.06	27	0.01	78	0.03	27	0.01

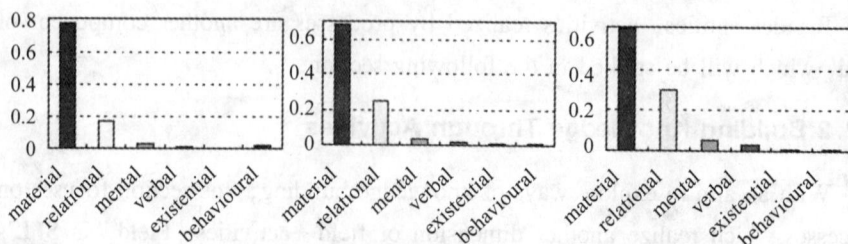

Figure 4.12　Processes at Three Levels of Physics Textbooks

As Table 4. 44 and Figure 4. 12 present, material, relational and mental processes play a very important role in building physical knowledge. For textbooks of Level 1, the total percentage of material processes and relational processes reaches 94%, with 77% to the former and 17% to the latter. For textbooks of Level 2, the total percentage of material processes and relational processes is 93%, with 68% to the former and 25% to the latter. For textbooks of Level 3, the total percentage of material processes and relational processes shows 89%, with 59% to the former and 30% to the latter.

Halliday (1994: 107) points out that "[M]aterial, mental and relational are the three main types of process in the English transitivity system". However, this research shows that material processes occur the most frequently in physics textbooks, and that mental ones take up less percentage. This means that, in the whole field of school physics, the domain model features figures of "doing" and "being" although there is a percentage variation between them across the three levels of textbooks. In other words, material processes and relational processes which are mainly composed of the activity sequences help construing the school physics field.

Second, each type of processes shows a regular occurrence tendency (either increasing or decreasing or constant) across the three levels of physics textbooks, which reflects the differences among the three school physics sub-fields.

Material processes keep their frequency going down from school physics Level 1 to school physics Level 3, in the order of 77%, 68%, 59%, while relational processes have their occurrence rising from17% to 25% to 30%. This is illustrated by Figure 4. 13 and Figure 4. 14.

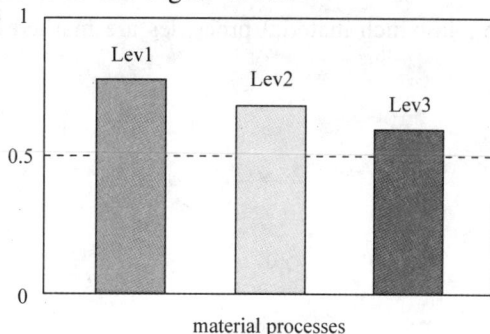

material processes

Figure 4. 13　Frequency Change of Material Processes in Physics Textbooks

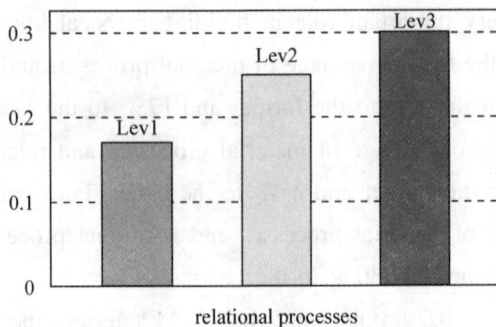

Figure 4.14   Frequency Change of Relational Processes in Physics Textbooks

The different occurrences of material and relational processes at three levels of textbooks show that the three sub-fields of school physics distinguish each other by activities. From the perspective of knowledge building, the differences among the three sub-fields of physics means that figures of "doing" is gradually less focused on and figures of "being" is more emphasized from the lower-level textbooks to the higher-lever textbooks.

The reason for more figures of "being" than those of "doing" at the higher school level lies in that ways for building the knowledge "force and motion" vary across the three physics levels. At the lower primary school level, the abstract concept "force and motion" is not described and explained directly to students, but it is introduced to students indirectly with more daily life experience. The concept "force and motion" is mainly construed in "doing" processes to help students sensing the effects of force. This can be shown by the excerpt in Table 4.45, in which material processes are marked in bold and other processes in italics.

Table 4.45   Excerpt of Material Processes in Textbooks of Level 1

[*Force and Motion*] (**from Royston, 2002: 18-21**)

Getting Faster

The harder you **push** something, the faster **it moves**. This girl **is pushing** a toy train across the floor. If she **gives** it a bigger push, it **will move** faster.

These runners **are working** hard **to run** as fast as they **can**. Their feet **push** down and backward on the ground. This **pushes** them up and forward.

Slope

A slope **can change** how fast something moves. This girl **is skateboarding** down a slope. The steeper the slope [*is*], the faster she **will move**.

This girl **is pushing** her wheelbarrow up a slope. She will **have to push** harder than she **did** on flat ground.

The above short text is showing to students the phenomenon which can be explained in Newton's second law: the acceleration depends on mass and force, that is, how heavy the object is and how hard it is being pushed or pulled. As the text shows, all the clauses are taking material processes except the clause "[T]he steeper the slope is" which is relational. In this way, students can have a clear understanding of the relationship between force and motion although not in strict terms of Newton's law, that is, harder push will cause something move faster. The abstract concept force is transformed into a common-sense experience of pushing, and the state of motion into a sensible phenomenon of moving faster. This makes the abstract physical knowledge accessible to students. In a word, more material processes are used to construe the daily-life "doing" activities at the lower level of school physics, which helps students understand the abstract scientific knowledge.

In the upper primary school physics field, students get access to the concept "force and motion" mainly by means of participating in the experiment, which still needs be construed in "doing" processes, but this abstract concept is described and explained on its own more and more in terms of other processes. This can be shown by the following excerpt in Table 4.46, in which material processes are marked in bold and other processes in italics.

Table 4.46   Excerpt of Material and Other Processes in Textbooks of Level 2

[*Science—Forces and Motion*] (**from Wilson, 2001: 14**)

Air pressure

The force of the air **pressing** on things *is called* air pressure. Although you *can't see* air pressure, you *can see* its effect with this quick experiment.

1. **Fill** the tumbler right up to the brim with water and slide the card over the top.

2. **Hold** the card against the tumbler with your other hand. **Get hold of** the tumbler with your other hand.

You *will need*

A plastic tumbler

A sink

A sheet of thin, stiff plastic or unwanted postcard

3. **Holding** the card in place, **turn** the tumbler upside down over the sink. **Let go of** the card. It should **stay put**, **held up** by nothing but air pressure!

What's **going on**?

Air pressure **pushes** in all directions, including upwards. It *is* easily strong enough **to hold up** the weight of the water in a tumbler. The card *acts* as a seal, *keeping* the air out of the tumbler as you **turn** it upside down. In fact, the air **is pressing** in on every square centimeter of your body with a force of about 10N, the same as the weight of a 1kg bag of sugar. You **are not crushed** because your body **is pushing** back with an equal, opposite force.

The above short text, which is chosen from one of the textbooks of Level 2, is explaining to students one of the forces "air pressure" by means of a quick experiment. Besides material processes, relational and mental processes exist in the text. The material processes construe the experience of doing the test, the relational processes are used in defining the concept "air pressure" and explaining the result of the experiment, and the mental processes orientate students to the effects of "air pressure" in the experiment. In this way, students can have a general understanding of the abstract concept "air pressure" which cannot be sensed by them directly but can indirectly through observing its effects shown in the experiment. On the whole, figures of "doing" realized by material processes at the upper-level school physics are still used for helping students understanding the abstract scientific knowledge by means of experiments, while figures of "being" realized by relational processes are mainly for explaining the abstract

158

concept itself.

At the junior school physics level, although experiments are still indispensable in helping students understanding the concept "force and motion", more technical meanings and taxonomical relationships among them need to be construed in "being" processes. This can be shown by the following excerpt in Table 4. 47, in which material processes are marked in bold, relational processes in bold italics, mental processes in italics and behavioral processes in bracket.

Table 4.47   Processes at the Junior School Physics Level

[*Exploring: Forces and Structure*] (**from Spiders, 1991: 8-9**)

Forces all around us

Different forces *produce* different effect. They *are* easy **to spot** when you *know* what to (look for).

Gravity *is* the name we **give** to the force that **pulls** everything towards the Earth. This force **causes a book to fall** when it **is pushed** over the edge of a table, and a ball **to roll** downs a hill. It *is* also the force that **enables us to keep our feet planted** firmly on the ground.

When surfaces **rub** against each other, they *create* a force *called* friction. The friction between your shoes and the floor **stops you from slipping** when you **run** about , but it also **makes the soles and heels of your shoes wear out** (see page 22).

When two people **play** "tug-of-war" with a rope, they **are putting** the rope under tension. This *is* another force. The person *causing* the most tension **will win** the game. The opposite force to tension *is called* compression and *to exert* this force you **have to push** rather than pull. If you **squash** an empty can, you **have compressed** it.

Magnetic force, as the name *suggests*, *is to do* **with** magnets and the pushes and pulls they *can produce*. The Earth has lines of magnetic force **running** around it and we **use** them when **finding** direction with a compass (see page 14).

Static electricity *causes* electrostatic force. Sometimes, when you **are taking off** a nylon garment, you *can feel* the tiny hairs on your arms **stand up**. It *is* electrostatic force that **is making them do** this (see page 16). Forces often *go* unnoticed because they act against each other. A book (resting) on a table *will stay* there without moving for as long as you **leave it**. We *know* that gravity **is trying to pull** the book towards the Earth, so why does it **not move**? The answer *is* that the table itself **exerts** a force. This force **acts upwards to balance** exactly the weight of the book. In other words, as the book **pushes** down, the table **pushes** back and the book *stays* where it *is*. Of course, if the book **exerts** too much force, the table **will break**!

续表

ACTIVITY

YOU *NEED*

- **a large piece of Plasticine**

1. **Warm** the Plasticine in your hands so that it *is* soft. **Roll** it into three identical balls.

2. **Drop** one of the balls of Plasticine on to the floor from the height of your knee.

3. **Pick up** the Plasticine carefully and (examine) it. What **has happened** to the Plasticine? What forces **have acted** on the Plasticine to **make this happen**?

4. **Drop** the second ball of Plasticine from the height of your shoulder.

5. **Drop** the third ball from as high as you **can reach**.

6. (Compare) all three balls carefully. What do you *notice*? Why *are* they different?

TEST YOURSELF

1. What type of force *results from* surfaces **rubbing** against each other?

2. What *causes* electrostatic force?

3. If two equal forces **work** against each other, what **will happen**?

The above text, which is chosen from one of the physics textbooks at the junior school level, is explaining to students several types of forces (gravity, friction, tension, compression and electrostatic force) and the effects they produce. When these specific kinds of forces are defined, the relationship between them and force must be described, which is usually construed by figures of being realized in relational processes. As the example illustrates, relational processes are used for their definition and for explaining their effects. Material processes are used again for construing the experience of doing the test and illustrating the concepts. Behavioral and mental processes elaborate the abstract knowledge by ways of concrete examples.

In a word, as more and more abstract knowledge is required to be constructed in higher-level physics textbooks, more relational processes must be needed to construe the complex relationships among the concepts, and few material processes will occur. This is because the scientific knowledge constructed across the three school physics levels is getting more complex with the development of the systematic technical taxonomies required in physical knowledge accumulation, which can be illustrated by Figure 4.15.

160

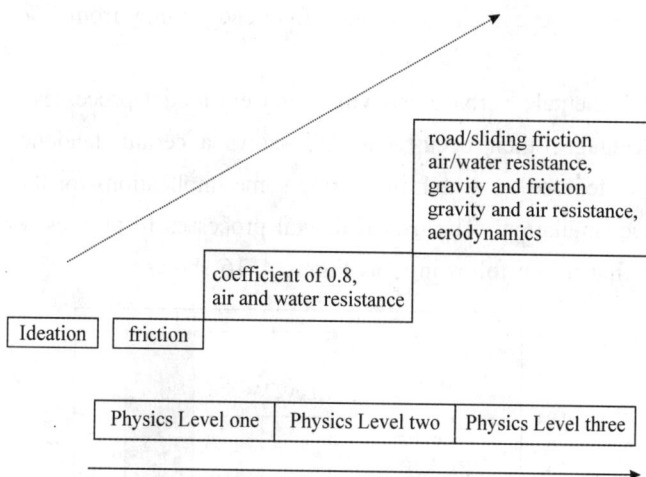

Figure 4.15　The Development of the Concept "Friction"
Across the Three Levels of Physics Textbooks

Figure 4.15 shows the development of the concept "friction" throughout the three levels of physics textbooks. In textbooks of Level 1, the concept of *friction* is elaborated on by itself. In textbooks of Level 2, two specific types of friction, that is, air and water resistance, and the measurement of its amount-coefficient of 0.8, are introduced. In textbooks of Level 3, the relationship between friction and gravity is further focused on. In addition, aerodynamics is mentioned. It is about the study of motion through air and the reduction of air resistance.

With more and more concepts are introduced in higher-level textbooks, one concept must be defined relating to others. As Halliday (1989) points out that, technical taxonomies are one of the main characteristics of scientific English. He (1985a) emphasizes that, although the grammar embodies a range of ways of defining or elaborating terms, the most familiar and probably the most frequently used is to define technical terms through an identifying relational clause. In addition, Wignell et al. (1993) point out that a technical taxonomy is typically based on two fundamental semantic relationships: "a is a kind of x" (superordination) and "b is a part of y" (composition). In other words, the definition of concepts and the complex relationship among the related concepts have to be expressed mainly by figures of "being" which are often construed by relational processes at the lexico-grammatical strata of language. This explains why the re-

161

lational processes have their occurrence frequency rising from17% to 25% to 30%.

Although mental, verbal, behavioral and existential processes together take a small percentage, their occurrence still shows a certain tendency across the three levels of textbooks, which may bring some implications for the ways of the knowledge accumulation. The use of mental processes in physics textbooks will be explored first in the following, as Figure 4. 16 shows.

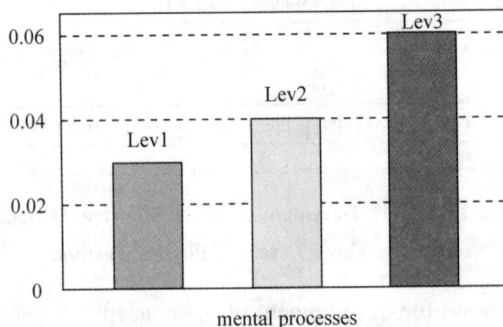

Figure 4. 16   Frequency Change of Mental Processes in Physics Textbooks

It is shown that mental processes keep their frequency going up from the lower primary school physics through the upper primary school physics to the junior school physics, with respective percentages of 3% , 4% , and 6%.

Mental processes which are construing internal experiences mainly perform three kinds of functions at the three levels of physics textbooks. First, they are used to motivate students for further thinking, which can be shown by the example "Can you **think of** three more pulls?" (Riley, 2001: 11). Second, they are used to state some knowledge to students, as is illustrated in the sentence "**Remember** that moving things will always go in a straight line unless there is a force tugging them off course" (Wilson, 2001: 34). Third, they are used for instructing the experiments, which may be seen in this excerpt "Any squares that are less that half-shaded **should be ignored** and any that is half or over should be counted as whole" (Spiders, 1991: 43). At school physic Level 1, only the first type of function exists.

Verbal processes occur in an increasing tendency across the three levels of physics textbooks, as Figure 4. 17 displays.

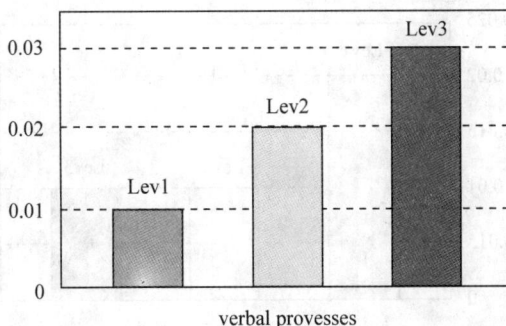

Figure 4.17   Frequency Change of Verbal Processes in Physics Textbooks

It is shown that verbal processes keep their frequency going up from textbooks of Level 1 to textbooks of Level 3, with respective percentages of 1%, 2%, and 3% for the latter.

Verbal processes mainly perform three kinds of functions at the three levels of physics textbooks. First, they are used to guide students for experiments, which can be shown by the example "**Ask** an adult to help you stick a strip of magnetic tape onto the bottom of the ball" (Nunn, 2003: 7). Second, they are used to state some knowledge to students, as is illustrated in the sentence "The Second Law **says** that the acceleration depends on mass and forcethat is, how heavy the object is and how hard it is being pushed or pulled" (Fardon, 2003: 15). Third, they are used to motivate students for theoretical thinking, which may be seen in this excerpt "**Explain** why cars are no longer the square box shapes they used to be?" (Shadwick & Barlow, 2003: 214). In textbooks of Level 1, the verbal processes perform only the first type of function. In textbooks of Level 2, the first two types of functions are played. In textbooks of Level 3, all the three types of functions are needed.

Behavioral processes are not used often in physics textbooks, which can be seen in Figure 4.18.

As Figure 4.18 expresses, the frequency of behavioral processes is respectively 2% in textbooks of Level 1, 1% in textbooks of Level 2 and 1% in textbooks of Level 3. Behavioral processes mainly perform three kinds of functions in physics textbooks. First, they are used instructing students to do the experiments, which can be shown by the example "Rub a plastic rod with the woolen

163

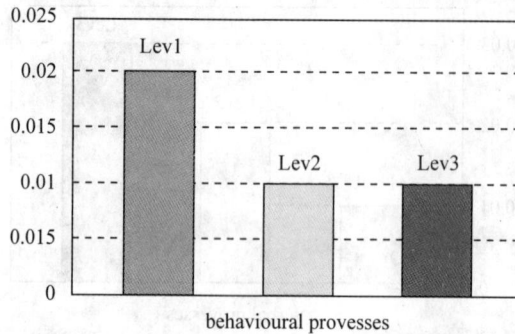

Figure 4.18 Frequency Change of Behavioural Processes at Three School Physics Levels

cloth, place it close to the detector and **watch** what happens" (Spiders, 1991: 17). Second, they are used to guide students to pay attention to some phenomenon, as is illustrated in the sentence "**Look at** the different ways that things are moving" (Nunn, 2003: 5). Third, they are used as an example explaining some theory, which may be seen in this excerpt "Balancing Something does not have to be moving to have a force acting on it. Gravity is pulling on you now, even if you **are sitting** still" (Wilson, 2001: 12).

Existential processes keep their occurrence frequency constant as 1% throughout the three levels of physics.

To summarize the major claims of this discussion thus far, it has been argued that mainly at work in school physics context are material, relational and mental processes, and the various organizations among them help construct a particular sub-field. More material processes and few relational and mental processes are characteristics of the lower primary school physics sub-field. With the development of physics into higher level sub-fields, material processes become fewer, at the same time, relational and mental processes occur more. Each type of processes plays their special functions in constructing the scientific knowledge.

4.2.3 Taxonomic Relations of Physical Knowledge in School Physics

The following section discusses the chains of taxonomic relations between technical terms in physics textbooks. The analysis is based on the adapted model developed in Figure 3.9 in Chapter 3.

Technical terms in physics are the important knowledge carriers of this subject. Those technical terms in one topic are not independent of each other, and construe the knowledge through the interaction among them. Each technical term in the physics text expects further technical terms to follow that are related to it in one of these six general ways: repetition, synonyms, contrast, class, part and causation.

The patterns of taxonomic relations between technical terms help construing the physics field. As Martin and Rose (2007: 81) state, "[A] lexical item initiates or expands on the field of a text, and this field expects a predictable range of related lexical items to follow".

As a text unfolds from one clause to the next, the chains of taxonomic relations between these technical terms build up a picture of them. Therefore, through an analysis of taxonomic relations between technical terms, a general picture of knowledge built at each level of physics textbooks may be illuminated. Furthermore, the comparision of the chains of taxonomic relations between technical terms at different levels of textbooks may throw light on the formation of hierarchical physical knowledge structure.

It is assumed that one technical term is connected to another by taxonomic relations, in other words, all the technical terms are related to each other in one topic (such as *force and motion* chosen in this topic) at each level or across all levels of physics textbooks. Therefore, it is important to classify the taxonomic relations between technical terms. Two steps are necessary for classifying taxonomic relations in the author's opinion: pick out all the entities in the form of technical terms, and group them in different categories of taxonomic relations.

4.2.3.1 Types of Taxonomic Relations at the Lower Primary School Physics

Based on the above two steps to classify the taxonomic relations of technical terms, a general picture of knowledge constructed in lower primary school physics textbooks can be shown as Figure 4.19.

As Figure 4.19 shows, the taxonomic relations of all technical terms at the lower primary school physics are quite simple, presenting us a picture of "force" including its three attributes: force effect, force type and direction of force. Force type is further divided into a scientific type and a common-sense type, each of them includes several sub-types. The main taxonomic relation between these technical terms is the category of class with its two sub-categories: class-

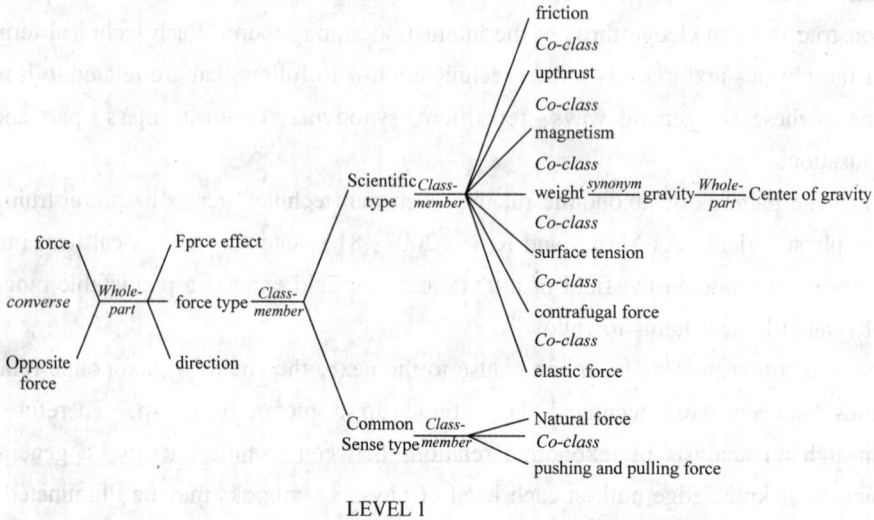

LEVEL 1

**Figure 4. 19   Types of Taxonomic Relations of Force
Itself at the Lower Primary School Physics**

member (3 occurrences) and co-class (7 occurrences). In addition, other taxonomic relations are found: synonym (1 occurrence), converse in contrast (1 occurrence), and whole-part in part exist (2 occurrences). On the whole, the
knowledge about force and motion at this level of textbooks is constructed in a
simple introductive way, which makes students just have a rough sensing of its
effect.

4. 2. 3. 2 Types of Taxonomic Relations at the Upper Primary School Physics

The knowledge of force and motion constructed in physics textbooks of Level 2 is getting more complicated, which is reflected in the taxonomic relations of
technical terms at this level of school physics. This can be seen from the following five figures. The taxonomic relations of technical terms in Figure 4. 20 are
mainly developed around the types of force, those in Figure 4. 21 around types of
physical quantities, those in Figure 4. 22 around the causative relationship between force and velocity, Figure 4. 23 around the causative relationship between
force and energy, and Figure 4. 24 around the relationship between force and motion, which will be examined in detail in this section.

Like Figure 4. 19, Figure 4. 20 offers a picture of "force" itself as well in

166

friction —$\dfrac{Whole\text{-}}{part}$— Coefficient of friction —$\dfrac{Class\text{-}}{member}$— resistance —$\dfrac{Class\text{-}}{member}$— Air and water resistance

Co-class
upthrust

Co-class
weight —$\dfrac{synonym}{}$— gravity —$\dfrac{Cause\text{-}}{effect}$— acceleration —$\dfrac{Whole\text{-}}{part}$— Center of gravity

Co-class
buoyant force —$\dfrac{Effec\text{-}}{factor}$— density

Co-class
pressure —$\dfrac{Whole\text{-}}{part}$— air pressure

Co-class
resultant

Scientific type —$\dfrac{Class\text{-}}{member}$—

Law of action and reaction

force —$\dfrac{Whole\text{-}}{part}$— force type —$\dfrac{Class\text{-}}{member}$—

Co-class

direction

Common Sense type —$\dfrac{Class\text{-}}{member}$—
drag
Co-class
pushing and pulling force

LEVEL 2 (1)

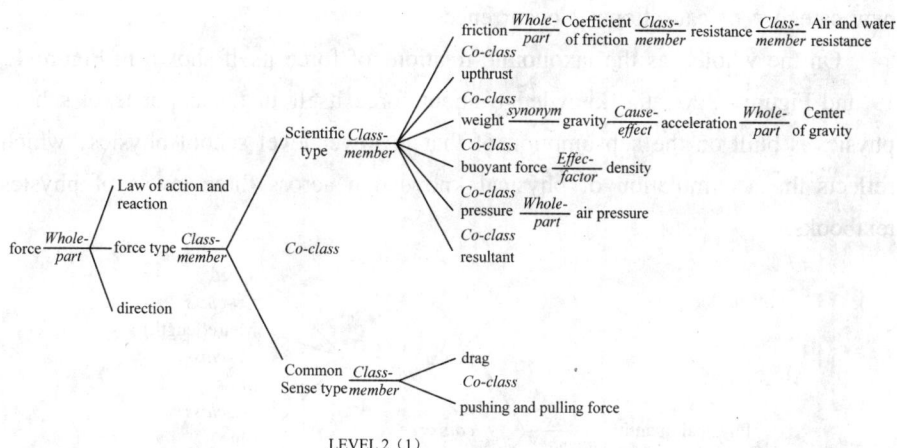

Figure 4. 20　Taxonomic Relations of Force Itself at the Upper Primary School Physics

terms of law of action and reaction, force types and the direction of force. There are some similarities and differences between the taxonomic relations shown by Figure 4. 19 and Figure 4. 20.

On the one hand, there are three similarities between the taxonomic relations shown by these two figures. First, force type is also further divided into scientific and common-sense subtypes in Figure 4. 20, which include their own subtypes. Second, there is some overlapping between the subtypes of force in these two figures. In terms of the scientific force type, friction, upthrust and weight are explained again, while for the common-sense force type, pushing and pulling force is picked up again in Figure 4. 20. Third, the taxonomic relations between these technical terms shown in Figure 4. 20 are also set up mainly by the category of class with its two sub-categories: class-member (5 occurrences) and co-class (7 occurrences). Furthermore, the taxonomic relations of synonym (1 occurrence) and whole-part in part (4 occurrences) also occur.

On the other hand, there are two differences between the taxonomic relations shown by these two figures. First, new force types are introduced into scientific and common-sense subtypes. In terms of the scientific force type, buoyant force, pressure and resultant are new categories in Figure 4. 20. However, for common-sense force types, drag is introduced for the first time. Second, the taxonomic relations between these technical terms shown in Figure 4. 20 include a

167

new category of causation (2 occurrences).

On the whole, as the taxonomic relations of force itself shown in Figure 4. 19 and Figure 4. 20, the knowledge about force itself in the upper-level school physics is built on the subsumption of that in lower-level school physics, which reflects the accumulation of physical knowledge across three levels of physics textbooks.

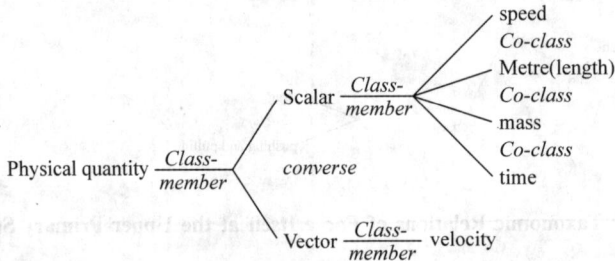

Figure 4. 21   Taxonomic Relations of Physical Quantities at the Upper Primary School Physics

Figure 4. 21 shows taxonomic relations of physical quantities in the upper primary school physics. Physical quantities can be described as two types, scalars at this school physics level including speed, meter, mass and time, and vectors shown by velocity. The taxonomic relations between these technical terms mainly belong to the category of class with its two sub-categories of class-member (3 occurrences) and co-class (3 occurrences), and the relation of converse shows itself once.

These taxonomic relations of physical quantities are realized by four levels. The first level is a class-member taxonomic relation between physical quantities and its two types, scalar and vector ones. The two types form the second level of these taxonomic relations, that is, converse. The third level refers to the class-member taxonomic relations between physical quantities of scalar and vector and their members. The fourth level is the co-class taxonomic relations among the members of scalar quantities.

Figure 4. 22 shows how knowledge about the relationship between force and velocity is constructed by means of a causation taxonomic relation among them. Force is the cause of acceleration and deceleration, and acceleration or deceleration brings about velocity including initial, ultimate and instantaneous ones.

force $\dfrac{Cause\text{-}}{effect}$ 〈 acceleration / converse / deceleration 〉 $\dfrac{Cause\text{-}}{effect}$ velocity $\dfrac{Class\text{-}}{member}$ 〈 Initial velocity / Co-class ultimate velocity / Co-class instantaneous velocity 〉

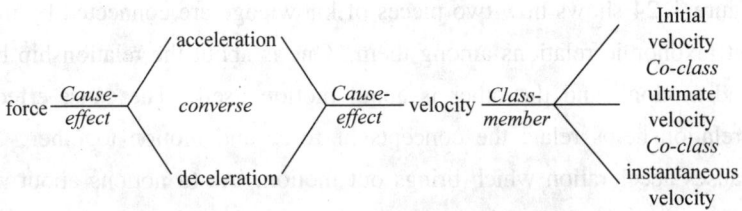

Figure 4. 22   Taxonomic Relations Around Force and Velocity

at the Upper Primary School Physics

force $\dfrac{Cause\text{-}}{effect}$ motion $\dfrac{Cause\text{-}}{effect}$ energy $\dfrac{Class\text{-}}{member}$ 〈 mechanical energy $\dfrac{Class\text{-}}{member}$ 〈 Potential energy / Co-class / Kinetie energy $\dfrac{Effect\text{-}}{factor}$ 〈 speed / mass 〉 〉 / Hear energy 〉 Co-class

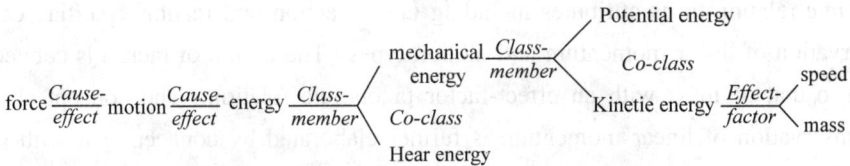

Figure 4. 23   Taxonomic Relations Around Force and Energy

at the Upper Primary School Physics

Figure 4. 23 shows two points of knowledge: knowledge about the relationship between force, motion and energy, and knowledge about energy. The concepts of force, motion and energy are connected by means of a causation taxonomic relation among them, that is, force causes motion which brings out energy, while the notions about energy are mainly explored through two subcategories of class taxonomic relations: that of co-class and that of class-member. In addition, a causation taxonomic relation construes the relationship between kinetic energy and two factors affecting its quantity, speed and mass.

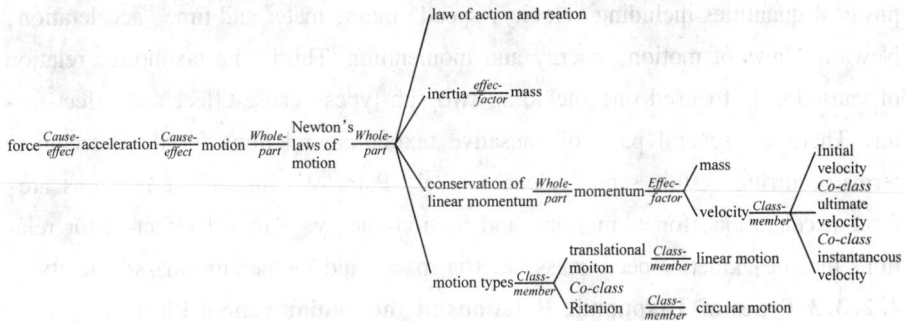

force $\dfrac{Cause\text{-}}{effect}$ acceleration $\dfrac{Cause\text{-}}{effect}$ motion $\dfrac{Whole\text{-}}{part}$ Newton's laws of motion $\dfrac{Whole\text{-}}{part}$ 〈 law of action and reation / inertia $\dfrac{effec\text{-}}{factor}$ mass / conservation of linear momentum $\dfrac{Whole\text{-}}{part}$ momentum $\dfrac{Effec\text{-}}{factor}$ 〈 mass / velocity $\dfrac{Class\text{-}}{member}$ 〈 Initial velocity / Co-class ultimate velocity / Co-class instantcous velocity 〉 〉 / motion types $\dfrac{Class\text{-}}{member}$ 〈 translational moiton $\dfrac{Class\text{-}}{member}$ linear motion / Co-class Ritanion $\dfrac{Class\text{-}}{member}$ circular motion 〉 〉

Figure 4. 24   Taxonomic Relations Around Force and Motion

at the Upper Primary School Physics

Figure 4. 24 shows how two pieces of knowledge are connected by means of different taxonomic relations among them. One is about the relationship between force and motion, and the other is about motion itself. The cause-effect taxonomic relation helps relate the concepts of force and motion together, that is, force causes acceleration which brings out motion. As to notions about motion, they are connected with each other by means of various taxonomic relations, those of whole-part, effect-factor, class-member and co-class. In explaining motion, Newton's laws of motion are focused on, which shows a whole-part taxonomic relation to its attributes including law of action and reation, inertia, conservation of linear momentum and motion types. The notion of inertia is connected to that of mass with an effect-factor taxonomic relation. The concept about conservation of linear momentum is further elaborated by connecting it with the notion of momentum through a whole-part taxonomic relation. The notion of momentum is then put together with mass and velocity by an effect-factor relation. For velocity, it sets a class-member taxonomic relation with its subtypes, such as initial velocity, ultimate velocity and instantaneous velocity which forms a co-class taxonomic relation. Motion types and their subtypes, including translational motion and rotation, stand in a class-member relationship.

As the above analysis shows, the taxonomic relations of technical terms in the upper primary school physics are much more complex than that in the lower primary school physics in several aspects. First, new types of force—buoyant force, pressure and resultant in scientific category and drag in common-sense category, are added. Second, more concepts connected with force are introduced, such as physical quantities including velocity, speed, mass, meter and time, acceleration, Newton's laws of motion, energy and momentum. Third, the taxonomic relation of causation is focused on, including two sub-types: cause-effect and effect-factor. There are several pairs of causative taxonomic relations for these technical terms occurring at this school physics level. Pairs of cause-effect relations are: force-acceleration, force- motion, and motion-energy. Pairs of effect-factor relations include: kinetic-speed/mass, inertia-mass, and momentum-mass/velocity.

4. 2. 3. 3 Types of Taxonomic Relations at the Junior School Physics

The taxonomic relations of technical terms in physics textbooks of Level 3 reflect a much deeper elaboration of the knowledge about force and motion, which can be seen from the following three figures. The taxonomic relations of technical terms in Figure 4. 25 are mainly developed around the relationship between force, motion and energy, those in Figure 4. 26 around the concept of acceleration, and those in Figure 4. 27 around the notion of force itself, which will be examined in detail in this section.

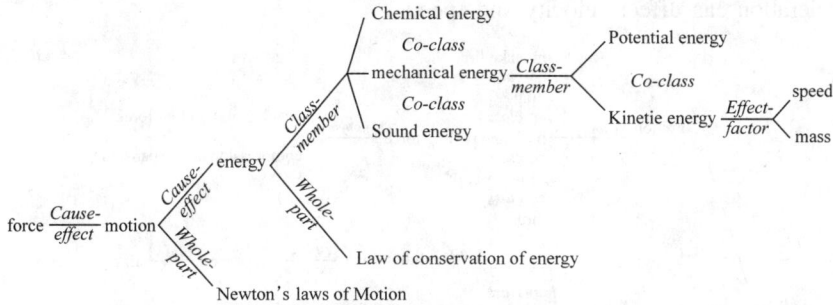

Figure 4. 25　Taxonomic Relations Around Force, Motion and Energy in Junior School Physics

The knowledge construed by taxonomic relations of technical terms in Figure 4. 25 is similar to that in Figure 4. 23, that is, the relationship between force, motion and energy, and the knowledge about energy. Specifically, there are two similarities between the taxonomic relations shown by these two figures. First, the taxonomic relation between concepts of force, motion and energy is also causation, that is, force causes motion which brings out energy. Second, energy is elaborated by its subtypes, and the taxonomic relation between them is again class-member.

However, there are some differences between the taxonomic relations in the upper primary school physics shown by Figure 4. 23 and those in the junior school physics shown by Figure 4. 25. Two more subtypes of energy are added, that is, chemical energy and sound energy, which again reflects the accumulation of physical knowledge in physics textbooks.

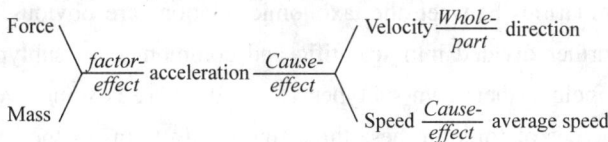

Figure 4. 26　Taxonomic Relations Around Acceleration at Junior School Physics

As Figure 4.26 shows, the concept of acceleration is explored further by relating to other concepts through two types of causation taxonomic relations, factor-effect and cause-effect. Force and mass are functioning as factors to bring about the acceleration of an object. Force is in directly proportional to the acceleration, and mass is in inversely proportional to the acceleration. Furthermore, acceleration can affect velocity and speed.

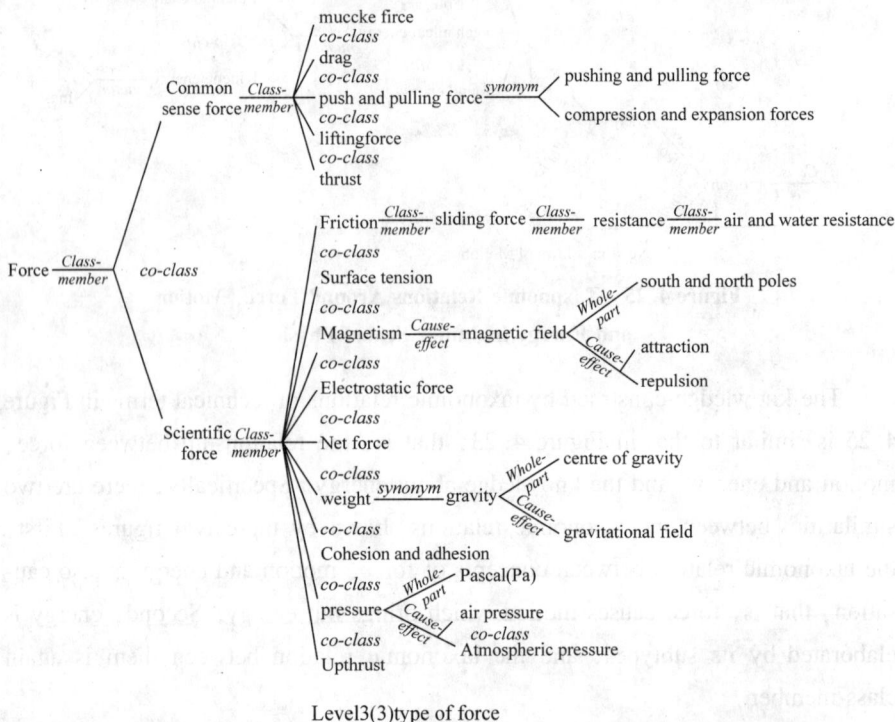

Level3(3)type of force

Figure 4.27   Taxonomic Relations Around Force Itself at Junior School Physics

Like Figure 4.19 and Figure 4.20, Figure 4.27 offers a picture of "force" itself as well in terms of force types. There are some similarities and differences between the taxonomic relations shown by these three figures.

Three similarities between the taxonomic relations are obvious. First, force type is also further divided into scientific and common-sense subtypes in Figure 4.27, which include their own subtypes. Second, there is some overlapping between the subtypes of force in these three figures. In terms of the scientific force type, the concepts of friction, suface tension, magnetism, weight, pressure and

172

upthrust occurr again, while for the common-sense force type, the notions of drag and pushing and pulling force are picked up again. Third, the taxonomic relations between these technical terms shown in Figure 4. 27 are also set up mainly by the category of class with its two sub-categories: class-member (7 occurrences) and co-class (14 occurrences). Furthermore, the taxonomic relations of synonym (2 occurrences), causation (3 occurrences) and whole-part in part (3 occurrences) also occur.

On the other hand, there are two differences between the taxonomic relations shown by these three figures. First, new force types are introduced into scientific and common-sense subtypes. In terms of the scientific force type, electrostatic force, net force, cohesion and adhesion are new categories in Figure 4. 27, while for common-sense force types, musle force, lifting force and thrust are explained for the first time. Second, the already mentioned concepts at the other two school physics are further elaborated, such as the concepts of friction and pressure. Take the concept *friction* for example, its sub-type *sliding force* is explained by introducing its sub-type *resistance* which is further elaborated by its sub-type *air and water resistance* in turn.

On the whole, the comparison of taxonomic relations of force itself shown in Figure 4. 19, Figure 4. 20 and Figure 4. 27 proves again that the knowledge about force itself in the higher-level school physics is built on the subsumption of that in the lower-level school physics, which reflects the accumulation of physical knowledge in physics textbooks.

As the above analysis shows, technical terms in the junior school physics are coming into more complex taxonomic relations. The already mentioned concepts introduced at previous textbooks are elaborated deeper and in much more detail. In addition, more new technical concepts are introduced into this level of physics.

4. 2. 3. 4 Hierarchinal Knowledge Structure in Physics

One of the features of hierarchical knowledge structure is its function of the subsumption and integration of existing ideas within more overarching proposition. The taxonomic relations between physical technical terms perform the role of intergrating and subsuming small notions into a general theory, which signifies the vertical nature of ways of school physics knowledge building.

The taxonomic relations of technical terms are getting more and more complex up the three levels of physics textbooks. The relation of causation is more emphasized in higher-level textbooks. Taxonomic relations between these techni-cal terms connected with *force and motion* help to construe a corresponding phys-ics field for scientific knowledge building and integrate these concepts into a gen-eral one. As students understand a technical term, it is interpreted in terms of the field, that is, under the overall basis of the theory. For example, there is a cause-effect relation between force and acceleration, and its interpretation de-pends on the understanding of the technical term force which shows itself as a physical concept. In a word, taxonomic relations among technical terms help to construe a scientific field and realize the vertical nature of the knowledge as a text unfolds by connecting one technical term with another through some expectant re-lations.

4.2.4 Summary

This research reported on here focuses on ideational resources of natural lan-guage which realize the field in school physics. In studying school physics, it is understandings of field which are most highly valued and which "set the scene" for the development of knowledge. The development of knowledge building in physics textbooks can be seen from the analysis of field in terms of entities, processes and taxonomic relations of technical terms.

Besides language, images also play important roles in school physics, which will be explored in the following section.

4.3 Building Knowledge Through Visual Images

Field is taken as construing through a complementarity of genres and modal-ities. Therefore, it is necessary to make an analysis of meaning-making through other modalities than language. In fact, the verbal texts and visual images are in-seperated from each other in building knowledge, and "[I]n any textbook there is a complex set of relations between verbal and visual components of such multi-modal texts, that may be left implicit for the reader to infer" (Martin & Rose, 2008: 167). Adopting tools of multimodal analysis discussed in Chapter 3 (see Figure 3.11 & Figure 3.12), the following section will focus on the ideational meanings construed by visual images and on the intersemiotic meanings between language and images in physics textbooks.

4.3.1 Ideational Meanings Construed by Visual Images

In the perspective of SFL, language realizes three types of meanings, ideational, interpersonal and textual. Scholars in SF-MDA hold the idea that images also construe three kinds of meanings similar to language. Since the research purpose is concerned with ways of knowledge building, only ideational meanings construed by visual images are focused on in this study. The following section first examines ideational meanings construed by visual images at each level of physics textbooks, and then discusses the development of ideational meanings construed in images across three levels of physics textbooks.

4.3.1.1 Ideational Meanings Construed by Visual Images in Textbooks of Level 1

There are 160 pieces of visual images in textbooks of Level 1. Based on the analytical tool of ideational meanings construed by visual images (see Figure 3. 11), the author analyzes all the pictures one by one and groups them in terms of phenomenon focus, category and representation. The study identifies six types of visual images, that is, implicit iconic single activity images, explicit iconic single activity images, explicit iconic classifying images, implicit iconic classifying images, explicit iconic compositional images, and implicit iconic compositional images, as is shown in Table 4.48 with their occurrence and frequency.

Table 4.48　Ideational Meanings Construed by Images in Textbooks of Level 1

Sum of images	Types of images	Occurrence-frequency	
160	Implicit iconic single activity images	101	63%
	Explicit iconic single activity images	30	19%
	Explicit iconic classifying images	8	5%
	Implicit iconic classifying images	9	6%
	Explicit iconic compositional images	8	5%
	Implicit iconic compositional images	4	3%

As Table 4.48 illustrates, there are some common features shown by the visual images in physics textbooks of Level 1. First, the focus of visual images in scientific texts at this school level is mainly on activities-exclusively a single activity (simple). That is, most of the visual images (81%) are construing a single activity. Second, there are some images whose categories are explicitly labeled, but most images (72%) are implicit for the reader to infer-from the accompanying verbal text or assumed knowledge of the field. Third, no indexical or symbolic images occur in the texts of this school level, and all the images are iconic representations of an entity or activity, such as a photograph or a realistic drawing.

On the other hand, there is an occurrence variation among the six types of visual images, the frequency of which is as follows: implicit iconic single activity images 63%, explicit iconic single activity images 19%, implicit iconic classifying images 6%, explicit iconic classifying images 5%, explicit iconic compositional images 5%, and implicit iconic compositional images 3%. It can be seen that implicit iconic single activity images are predominating in physics textbooks of Level 1.

(1) *Implicit Iconic Single Activity Images*

Most of visual images in textbooks of Level 1 belong to this type occupying a percentage of 63%. They show a single activity which is implicit and iconic, which can be illustrated by Figure 4. 28.

Figure 4. 28   Implicit Vectors Construing Simple Activities (Push &Pull, 2001: 12)

As Figure 4. 28 shows, three simple activities are construed by the three con-figurations of the images in the picture: this girl's pushing of her car, this boy's pushing of his car, and the boy's car going further than the girl's. With a realistic photograph, the representations of these three simple activities are clearly iconic.

According to Martin and Rose (2008), activities are construed in technical images by means of vectors in two ways, they are either made explicit in techni-cal diagrams with lines and arrows with labels, or implied by the direction of a body or gaze. In the photograph, the vectors for construing activities belong to the latter, implicitly shown by not only the direction of a body or gaze but also any such kind of symbols. As the images show, the girl's stretching hand is di-rected by two lines towards her toy car going before her, the boy's more stretc-hing hand is directed by three lines towards his toy car going further before him, and there is a distance between the two cars. The two children's stretching hands, the lines directing from the hands towards the toy cars and the distance between two cars, they are all vectors relatively construing three simple activities which are explicated by the accompanying verbal text.

In a word, as it construes single activities, this visual image is a simple ac-tivity image that is implicit for lacking of explicit labeled vectors and that is icon-ic because of its representation by a photograph.

(2) *Explicit Iconic Single Activity Images*

This type is the second most often-occurring with a percentage of 19%. Contrast to the unlabeled vectors in implicit iconic single activity images, the vectors in explicit iconic activity images should be marked be verbal titles clear-ly. Some visual images in physics textbooks of Level 1 belong to this type, showing a single activity which is explicit and iconic. In physics at this level, the vectors for construing activities are still represented by the features of the image, but they are labeled with verbal texts. For example, in Figure 4. 29, the posture

Figure 4. 29   Explicit Iconic Single Activity Images (from Nunn, 2003: 6)

of the two hands and short wavy lines around the hands are functioning as a vector which is explicated by the label "Rubbing" in the image. As it construes a single activity, this photograph is a simple activity image that is explicit and iconic.

(3) *Implicit Iconic Classifying Image*

This type of images occurs with a percentage of 6%. Some iconic classifying images are implicit, as shown in Figure 4. 30. The image in Figure 4. 30 illustrates two opposite forces marked by the two arrows: one is the foot's downward push on the ground, and another is the ground's upwards push on the foot. These two forces are shown with realistic drawings but no labels.

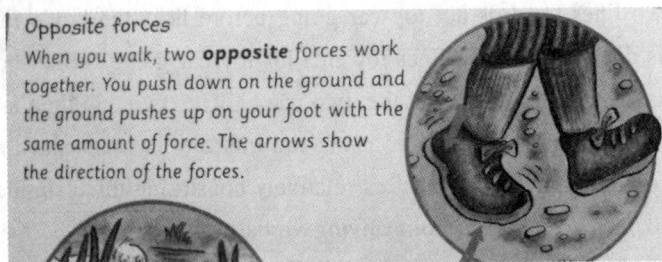

Opposite forces
When you walk, two **opposite** forces work together. You push down on the ground and the ground pushes up on your foot with the same amount of force. The arrows show the direction of the forces.

Figure 4. 30　Opposite Forces (from Nunn, 2003: 6)

(4) *Explicit Iconic Classifying Image*

This type of visual images occurs in physics textbooks of Level 1 with a percentage of 5%. A classifying image that is explicit and iconic is Figure 4. 31,

All Kinds of forces

Figure 4. 31　Different Ways that Things Are Moving (from Nunn, 2003: 4-5)

which classifies different forces in a common-sense way. These forces make things moving, which is illustrated with realistic drawings. Each force is labeled with a name showing the way of moving: *flying*, *bouncing*, *sliding*, *spinning*, *digging and etc.*.

(5) *Explicit Iconic Compositional Image*

This type occupies 5% in physics textbooks of Level 1. A compositional image which is explicit and iconic is displayed in Figure 4.32. It is chosen from one of this level's textbooks, indicating parts of the crane which is working in a photo, with labels for the jib and the cable.

This crane is lifting a heavy load. The engine makes a force that moves the jib. The jib pulls up the cable. The cable lifts the load.

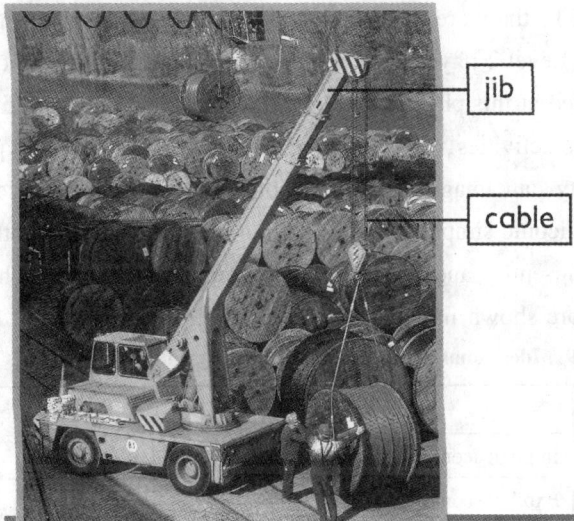

jib

cable

Figure 4.32   Explicit Compositional Image (from Royston, 2002: 7)

(6) *Implicit Iconic Compositional Image*

Besides explicit iconic compositional images, some compositional images with a percentage of 3% are implicit and iconic, as Figure 4.33 shows. The picture is about the composition of a pulley including both a rope and a wheel, which are not labeled explicitly.

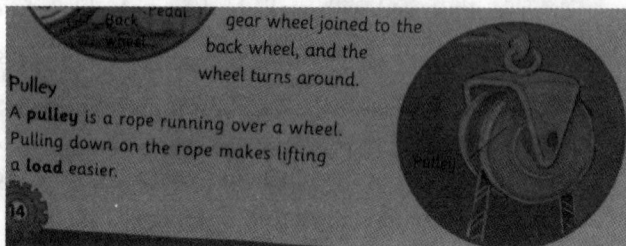

Figure 4. 33   Imlicit compositional image（from Nunn，2003：14）

4.3.1.2 Ideational Meanings Construed by Visual Images in Textbooks of Level 2

There are 124 pieces of visual images in physics textbooks of Level 2. After the analysis of these images，ten types are identified. Besides the four types of visual images（implicit iconic single activity images，explicit/implicit iconic classifying image，implicit iconic compositional image）shown in physics textbooks of Level 1，there are other options for visual images in construing ideational meanings in Level 2 physics textbooks. Therefore，another six types of images are further added at this physics level：explicit iconic complex activities，implicit iconic complex activities，explicit symbolic simple activity，explicit symbolic complex activity，an image construing both an explicit iconic classifying entity and an explicit iconic simple activity，and an image construing both an implicit iconic classifying entity and implicit iconic complex activities. The ten types of visual images are shown in Table 4.49 with their occurrence and frequency.

Table 4. 49   Ideational Meanings Construed by Images in Level 2 Textbooks

Sum of images	Types of images	Occurrence-frequency	
	Implicit iconic single activity images	73	59%
	Explicit iconic classifying images	6	5%
	Implicit iconic classifying images	8	6%
124	Implicit iconic compositional images	2	2%
	Explicit symbolic simple activity images	2	2%
	Explicit symbolic complex activity images	2	2%
	Images construing both an explicit iconic classifying entity and an explicit iconic simple activity	1	1%

续表

Sum of images	Types of images	Occurrence-frequency	
124	Images construing both an implicit iconic classifying entity and an implicit iconic complex activities	1	1%
	Images construing implicit iconic complex activities	28	23%
	Images construing explicit iconic complex activities	1	1%

As Table 4.49 expresses, some new features are shown by visual images in construing ideational meanings in physics textbooks of Level 2. First, phenomenon focus of an image expands from single activities to activity sequences. Second, images are not only relatively iconic representations of an activity, such as a photograph or realistic drawing, but also symbolic representations such as diagrams. Third, images are not always purely focusing on an entity or an activity but sometimes focusing on both an entity and an activity.

On the other hand, the occurrence of the ten types of visual images also varies. Their frequency is as follows: implicit iconic single activity images 59%, images construing implicit iconic complex activities 23%, implicit iconic classifying images 6%, explicit iconic classifying images 5%, implicit iconic compositional images 2%, explicit symbolic simple activity images 2%, explicit symbolic complex activity images 2%, images construing both an explicit iconic classifying entity and an explicit iconic simple activity 1%, images construing both an implicit iconic classifying entity and an implicit iconic complex activities 1%, and images construing explicit iconic complex activities 1%.

Since the four types of visual images (implicit iconic single activity images, explicit iconic classifying image, implicit iconic classifying image, implicit iconic compositional image) have been described at school physics Level 1, the following analysis just focuses on the remaining six types.

(1) *Implicit Iconic Complex Activities*

With a percentage of 23%, this type of visual images is a main one occur-

ring at this school level. The image in Figure 4.34 expresses how to make a pa-per glider in five steps each of which is a simple activity. The five activities to-gether make up an activity sequence. The dotted lines in each picture act as a vector showing the activity in this step. Since there is no explicit verbal exposi-tion for each vector, the images are represented in an implicit way.

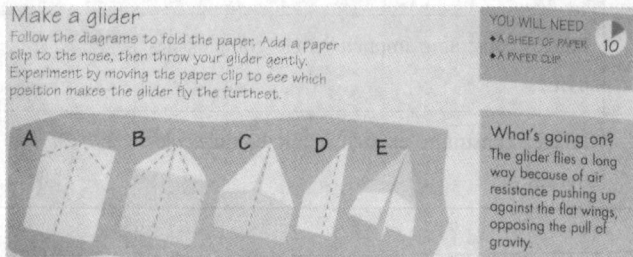

Make a glider
Follow the diagrams to fold the paper. Add a paper clip to the nose, then throw your glider gently. Experiment by moving the paper clip to see which position makes the glider fly the furthest.

YOU WILL NEED
♦ A SHEET OF PAPER
♦ A PAPER CLIP
10

What's going on?
The glider flies a long way because of air resistance pushing up against the flat wings, opposing the pull of gravity.

Figure 4.34   Implicit Iconic Complex Activities (from Wiston, 2001: 29)

(2) *Explicit Symbolic Simpe Activity*

Some symbolic images begin to play their functions in textbooks of Level 2. This type of explicit symbolic simple activity has a percentage of 2% at school physics Level 2, which can be illustrated by Figure 4.35.

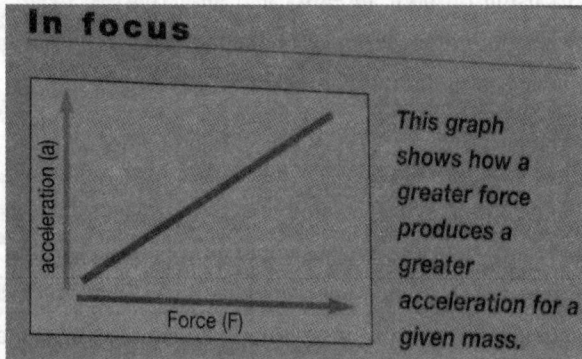

In focus

This graph shows how a greater force produces a greater acceleration for a given mass.

Figure 4.35   Explicit Symbolic Simpe Activity (from Fardon, 2003: 19)

The above image is a mathematical graph with the red upward oblique line functioning as the vector construing a relational process in which a greater force produces a greater acceleration for a given mass. The yellow and the blue arrow are not playing the role of vector, but represent the two entities *acceleration* and *force*. These two arrows help the vector shown by the red upward oblique line to construe a simple activity explicitly with clear labels *acceleration* (a) and *Force* (F).

(3) *Explicit Symbolic Complex Activity*

Besides the images of explicit symbolic simple activity, some symbolic images focus on complex activities in textbooks of Level 2. This type of images, as Figure 4. 36 shows, occupies 2%.

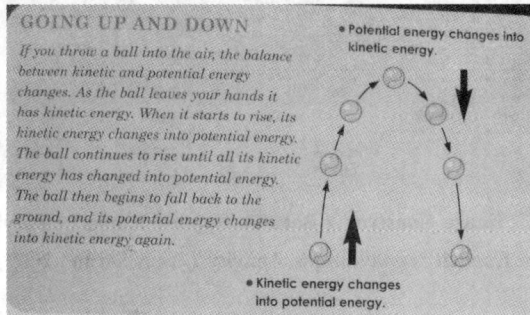

Figure 4. 36   Explicit Symbolic Complex Activity (from Sarah, 2009: 19)

The above symbolic image in Figure 4. 36 construes an activity sequence, showing the balance change between kinetic and potential energy of a ball when it is thrown into the air. The upward big arrow at the bottom of the image is the vector construing the activity of the kinetic energy of the ball changing into the potential energy when it starts to rise, and the downward big arrow construes the activity of the potential energy of the ball changing into the kinetic energy. All the other arrows connecting the symbol of the ball also function as vectors construing the continuous changes between the two types of energies. The verbal expositions accompanying the two main vectors make the symbolic image an explicit one.

(4) *Images Construing both an Explicit Iconic Classifying Entity and an Explicit Iconic Simple Activity*

This image type shown in Figure 4. 37 occurs only once in the upper primary school physics, but it is important in construing knowledge. In introducing the opposite forces in the following image shown in Figure 4. 37, an iconic representation of a plane is used as an example. Two pairs of forces are classified and shown explicitly, "gravity and lift" and "thrust and drag", which are produced when an aeroplane zooms across the sky. At the same time, the four arrows act

as vectors construing four simple activities respectively. In a word, with a definite verbal explanation for the four vectors, this image focuses on both entities and activities in an explicit way.

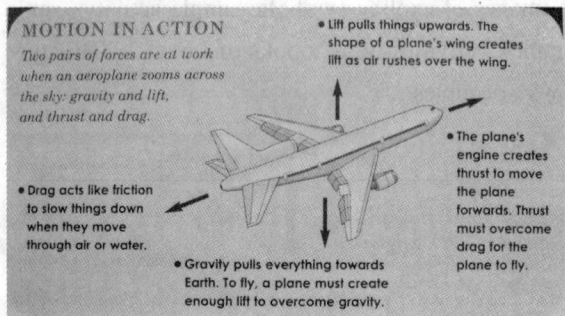

Figure 4.37   Image Construing Both an Explicit Iconic Classifying Entity and an Explicit Iconic Simple Activity（from Sarah, 2009：5）

（5）*Image Construing Both an Implicit Iconic Classifying Entity and Implicit Iconic Complex Activities*

This image type occurs once, which is shown in Figure 4.38, four types of

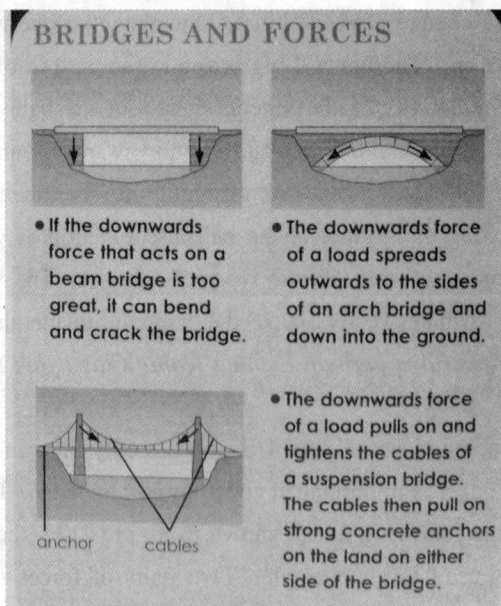

Figure 4.38   Image Construing Both an Implicit Iconic Classifying Entity and Implicit Iconic Complex Activities（from Sarah, 2009：26）

bridges can be identified by the iconic pictures of them, and the arrow vectors marked out in each bridge picture construe an activity sequence. It shows how the forces caused by the weight on the bridge are transferred by means of the different shapes into the ground.

(6) *Explicit Iconic Complex Activities*

One visual image in the upper primary school physics belongs to this type, showing an activity sequence in iconic representation with explicit vectors. In Figure 4.39, an activity sequence is construed by two vectors shown by the turning arrow and the straight arrow in the image. This activity sequence shows how a screw works. The turning arrow labeled by the title *turning motion* shows the activity that the screwdriver is turning the scew, and the straight arrow marked by the title *forward motion* means that the scew is pushed into a surface by a forward pushing moition which is changed from the turning motion of the scewdriver. That is, the turning motion of the screwdriver causes the forward motion of the scew, which is construed explicitly by two vectors as complex activities.

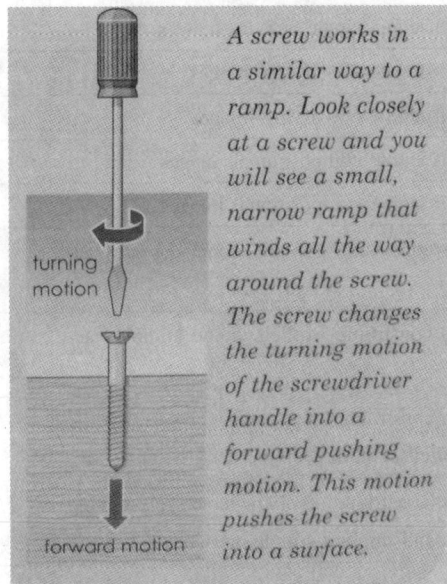

turning
motion

A screw works in
a similar way to a
ramp. Look closely
at a screw and you
will see a small,
narrow ramp that
winds all the way
around the screw.
The screw changes
the turning motion
of the screwdriver
handle into a
forward pushing
motion. This motion
pushes the screw
into a surface.

forward motion

Figure 4.39   Explicit Iconic Complex Activities (from Sarah, 2009: 9)

4.3.1.3 Ideational Meanings Construed by Images in Textbooks of Level 3

129 pieces of visual images construing ideational meaning are analyzed in

textbooks of Level 3, and 12 types are classified. Besides the six types of visual images (explicit/implicit iconic classifying image, explicit/implicit iconic compositional image, explicit/implicit iconic single activity images) shown in textbooks of Level 1 and the other two types (explicit iconic complex activities, implicit iconic complex activities) occurring in textbooks of Level 2, there are other options for visual images in construing ideational meanings in textbooks of Level 3. Therefore, another four types of images are further added at this physics level: explicit iconic entity and implicit symbolic simple activity, explicit iconic classifying and implicit simple activities, implicit iconic classifying and implicit complex activities, and images construing a compositional explicit entity by means of mathematical symbols. The twelve types of visual images are shown in Table 4.50 with their occurrence and frequency.

Table 4.50   Ideational Meanings Construed by Visual Images in Textbooks of Level 3

Sum of images	Types of images	Occurrence-frequency	
129	Implicit iconic single activity images	74	57%
	Explicit iconic single activity images	9	7%
	Explicit iconic classifying images	9	7%
	Implicit iconic classifying images	3	2%
	Explicit iconic compositional images	2	2%
	Implicit iconic compositional images	6	5%
	Images construing implicit iconic complex activities	15	12%
	Images construing explicit iconic complex activities	1	1%
	Images construing an explicit iconic entity and an implicit symbolic simple activity	1	1%
	Images construing explicit iconic classifying entities and implicit simple activities	1	1%
	Images construing implicit iconic classifying entities and implicit complex activities	2	2%
	Images construing a compositional explicit entity by means of mathematical symbols	6	5%

　　As Table 4. 50 indicates, some new features are displayed by the visual images in construing ideational meanings in textbooks of Level 3. First, the image shows a single activity in two forms of representations and categories, that is, an explicit iconic entity and implicit symbolic simple activity. Second, there are more choices for an image showing the combination between entities and activities, for example, an image showing an explicit iconic classifying and implicit simple activities, or an image showing implicit iconic classifying and implicit complex activities. Third, the entity or activity in an image is often made into a compositional explicit entity by means of mathematical symbols.

　　On the other hand, the occurrence of the twelve types of visual images also varies. Their frequency is as follows: implicit iconic single activity images 57%, images construing implicit iconic complex activities 12%, explicit iconic single activity images 7%, explicit iconic classifying images 7%, implicit iconic compositional images 5%, images construing a compositional explicit entity by means of mathematical symbols 5%, implicit iconic classifying images 2%, explicit iconic compositional images 2%, images construing implicit iconic classifying entities and implicit complex activities 2%, images construing explicit iconic complex activities 1%, images construing an explicit iconic entity and an implicit symbolic simple activity 1%, and images construing explicit iconic classifying entities and implicit simple activities 1%.

　　Since the six types of visual images (explicit/implicit iconic classifying image, explicit/implicit iconic compositional image, explicit/implicit iconic single activity images) have been described in textbooks of Level 1 and the other two types (implicit iconic complex activities and explicit iconic complex activities) in textbooks of Level 2 have been described in the above sections, the following analysis just focuses on the remaining four types.

　　(1) *Image Construing a Compositional Explicit Entity by Means of Mathematical Symbols*

　　This type occurs at this school level with a percentage of 5%. The following image, which is shown in Figure 4. 40, construes an abstract entity — the Law of Conservation of Momentum, explicitly by means of mathematical symbols in a symbolic way. The Law of Conservation of Momentum tells us that if two or more objects act on each other, their total momentum remains unchanged.

The objects are represented symbolically by the two cue balls in the image. The momentum of the cue is divided into two parts transferred to the two balls respectively, shown by the billiard cue and two arrows starting from the balls. At the same time, the mathematical calculating formulas of the three momenta are labeled explicitly. On the whole, this image construes a compositional explicit entity by means of mathematical symbols.

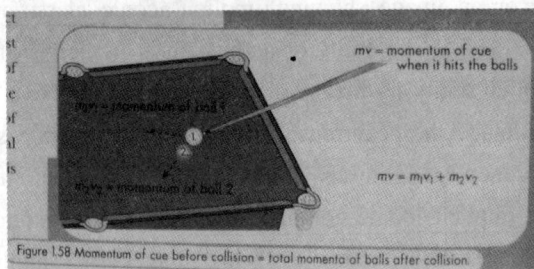

Figure 4.40   Image Construing a Compositional Explicit Entity by Means of Mathematical Symbols (from Janet, 1999: 22)

(2) *Image Constuing Implicit Iconic Classifying Enties and Implicit Complex Activities*

This type occurs with a percentage of 2%. The following image, as Figure 4.41 shows, construes a combination of implicit iconic classifying entities and implicit complex activities. It first construes implictit iconic classifying entities which can be identified clearly in the photograph although no labels are given to them. These entities are a classifying of materials needed in the experiment: toy cars, rulers and tables. This image also construes implicit complex activities,

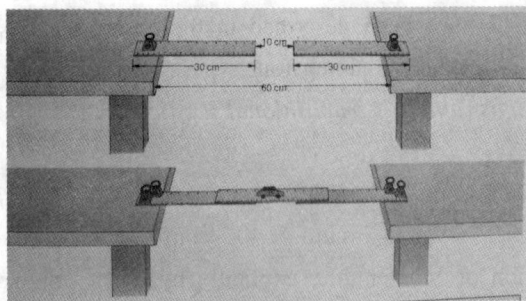

Figure 4.41   Image Construing Implicit Iconic Classifying and Implicit Complex Activities (from Spiders, 1991: 39)

showing how to make a structure of cantilever bridge to test how all the forces involved are acting to support the structure. The steps of doing this experiments can be inferred through the illustration.

(3) *Image Construing an Explicit Iconic Entity and an Implicit Symbolic Simple Activity*

This type occurs only once, as Figure 4.42 illustrates. This image is showing Hook's Law that there is a link between the stretch of a spring and the force causing it. This image is made up of two parts: the left part of which construes an explicit iconic entity, with five springs hanging different newtons' of weights and their stretching length marked; the right part of which construes an implicit symbolic simple activity, with a mathematical graph to show the relation between the stretch of a spring and the force causing it. If, for instance, a 1 N force causes a spring to stretch 2cm, and then a 2 N force will cause a 4cm stretch in the same spring. A 3 N force will cause a 6 cm stretch and so on.

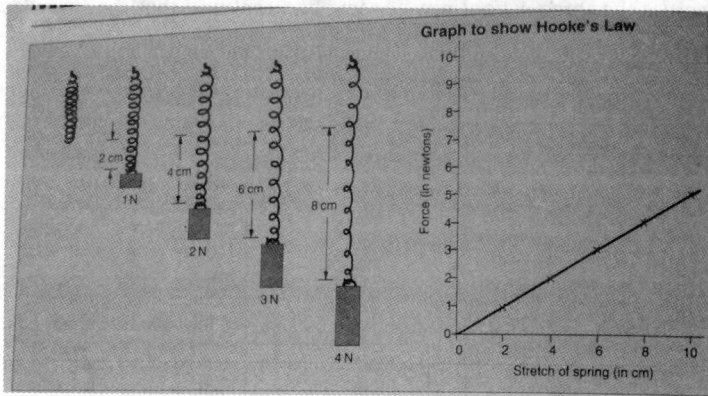

Figure 4.42   Image Construing Explicit Iconic Entity and Implicit Symbolic Simple Activity(from Spiders, 1991: 32)

(4) *Image Construing an Explicit Iconic Classifying and Implicit Simple Activities*

One image is found belonging to this type, which is shown in Figure 4.43. Four types of bridges are shown by the iconic pictures of them with explicit titles. The arrow vectors marked out in each bridge picture construe the activity sequence in an implicit way, showing how the forces caused by the weight on the bridge are transferred by means of different shapes into the ground.

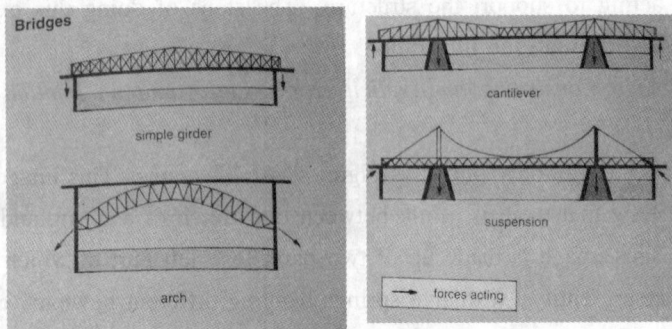

**Figure 4. 43　Image Construing an Explicit Iconic Classifying
and Implicit Simple Activities(from Spiders, 1991: 38)**

4.3.1.4 The Development of Ideational Meanings Construed by Visual Images

The ideational meaning construed by images is developing from simple to complex across the three school physics levels, implying that the knowledge constructed is more and more complex. This can be shown by Figure 4. 44, which summarizes the development of ideational meaning construed in images across three levels of physics textbooks.

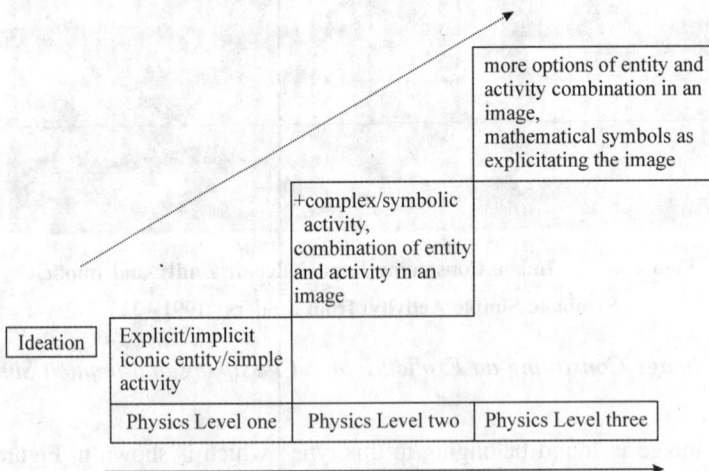

**Figure 4. 44　The Development of Ideational Meaning Construed
by Visual Images Across Three School Physics Levels**

190

In textbooks of Level 1, the knowledge is built in a more common-sense way, so what images construe are just an explicit/implicit iconic entity or a simple activity. In textbooks of Level 2, physical knowledge is introduced in a more scientific way so that what images construe are not only an explicit/implicit iconic entity or a simple activity, but a complex/symbolic activity or a combination of entity and activity. To meet the need to build physical knowledge in a much more scientific way in textbooks of Level 3, images have much more options for construing entities and activities: entity and activity often occurring simultaneously, and mathematical symbols used as explicating.

4.3.2 Intersemiotic Ideational Meanings Between Language and Images

The meaning of texts in physics textbooks is construed not only by written language, but also by images and mathematical symbols. Each of the three semiotic resources not only works individually in producing its independent special meaning with no bearing to each other, but together contributes to complement the others to produce a meaning from the text that is greater than the sum of its parts (Royce, 1998: 27). The meanings made across semiotic systems is known as *intersemiosis* (or, as Royce refers to it, intersemiotic complementarity). Based on the analysis tool for intersemiotic ideational meanings developed in Chapter 3 (see Figure 3.12), this section will outline the features of ideational meanings at the intersection of language and image across three levels of physics textbooks.

4.3.2.1 Intersemiotic Ideational Meanings in Textbooks of Level 1

120 pieces of visual images with verbal langage are identified in physics textbooks of Level 1. Based on the analysis tool for describing intersemiotic ideational meanings between language and images, the author analyzes all the pictures one by one and groups them in terms of redundancy, instantiation and exposition. This study identifies two types of intersemiotic ideational meanings between language and visual images at this level of textbooks, that is, redundancy and instantiation, as is shown in Table 4.51 with their occurrence and frequency.

**Table 4.51   Intersemiotic Ideational Meanings Between Language
and Images in Physics Textbooks of Level 1**

Sum of images	Types of intersemiotic ideational meanings	Occurrence-frequency	
120	Redundancy	79	66%
	Instantiation	41	34%

As Table 4.51 shows, all the images in textbooks of Level 1 are functioning as instantiations or redundancy of their relevant verbal language, which can make the scientific knowledge more accessible to young children who need depend on a concrete and vivid way of thinking. Redundancy with a frequency of 66% is found more often occurring than instantiation which has a frequency of 34%.

The following section explores these two types of image-text relations in textbooks of Level 1: instantiation and redundancy.

As Figure 4.45 shows, the image-text relation is one of instantiation. The language conveys the habitual nature of the activity, that is, two opposite forces work together, while the image indicates one instance. As the picture displays, one person is walking with his foot pushing down on the ground, and at the same time, the ground is pushing up on his foot. This image concurs with, and provides an instantiation of the text, that is, "When you walk, two opposite forces work together". The image clearly suggests additional meanings such as the opposite directions of the two forces, making this knowledge be able to be sensed more vividly.

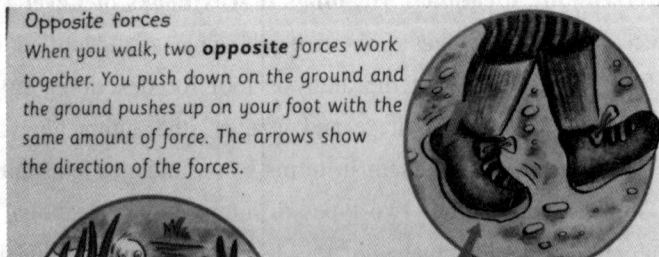

Opposite forces
When you walk, two **opposite** forces work together. You push down on the ground and the ground pushes up on your foot with the same amount of force. The arrows show the direction of the forces.

Figure 4.45   Example of Instantiation (from Nunn, 2003: 6)

Another important relationship between images and texts in textbooks of Level 1 is one of redundancy. This relation obtains when the image and the text are having an equivalent participant-process-phenomenon configuration. For example, the two images in Figure 4.46 can be transcoded respectively as "an engine pulls a train," and "a tractor pulls a trailer". This is redundant with the verbal texts, but this is not a simple inter-modal duplication of meaning. In both cases, significant additional meanings are added by the images, that is, visual images make students sense the pulling forces more easily and vividly.

Figure 4.46   Example of Redundancy (from Riley, 2001:10)

4.3.2.2 Intersemiotic Ideational Meanings in Textbooks of Level 2

By an analysis of 198 pieces of visual images with verbal langage in physics textbooks of Level 2, the research finds out three types of intersemiotic ideational meanings between language and visual images, that is, redundancy, instantiation, and exposition, as is shown in Table 4.52 with their occurrence and frequency.

Table 4.52   Intersemiotic Ideational Meanings Between Language and Images in Physics Textbooks of Level 2

Sum of images	Types of intersemiotic ideational meanings	Occurrence-frequency	
	redundancy	47	23.7%
198	instantiation	48	24.2%
	exposition	103	52.1%

The frequency of redundancy is decreasing from 66% in textbooks of Level

1 to 23. 7% in textbooks of Level 2, and that of istatiation from 34% in physics textbooks of Level 1 to 24. 2% at this level. As Table 4. 53 shows, besides redundancy and instantiation, another type of intersemiotic ideational meanings between language and images-exposition, is also found in textbooks of Level 2, which is predominating with 52. 1%.

Since redundancy and instantiation have been examined in textbooks of Level 1, the following section investigates only exposition.

Images in textbooks of Level 2 are not only represented by iconic photographs or realistic drawings, but shown by symbolic graphs. Martinec and Salway (2005: 350) describe such type of image-text relations as "exposition" — "where the image and the text are of the same level of generality". This kind of images can construe the scientific knowledge in a more abstract and concise way, making the verbal form of scientific knowledge condensed. As is shown in Figure 4. 47, the image-text relation is one of exposition.

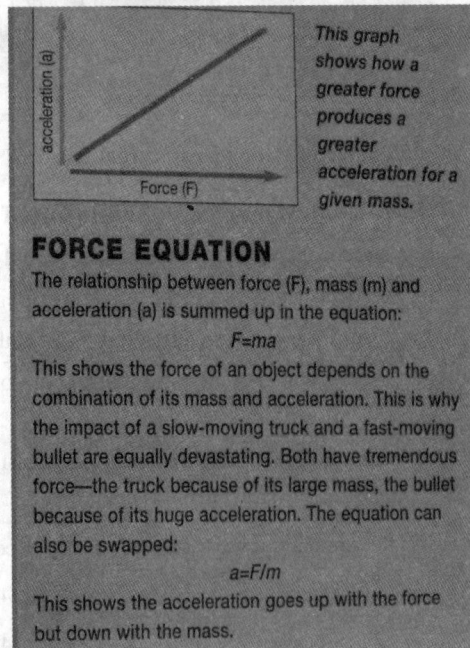

Figure 4. 47   Example of Exposition Relation (from Fardon, 2003:19)

The short verbal text at the right of the graph summarizes the meaning construed by this graph. The long verbal text below the graph elaborates on what is represented by it, that is, the relationship between force (F), mass (m) and acceleration (a). This relationship is summed up in two equations: $F = ma$ and $a = F/m$. All the knowledge constructed by the two parts of texts can be wrapped into the concise graph. The visual graph and its relevant verbal language is of the same level of the generality.

4.3.2.3 Intersemiotic Ideational Meanings in Textbooks of Level 3

There are 171 pieces of visual images with verbal language in physics textbooks of Level 3. Besides the above three types of intersemiotic ideational meanings between language and visual images, that is, redundancy, instantiation, and exposition, another type is a combination of instantiation with exposition in textbooks of Level 3, as is shown in Table 4.54 with their occurrence and frequency.

Table 4.54   Intersemiotic Ideational Meanings Between Language and Images at Physics Textbooks of Level 3

Sum of images	Types of intersemiotic ideational meanings	Occurrence-frequency	
171	redundancy	22	13%
	Instantiation	33	19%
	exposition	109	64%
	Instantiation + exposition	7	4%

As Table 4.54 shows, redundancy is decreasing to 13% and instantiation to 19%. On the other hand, exposition is increasing to 64%. In addition, the type of instantiation plus exposition shows itself with a frequency of 4%. Since redundancy, instantiation and exposition have been examined in textbooks of Level 1 and Level 2, the following section investigates only the type of instantiation plus exposition.

The relationship between images and verbal language in physics textbooks of the first two levels is simple, that is, one of instantiation, redundancy or exposition, while the relationship between images and verbal language is complex in textbooks of Level 3, that is, one including both instantiation and exposition. This type of intersemiotic ideational meanings between images and language is displayed in Figure 4.48.

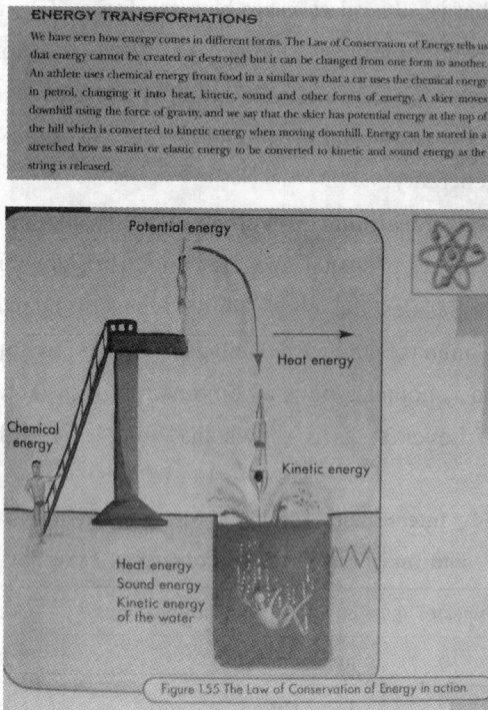

Figure 4.48   Example of Image-text Relation as Instantiation Plus Exposition
(from Janet, 1999: 21)

As Figure 4.48 shows, the image-text relation is one of instantiation plus exposition. The short verbal text above the image is about the Law of Conservation of Energy, which is elaborated on by means of the image with an athlete as instantiation. The knowledge is construed by the image and the text which are of the same level of generality.

4.3.2.4 Features of Intersemiotic Ideational Meanings

Features of intersemiotic ideational meanings are varying across three levels of physics textbooks, as Figure 4.49 shows.

In textbooks of Level 1, only instantiation and redundancy are found out to show the intersemiotic ideational meanings between language and images. In textbooks of Level 2, exposition is used for expressing the intersemiotic ideational meanings between language and images. In textbooks of Level 3, a new type

196

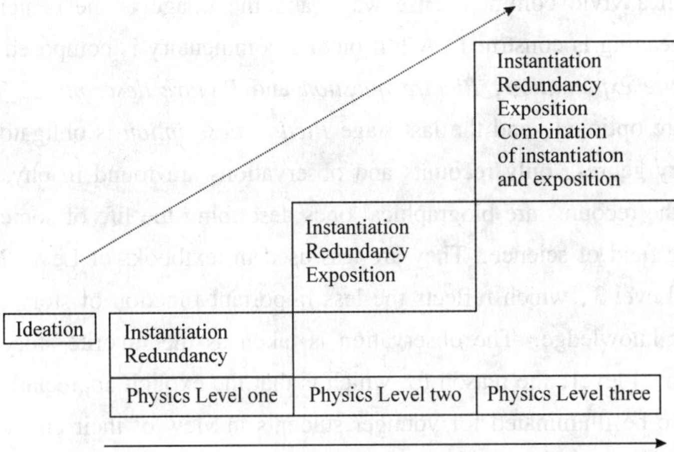

		Instantiation Redundancy Exposition Combination of instantiation and exposition
	Instantiation Redundancy Exposition	
Instantiation Redundancy		
Physics Level one	Physics Level two	Physics Level three

Ideation

Figure 4.49   Features of Intersemiotic Ideational
Meaning Across Three School Physics Levels

of intersemiotic ideational meanings is characterized by a combination of instantiation and exposition. On the whole, more and more intersemiotic relationships between language and images are abundant with school physics developing from lower primary schools through upper primary schools to junior schools.

4.4 Summary

In Chapter 4, the theoretical framework based on SFL, SF-MDA and the theory of knowledge structures in SE is used to provide an analysis of knowledge building aross three levels of physics textbooks in terms of genre, field and mulitimodality.

For genre analysis, story and two macro-genres which are experimental procedure and picture commentary are found in physics textbooks, and they are given a detailed description of generic structures with examples from the texts.

The general purpose of an experimental procedure equals the final aim of doing science which is to deepen students' understanding of scientific knowledge. It is this purpose which conditions its generic structure Theoretical warming-up ^ Experiment/Activity ^ (Theoretical summary)/Theoretical exploration.

The purpose of a picture commentary is to help students sense the scientific

197

knowledge in a vivid common-sense way, and the image is the center around which the meaning is construed. A full picture commentary is composed of three stages, *Picture explanation*, *Picture question* and *Picture description*. The first two stages are optional, and the last stage *Picture description* is obligatory.

For story genres, only recounts and observations are found in physics textbooks. All the recounts are biographical ones describing the life of some famous people in the field of science. They are less used in textbooks of Level 2 than in textbook of Level 3, which reflects the less important function of story in building scientific knowledge. The observation is taken as the favorite story type at the lower school level, the reason for which is that the explicit appreciation of the story needs to be illuminated for younger students in view of their cognition.

In terms of field analysis, the features and occurrence of both entities and processes are explored across the three school physics sub-fields: lower primary school physics sub-field, upper primary school physics sub-field and junior school physics sub-field.

The results show both some similarities and some variations in entitities in these sub-fields. In each sub-field, the top five types of entities occurring are the same, which are concrete everyday entities, generic entities, technical entities, pronouns and metaphoric process entities in order from a high frequency to a low frequency. At the same time, the occurrence of these entities varies as the school physics sub-fields develop from the lower level to the upper level, with a decreasing occurrence of common-sense entities and an increasing occurrence of uncommon-sense entities.

The analysis of processes also throws light on the features of three school physics sub-fields. First, each sub-field has the same top three often-occurring processes, which are material, relational and mental ones in order. The total occurrence of the first two types predominates in each sub-field. Second, each type of processes shows a regular occurrence tendency across the three levels of physics textbooks, which reflects the differences among the three school physics sub-fields. More material processes and few relational and mental processes are characteristics of the lower primary school physics sub-field, and vice versa.

Technical terms in each school physics sub-field are related to each other, forming different taxonomic relations in one of these six general ways: repetition, synonyms, contrast, class, part and causation. More complex taxonomic relations exist in the higher-level physics textbooks.

The analysis of field should include the meanings construed by other semiotics besides language. Both the ideational meanings construed by visual images and the intersemiotic meanings between language and images are getting from simple to complex across three levels of physics textbooks.

Chapter 5　A Linguistic Exploration of SD and SG in Physics Textbooks

As the analysis shows in the above chapter, the higher-level physics textbooks are construing a more abstract and uncommon-sense subfield than the lower-level ones. Therefore, the structure of knowledge is getting more and more vertical across the three levels of physics textbooks.

In this chapter, the verticality of knowledge constructed in each school physics sub-field will be explored from the linguistic perspective of SD and SG. The analysis is intended to show the development of SD and SG throughout the three levels of physics textbooks and the different patterns of SD and SG in introducing technical concepts at each level of physics textbooks. The tools and methods of analysis as developed in Chapter 3 will be adopted.

5.1 The Development of SG and SD in Physics Textbooks

In the following section, the study explores the variation of SG and SD by analyzing linguistic resources at the three levels of physics textbooks.

5.1.1 The Development of SG Across Three Levels of Physics Textbooks

The variation of SG in the three levels of physics textbooks can be explored in terms of three linguistic variables: deixis, arguability, and iconicity. For deixis, participants and processes need to be examined. The generic and specific participants, which are generic and concrete everyday entities at the stratum of context, are identified out. As to processes, they are investigated according to whether they refer to recurrent or particular events. As for arguability, it is analyzed in terms of finite or non-finite processes. About iconicity, grammatical metaphors are examined. The occurrence of these items at different levels of textbooks is shown in Table 5.1 and Table 5.2.

Table 5.1　The Occurrence of Deixis (participants) and Iconicity in Physics Textbooks

Textbooks	Sum of words	Occurrence-frequency (×1000)						
		Generic participants		Specific participants		Grammatical metaphors		
Level 1	4168	139	33.349	574	137.716	32	7.678	
Level 2	19658	920	46.8	1956	99.959	188	9.563	
Level 3	21332	1109	51.99	1679	78.708	331	15.516	

Table 5.2　Deixis (processes) and Arguability

Textbooks	Sum of words	Occurrence-frequency (×1000)							
		Non-finite		finite		recurrent		particular	
Level 1	523	54	10.33	469	89.67	16	3.1	507	96.9
Level 2	2396	289	12.06	2107	87.94	1312	54.8	1084	45.2
Level 3	2723	387	14.21	2336	85.79	2216	81.4	507	18.6

As Table 5.1 and Table 5.2 show, the SG is getting weaker and weaker from textbooks of Level 1 through textbooks of Level 2 to textbooks of Level 3, which can be seen from the change of occurrences in terms of deixis, arguability and iconicity.

First, the occurrences of two dimensions in deixis, participants and processes, signify a process of weakening SG from lower-level textbooks to higher-level textbooks.

The degree of genericity of participants, that is, generic or specific, decides the level of SG. The more generic the participants, the weaker gravity they give; the more specific the participants, the stronger gravity they have. Furthermore, the density of generic/specific participants is about to decide the strength of SG in a text. In other words, the more generic participants exist in a text, the weaker SG the text is; the more specific participants occur in a text, the stronger SG the text contains.

This study shows that there is an increasing tendency to the occurrence of generic participants and a decreasing tendency to that of specific participants with the textbooks are getting to a higher level. The occurrence of geneic participants is rising steadily with 33. 349/1000 in textbooks of Level 1, 46. 800/1000 in textbooks of Level 2 and 51. 99/1000 in textbooks of Level 3. On the other hand, the occurrence of specific participants is decreasing steadily with 137. 716/1000 in textbooks of Level 1, 99. 959/1000 in textbooks of Level 2 and 78. 708/1000 in textbooks of Level 3. In a word, the higher the level of textbooks are, the more generic participants and less specific participants occur, which causes a process of SG weakening.

At the same time, the degree of habituality of processes, that is, particular or recurrent, influences the strength of SG. Recurrent processes will cause weaker SG than particular processes. Furthermore, the density of recurrent/particular events is about to decide the strength of SG in a text. In other words, the more recurrent events come up in a text, the weaker SG the text is; the more particular events appear in a text, the stronger SG the text contains.

As this research shows, there is an increasing tendency to the occurrence of recurrent events and a decreasing tendency to that of particular events with the textbooks are getting to a higher level. The occurrence of recurrent events is rising steadily with 3. 1/% in textbooks of Level 1, 54. 8/% in textbooks of Level 2 and 81. 4/% in textbooks of Level 3. On the other hand, the occurrence of specific participants is decreasing steadily with 96. 9/% in textbooks of Level 1, 45. 2/% in textbooks of Level 2 and 18. 6/% in textbooks of Level 3. In a word, the higher the level of textbooks are, the more recurrent events and the fewer particular events occur, which causes a process of SG weakening.

Second, the occurrences of finite and non-finite processes which show arguability signify a weakening process of SG from the lower-level textbooks to the higher-level textbooks. A finite process results in a stronger SG, while a non-finite process leads to a weaker SG. Furthermore, the density of finite/non-finite processes is about to decide the strength of SG in a text. In other words, the more non-finite processes are used in a text, the weaker SG the text is; the more finite processes show themselves in a text, the stronger gravity the text contains.

As this research shows, there is an increasing tendency to the occurrence of non-finite processes and a decreasing tendency to that of finite processes with the textbooks are getting to a higher level. The occurrence of non-finite processes is rising steadily with 10.33% in textbooks of Level 1, 12.06% in textbooks of Level 2 and 14.21% in textbooks of Level 3. On the other hand, the occurrence of finite processes is decreasing steadily with 89.67% in textbooks of Level 1, 87.94% in textbooks of Level 2 and 85.79/% in textbooks of Level 3. In a word, the higher the level of the textbooks are, the more non-finite processes and the fewer finite processes occur, which causes a process of SG weakening.

Third, the occurrences of grammatical metaphors meaning iconicity also show a weakening process of SG from lower-level textbooks to higher-level textbooks. The degree of iconicity has a direct effect on SG. As there is a less iconical relationship between metaphorical expressions and the experience they construe, metaphorical forms mean weaker SG. Furthermore, the density of grammatical metaphors is about to decide the strength of SG in a text. In other words, the more grammatical metaphors there are in a text, the weaker SG the text is.

As this research shows, there is an increasing tendency to the occurrence of grammatical metaphors with the textbooks are getting to a higher level. The occurrence of grammatical metaphors is rising steadily with 7.678/1000 in textbooks of Level 1, 9.563/1000 in textbooks of Level 2 and 15.516/1000 in textbooks of Level 3. In a word, the higher the level of the textbooks are, the more grammatical metaphors are occurring, which causes a process of SG weakening.

5.1.2 The Development of SD Across Three Levels of Physics Textbooks

The variation of SD in the three levels of physics textbooks can be explored in terms of technicality. In this study, technicality includes both technical terms and physical and mathematical symbols. The occurrence of these items at different levels of textbooks is shown in Table 5.3.

Table 5.3   The Occurrence of Distillation in Physics Textbooks

Textbooks	Sum of Technicality	Occurrence-frequency (×1000)	
			Technicality
Level 1	4168	92	22.073
Level 2	19658	700	35.609
Level 3	21332	1061	49.74

As Table 5.3 shows, the SD is getting stronger and stronger from textbooks of Level 1 through textbooks of Level 2 to textbooks of Level 3, which can be seen from the change of occurrences in technicality.

The occurrences of technicality show a process of strengthening SD from the lower-level textbooks to the higher-level textbooks. Technicality, which is the distillation of meaning, has stronger SD than non-technicality. Furthermore, the density of technicality is about to decide the strength of SD in a text. In other words, the more technical terms and physical and mathematical symbols there are in a text, the stronger SD the text is.

As this book shows, there is an increasing tendency to the occurrence of technicality with the textbooks are getting to a higher level. The occurrence of technicality is rising steadily with 22.073/1000 in textbooks of Level 1, 35.609/1000 in textbooks of Level 2 and 49.74/1000 in textbooks of Level 3. In a word, the higher the level of the textbooks are, the more technicalities are occurring, which causes a process of SD strengthening.

5.1.3 Knowledge Building Through SG and SD in Physics Textbooks

As the above analysis shows, there is a process of weakening SG and a process of strengthening SD from the lower-level textbooks to the higher-level textbooks, which suggests that the physical knowledge is built in a more and more abstract and scientific way across school years.

Weakening SG means abstracting generalising principles from the concrete particulars of a specific context case. Therefore, the weakening process of SG implies that knowledge is built in a more concrete way in the lower-level textbooks, and that knowledge is constructed in a more abstract way in the higher-level textbooks.

On the other hand, strengthening SD refers to condensing a large range of meanings into symbols or technical terms. Hence, the process of strengthening SD shows that the knowledge built in higher-level textbooks is getting more scientific in contrast to that constructed in lower-level textbooks.

5.2 Patterns of SG and SD in Introducing Technical Concepts

The above section illustrates the general developing tendency of SG and SD across the different levels of physics textbooks. However, for a particular piece of knowledge, its construction must experience the ups and downs of both SG and SD. In other words, the successful introduction of a concept needs the waving of SG and SD. The three levels of physics textbooks, the texts of which chosen for the study are all about the concept of *force*, are used for different ages of students. Therefore, the patterns of SG and SD are assumed to be different in introducing the technical concept *force* at each level of the textbooks, which is explored in the following section.

5.2.1 The Pattern of SG and SD in Physics Textbooks of Level 1

School physics Level 1 is used for students of K-2 to have a simple sense of the scientific concept *force and motion*, so it is assumed that the concepts at this school level must be introduced in a way suitable to students' understanding and that the development of SD and SG in introducing concepts must agree with it. The topic chosen in this study is about force, therefore, in the following section, an excerpt, shown in Table 5.4 which explains the concept force, is taken as an example to explore the developing pattern of SD and SG in concept introduction at school physics Level 1.

Table 5.4　Example of Introducing the Concept "Force" at School Physics Level 1

[Push and Pull] (from Riley, 2001: 26-27)
You use a force every time you move something, change its direction or change its shape.
You push a pram/swing.
You pull a brush through your hair/a book from your bag.
A push/a pull is a force.
You use pushing and pulling forces to twist and turn things, too
Jessica tries to bend some things.
She uses pushing and pulling forces.

5.2.1.1 The Pattern of SG in Physics textbooks of Level 1

For the introduction of the concept "force", there are six steps in the development of SG, as shown in Figure 5.1.

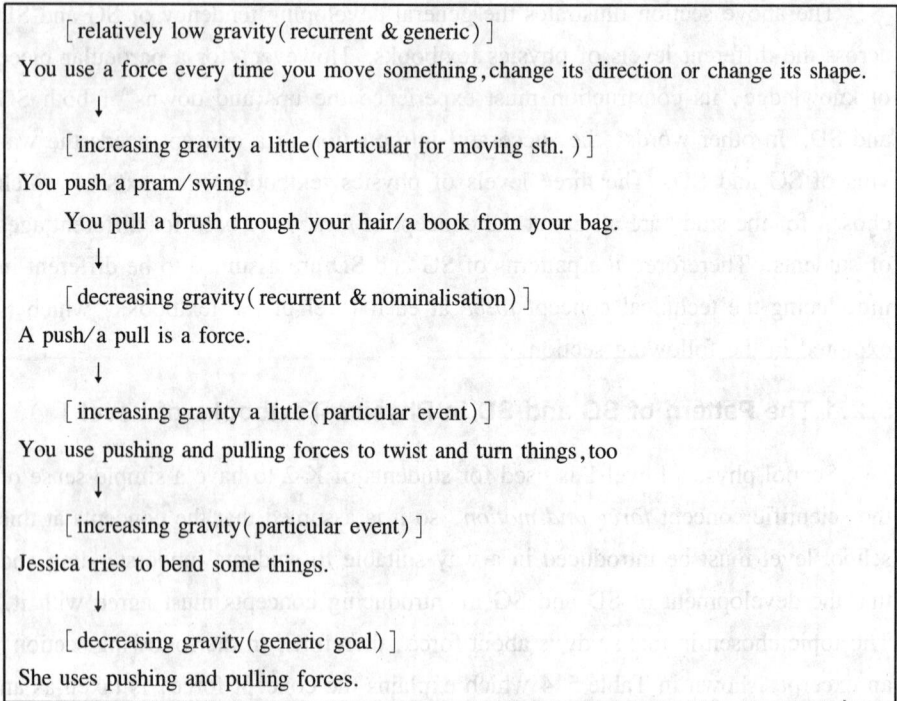

[relatively low gravity(recurrent & generic)]

You use a force every time you move something, change its direction or change its shape.

↓

[increasing gravity a little(particular for moving sth.)]

You push a pram/swing.

　You pull a brush through your hair/a book from your bag.

↓

[decreasing gravity(recurrent & nominalisation)]

A push/a pull is a force.

↓

[increasing gravity a little(particular event)]

You use pushing and pulling forces to twist and turn things, too

↓

[increasing gravity(particular event)]

Jessica tries to bend some things.

↓

[decreasing gravity(generic goal)]

She uses pushing and pulling forces.

Figure 5.1　Analysis of SG of force

In the first step, the concept "force" is presented directly without definition. Some recurrent activities, which are offered for illustrating the situations in which "force" is used, and generic participant "you" lift the meaning of "force" somehow above the concrete particulars of specific contexts. That is, there is a relatively low degree of SG to which the interpretation of the meaning "force" is less dependent on its context. In the second step, the SG of the concept "force" is strengthened in that the condensed abstract concept "force" is moving down to its concrete examples. The examples of "You push a pram/ swing" and "You pull a brush through your hair/a book from your bag" are particular instances of moving something in the above step. In the third step, the meaning of "force" is again lifted above the concrete particulars of specific contexts by nominalisation of "push" and "pull" and recurrent nature expressed with "is", which causes a weakening of SG. In the fourth step, although recurrent activities and the generic participant "you" are shown, SG of this concept is increased a little because of particular activities "twist and turn things" used to illustrate the concept "pushing and pulling forces". In the fifth step, there is a continuous increasing of SG, with the particular event "Jessica tries to bend some things" as a concrete example of the recurrent activities "twist and turn things" in the fourth step. In the sixth step, the SG of the meaning is decreasing with the concrete particulars of a specific case "Jessica tries to bend some things" are abstracted into a generalising principle "She uses pushing and pulling forces".

The six steps, which realize the development of SG in the introduction of the concept "force", can be put in a form of wave, as Figure 5.2 shows.

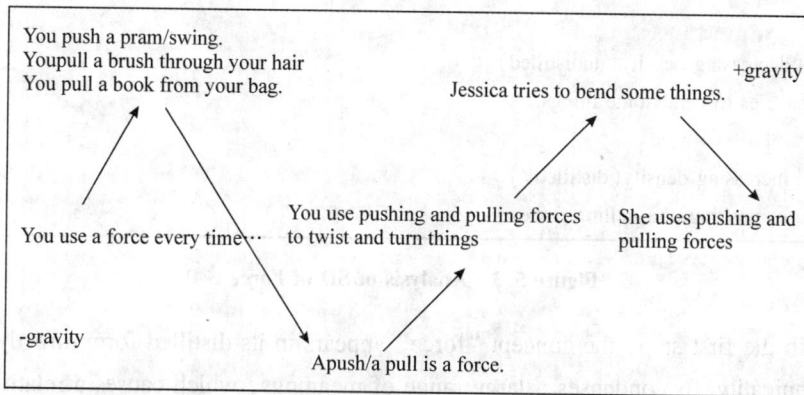

Figure 5.2   Logogenetic Shunting (+ - SG) of the Concept Force

As the wave of SG in Figure 5.2 shows, there are two characteristics about the the development of SG in introducing the concept "force" in textbooks of Level 1. First, there is one complete SG wave with the other two half ones. The third step expressed by the sentences "A push is a force" and "A pull is a force" is at the bottom of the complete SG wave, and the second step and the fifth step which include several concrete examples are at the tops of the two half SG waves. Second, the explanation of the concept "force" both begins and ends at the half way of the wave.

5.2.1.2 The Pattern of SD in Physics Textbooks of Level 1

Parallel to the six steps of SG for the introduction of the concept "force", there are also six steps in the development of SD, as shown in Figure 5.3 .

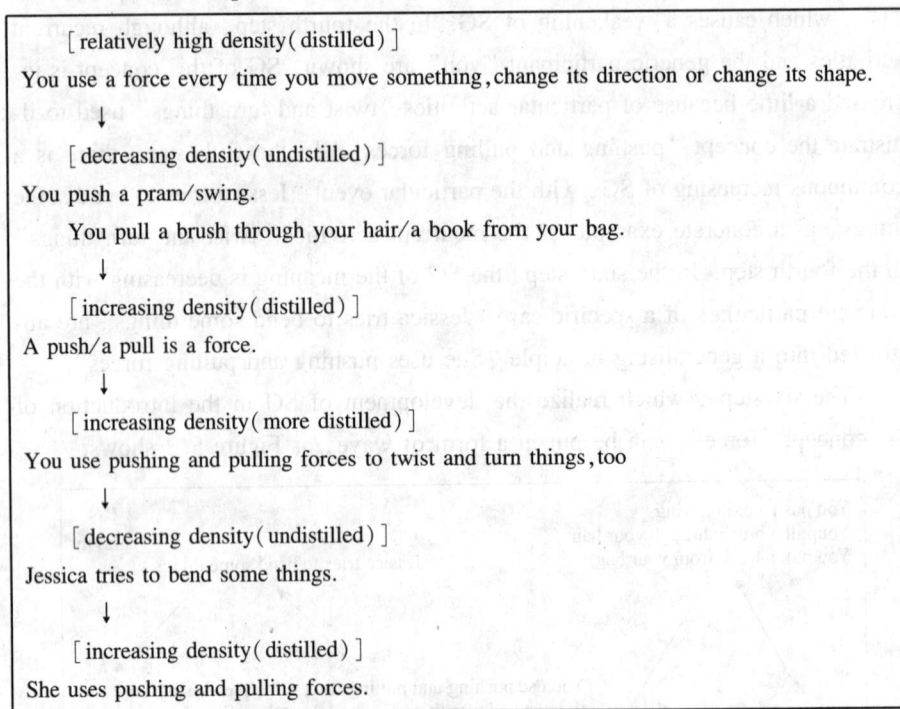

[relatively high density(distilled)]

You use a force every time you move something, change its direction or change its shape.

↓

[decreasing density(undistilled)]

You push a pram/swing.

You pull a brush through your hair/a book from your bag.

↓

[increasing density(distilled)]

A push/a pull is a force.

↓

[increasing density(more distilled)]

You use pushing and pulling forces to twist and turn things, too

↓

[decreasing density(undistilled)]

Jessica tries to bend some things.

↓

[increasing density(distilled)]

She uses pushing and pulling forces.

Figure 5.3   Analysis of SD of Force

In the first step, the concept "force" appears in its distilled form directly as a technicality. It condenses a large range of meanings, which causes a relatively high SD. In the second step, the SD of the concept "force" is weakened in that this dense concept is unpacked into everyday language with concrete examples "You push a pram/swing" and "You pull a brush through your hair/a book from your bag". In the third step, the meaning expressed in the above examples "You push a pram/swing" and "You pull a brush through your hair/a book from your bag" is condensed into the nominalization "push" and "pull" and further into the technical term "force", which is strengthening the SD. In the fourth step, the meaning construed in the above step by "A push/pull is a force" is taken in a more condensed expression of "pushing and pulling forces". That is, SG is increasing more. In the fifth step, there is a decreasing of SD compared to SD in the above step, with the particular event "Jessica tries to bend some

208

things" in its undistilled expression to unpack the meaning condensed in "push-ing and pulling forces" in the above fourth step. In the six steps, SD is increas-ing again. The undistilled meaning of a specific case "Jessica tries to bend some things" is packed into its corresponding technical terms "She uses pushing and pulling forces".

The six steps in realizing the development of SD can be put in a form of wave, as Figure 5.4 shows.

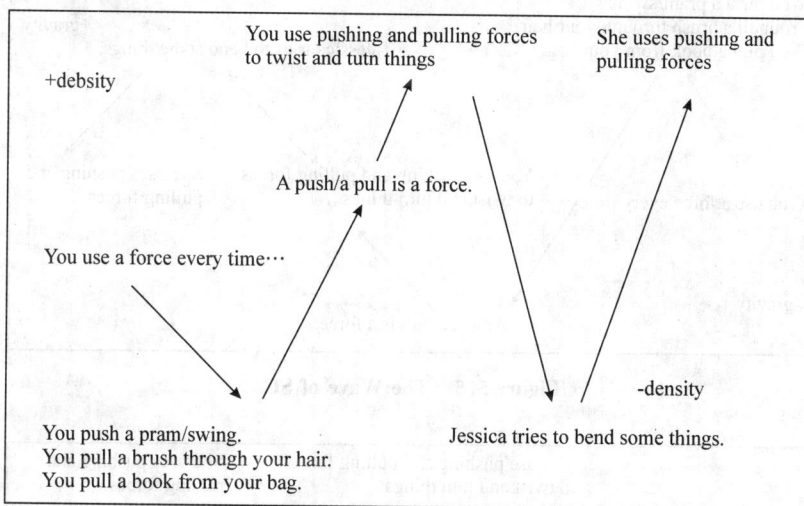

You use pushing and pulling forces to twist and tutn things

She uses pushing and pulling forces

+debsity

A push/a pull is a force.

You use a force every time···

You push a pram/swing.
You pull a brush through your hair.
You pull a book from your bag.

-density

Jessica tries to bend some things.

Figure 5.4   Logogenetic Shunting (+-SD)

As the wave of SD in Figure 5.4 shows, some features also characterise the development of SD in introducing the concept "force" in textbooks of Level 1. First, there are two complete SD waves with another half one. The second and the fifth steps which include several concrete examples are at the bottoms of the two complete SD waves. The fourth and the sixth steps introducing "pushing and pulling forces" are at the tops of the two complete SD waves. Second, the ex-planation of the concept "force" begins at the half way of the half wave. Third, the third step, which is about the definition of the concept "force" ("A push/ pull is a force") , has a higher SD than the first step about the introduction of the concept "force".

5.2.1.3 The Relationship Between SG and SD in Physics Textbooks of Level 1

Generally speaking, the degree of SG is at negative relevance with that of

SD, that is, a stronger SG is usually with a weaker SD, and vice versa. However, the correspondence between them is not at the same degree. The strongest/weakest SG may correspond to a weaker/stronger SD, but not necessarily to a weakest/stongest SD, although sometimes it is. The relationship between SG and SD in textbooks of Level 1 can be shown in Figure 5.5 and Figure 5.6.

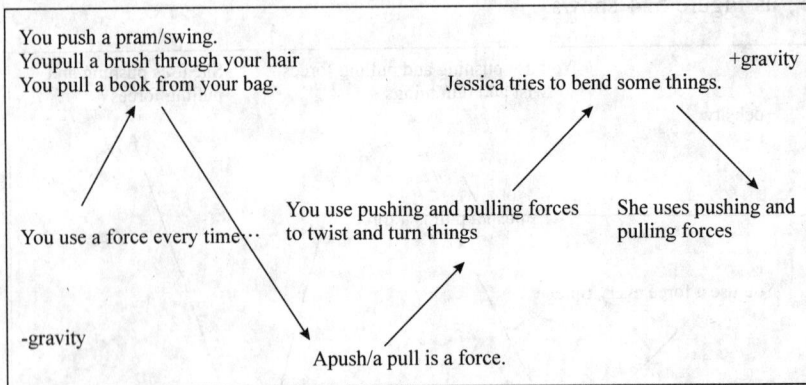

Figure 5.5   The Wave of SG

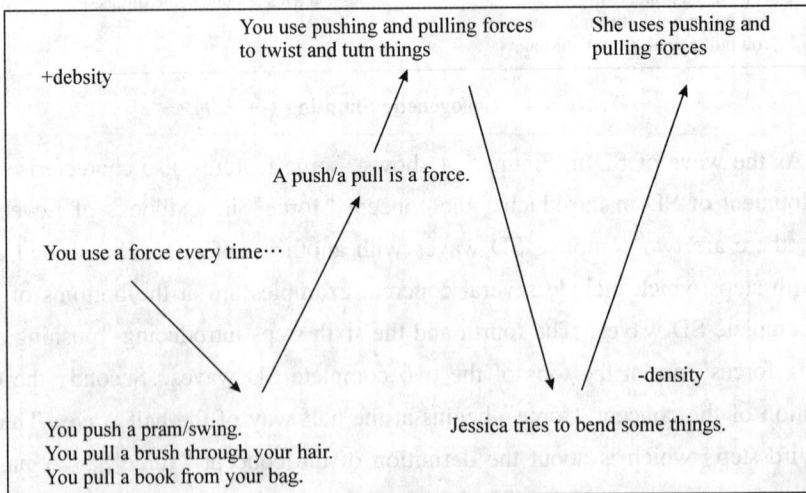

Figure 5.6   The Wave of SD

As Figure 5.5 and Figure 5.6 illustrate, there are completely conversing correspondences between the degree of SG and that of SD in textbooks of Level

1. On the one hand, the SG degree suggested by the highest tops of SG wave is the same to that implied by the lowest bottoms of SD. For example, in the first step in introducing the concept 'force' the degree of SG lowerness is the same to that of SD higherness. On the other hand, not all the examples show the completely conversing correspondences between SG and SD in textbooks of Level 1. The SG degree suggested by the lowest bottom of SG wave is not shown at the highest top in SD wave, although it is at a higher Level of SD. The two highest tops of SD involve lower SG but not the lowest. On the whole, the degree of SG is on the contrary direction of that of SD although they are sometimes not at the same level.

5.2.2 The Pattern of SD and SG in Physics Textbooks of Level 2

School physics Level two is used for upper primary school students of years 2-6, further presenting the scientific concept *force and motion*, and it is assumed that the concepts at this school level must be introduced in a way different from that at Level 1 and that the development of SD and SG in introducing concepts must agree with it. In the following section, an excerpt, shown in Table 5.5 which explains the concept *force*, will be taken as an example to explore the developing pattern of SD and SG in concept introduction in textbooks of Level 2.

Table 5.5   Example of introducing the concept 'Buoyant force' at school physics Level 2

[*What are Forces and Motion*?] (from Sarah, 2009: 22)   **Buoyant Force**   When an object is lowered into water, it displaces (pushes aside) some of the water.   That is why the water level rises when you get into the bath.   The water pushes upwards against the object, and may even hold it up.   The pushing force of a liquid such as water is called buoyant force.   The buoyant force is equal to the weight of liquid displaced by the object.   The bigger an object is, the more liquid it displaces, and the greater the buoyant force is.

5.2.2.1 The Pattern of SG in Physics Textbooks of Level 2

For the introduction of the concept "buoyant force", there are five steps in the development of SG, as shown in Figure 5.7.

[relatively low gravity(recurrent & generic)]

When an object is lowered into water, it displaces(pushes aside) some of the water.

↓

[increasing gravity a little(particular & specific contrast to the above.)]

That is why the water level rises when you get into bath.

↓

[decreasing gravity(recurrent & generic)]

The water pushes upwards against the object, and may even hold it up.

↓

[decreasing gravity more(generic & recurrent)]

The pushing force of a liquid such as water is called buoyant force.

The buoyant force is equal to the weight of liquid displaced by the object.

[increasing gravity a little(specific contrast to the above)]

↓

The bigger an object is, the more liquid it displaces, and the greater the buoyant force is.

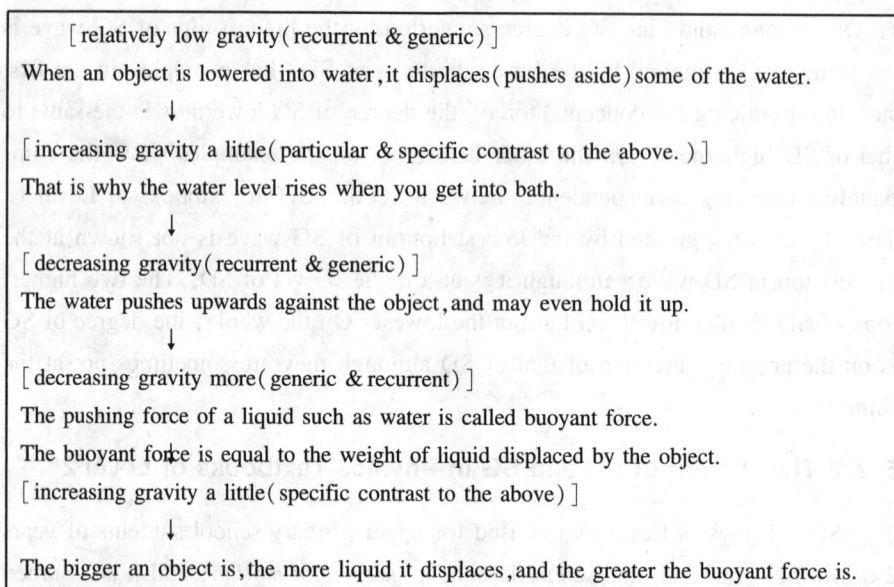

Figure 5.7   Analysis of SG of Buoyant Force

In the first step, the sentence contains a relatively weak degree of SG because the recurrent feature of the event implied by "when" clause and the generic participant "an object" lift the meaning somehow above the concrete particulars of specific contexts. In the second step, the SG gets strengthened in that the condensed abstract concept expressed by "when" clause and the generic participant "an object" is moving down to its concrete examples. The example of "That is why the water level rises when you get into the bath" is a particular instance illustrating the experience construed by "When an object is lowered into water, it displaces (pushes aside) some of the water". In the third step, the meaning construed in the sentence "The water pushes upwards against the object, and may even hold it up" is again lifted above the concrete particulars of specific contexts by the generic participant "object" and the recurrent process expressed by the present tense, which causes a weakening of SG. In the fourth step, there is a continuous decreasing of SG from compared to the SG in the above step, which is caused by two linguistic features. First, the experience "The water pushes upwards against the object, and may even hold it up" in the fourth step is construed in a more generic way as "pushing force" which is then defined as "buyant force". Second, the present tenses construe these processes again as recurrent activities. In the fifth step, the SG in the sentence is increasing because the experience construed in the sentence "The bigger an object is, the more liquid it displaces, and the greater the buoyant force is" functions as a specific case illustrating the generalising principle expressed by the sentence "The buoyant force is equal to the weight of liquid displaced by the object" in the above step.

The five steps, which realize the development of SG in the introduction of the concept 'buoyant force' can be put in a form of wave, as Figure 5.8 shows.

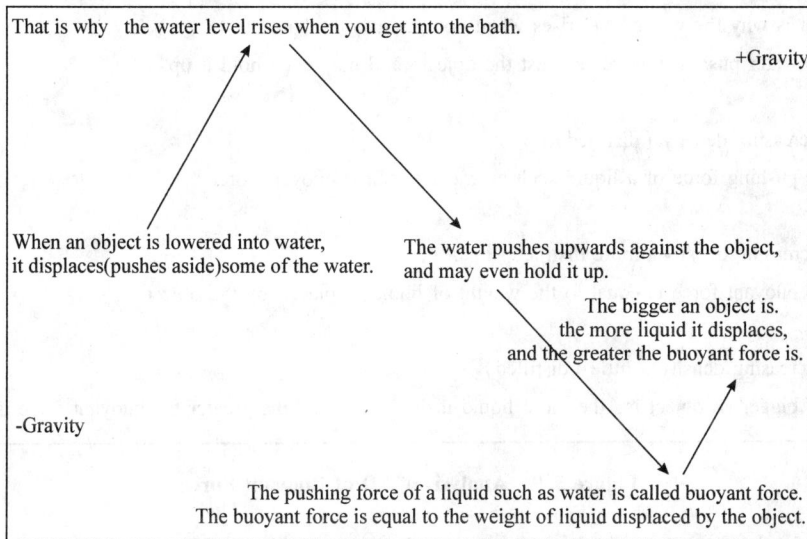

That is why   the water level rises when you get into the bath.

+Gravity

When an object is lowered into water,
it displaces(pushes aside)some of the water.

The water pushes upwards against the object,
and may even hold it up.

The bigger an object is.
the more liquid it displaces,
and the greater the buoyant force is.

-Gravity

The pushing force of a liquid such as water is called buoyant force.
The buoyant force is equal to the weight of liquid displaced by the object.

Figure 5.8   Logogeneric Shunting (+ -SG) of Buoyant Force

As the wave of SG in Figure 5.8 shows, there are two characteristics about the development of SG in introducing the concept "buoyant force" in textbooks of Level 2. First, this SG seems to have two waves with the highest top and the lowest bottom, but it is not so in a strict sense in that the wave begins from half way and ends also at half way. The fourth step expressed by the sentences "The pushing force of a liquid such as water is called buoyant force" and "The buoyant force is equal to the weight of liquid displaced by the object" is at the bottom of the SG wave, and Step two which offers a concrete example "That is why the water level rises when you get into the bath" is at the tops of the two half SG waves. Second, the explanation of the concept "buyant force" both begins and

213

ends at the half way of the wave, but the position of SG of the ending step is a little lower than that of the beginning step.

5.2.2.2 The Pattern of SD in Physics Textbooks of Level 2

There are five steps of SG for the introduction of the concept "buyant force", while the steps in the development of SD are adapted to four, as shown in Figure 5.9.

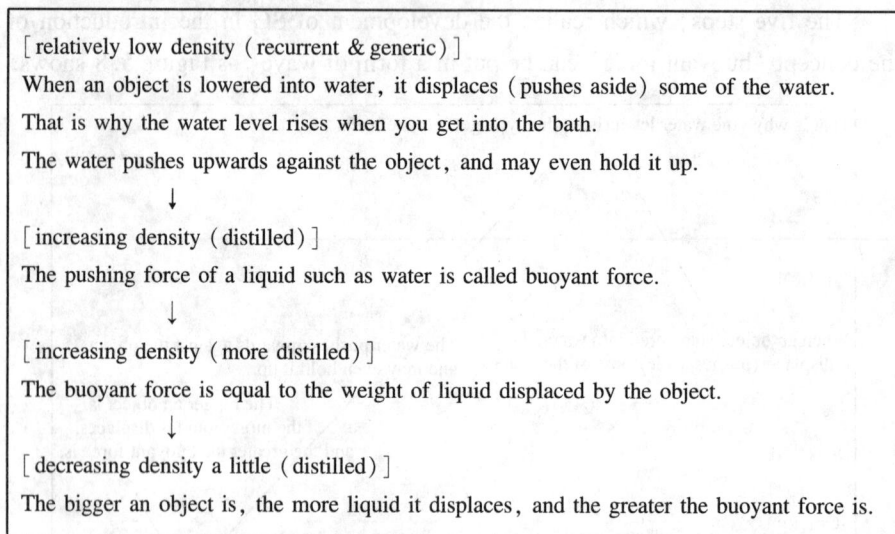

[relatively low density (recurrent & generic)]

When an object is lowered into water, it displaces (pushes aside) some of the water.

That is why the water level rises when you get into the bath.

The water pushes upwards against the object, and may even hold it up.

↓

[increasing density (distilled)]

The pushing force of a liquid such as water is called buoyant force.

↓

[increasing density (more distilled)]

The buoyant force is equal to the weight of liquid displaced by the object.

↓

[decreasing density a little (distilled)]

The bigger an object is, the more liquid it displaces, and the greater the buoyant force is.

Figure 5.9　Analysis of SD of Buoyant Force

In the first step, before presenting the technical term "buyant force", several concrete examples of this phenomenon are provided and explained in everyday language, which creates a relatively weak SD. In the second step, a large range of meanings construed in the above particular examples are distilled into a technicality "buyant force", which increases the SD. In the third step, the meaning construed in the above step by the sentence "The pushing force of a liquid such as water is called buoyant force" is further expressed as a principle "The buoyant force is equal to the weight of liquid displaced by the object" which condenses more meanings. That is, SD is increasing more compared to that in the above step. In the fourth step, there is a decreasing of SD compared to that in the above step, with the particular explanation "The bigger an object is, the more liquid it displaces, and the greater the buoyant force is" in its undistilled expression to unpack the meaning condensed in the principle of "The buoyant force is equal to the weight of liquid displaced by the object" in the above fourth step.

The four steps, which realize the development of SD in introducing the technical concept "buoyant force", can be put in a form of wave, as Figure 5. 10 shows.

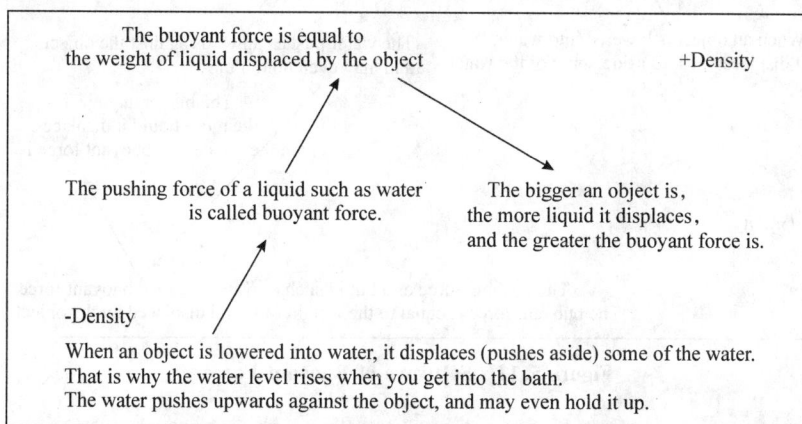

The buoyant force is equal to
the weight of liquid displaced by the object   +Density

The pushing force of a liquid such as water   The bigger an object is,
is called buoyant force.   the more liquid it displaces,
                                                             and the greater the buoyant force is.

-Density
When an object is lowered into water, it displaces (pushes aside) some of the water.
That is why the water level rises when you get into the bath.
The water pushes upwards against the object, and may even hold it up.

Figure 5. 10   Logogenetic shunting (+ − SD) of Buoyant Force

The analysis of the four steps reveals that some features characterize the development of SD at school physics Level 2. First, there is a SD wave with a quarter lacking. The first step which is showing several concrete examples is at the bottoms of the SD waves. The third step introducing the buoyant force principle "The buoyant force is equal to the weight of liquid displaced by the object" is at the tops of the SD waves. Second, the definition of the concept "buoyant force" and the unpacking of the buoyant principle "The bigger an object is, the more liquid it displaces, and the greater the buoyant force is" stay at the same level of SD degree. It is the meaning construed by this buoyant principle that ends at the half way of the SD.

5. 2. 2. 3 The Relationship Between SG and SD in Physics Textbooks of Level 2

The relationship of negative relevance between SG and SD at school physics Level 2 can be shown in Figure 5. 11 and Figure 5. 12.

As Figure 5. 11 and Figure 5. 12 illustrate, the steps of SG and those of SD are not the same although there is some overlapping. In addition, there are no completely conversing correspondences between the degree of SG and that of SD

That is why the water level rises when you get into the bath.

+Gravity

When an object is lowered into water, it displaces(pushes aside)some of the water.

The water pushes upwards against the object, and may even hold it up.

The bigger an object is.
the more liquid it displaces,
and the greater the buoyant force is.

-Gravity

The pushing force of a liquid such as water is called buoyant force.
The buoyant force is equal to the weight of liquid displaced by the object.

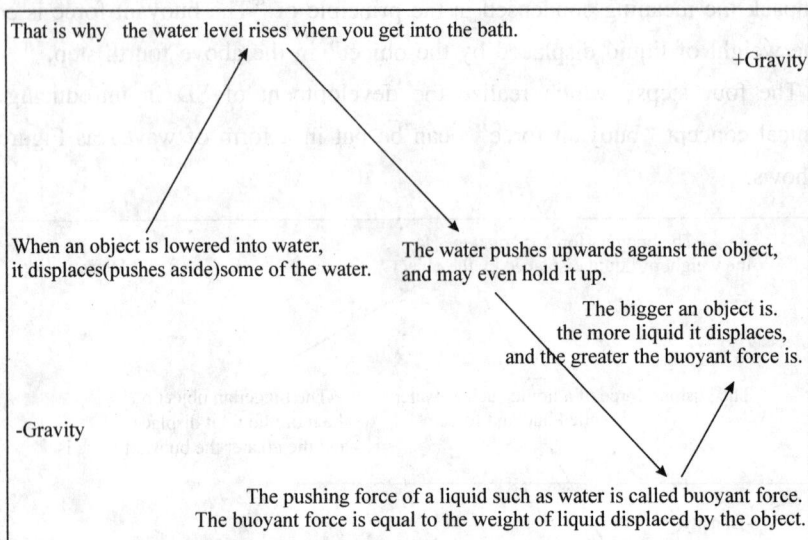

Figure 5. 11   SG wave of Buoyant Force

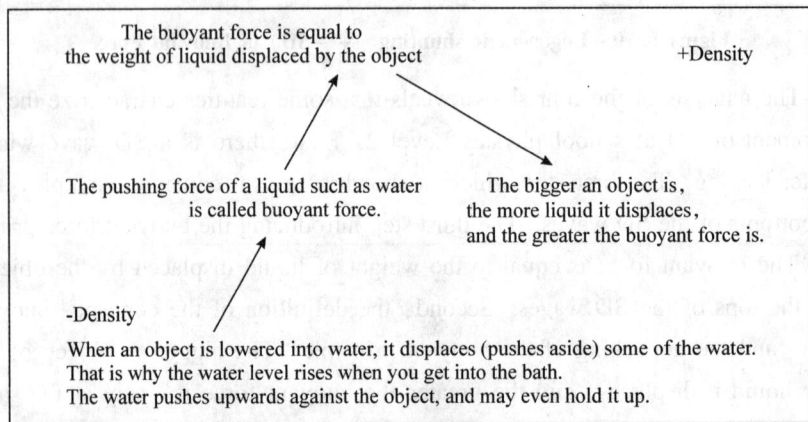

The buoyant force is equal to
the weight of liquid displaced by the object

+Density

The pushing force of a liquid such as water
is called buoyant force.

The bigger an object is,
the more liquid it displaces,
and the greater the buoyant force is.

-Density

When an object is lowered into water, it displaces (pushes aside) some of the water.
That is why the water level rises when you get into the bath.
The water pushes upwards against the object, and may even hold it up.

Figure 5. 12   SD wave of Buoyant Force

at the school physics Level 2. For example, the experience at the highest tops of SG wave only functions as one of the components of the experience at the lowest bottom of SD wave, and the experience at the lowest bottom of SG wave is further divided into two separated experiences acting respectively at the half way and the highest top of SD wave. The experience in the last step is the same, but its degree of SG is weaker than that of SD. The different criteria for deciding the developing steps of SG and SD necessitate the individual analysis of them.

5.2.3 The Development of SD and SG in Physics Textbooks of Level 3

School physics Level 3 is used for junior school students of years 7-10 for a deeper exploration of the scientific concept *force and motion*, so it is assumed that there are some differences in the way to introduce scientific concepts from the above two school physics levels, and that the development of SD and SG in introducing these concepts must have its own characteristics. In the following section, an excerpt, shown in Table 5.6, which explains the concept "force" will be taken as an example to explore the developing pattern of SD and SG in concept introduction at school physics Level 3.

Table 5.6　Example Explaining the Concept "force" at School Physics Level 3

[*Exploring-Force and Structure*] (**from Spiders, 1991: 6**) 　　What is a force? Have you ever felt "forced" to do something you did not intend or want to do? What about slipping on a frozen puddle and failing over, or having to chase something that has blown a-way on a windy day? We all experience forces constantly. Often we do not notice they are there, but at other times, such as when two cars collide, they are obvious. What is a force, and why do forces feature so strongly in our everyday lives? You cannot see forces but you can observe their effects. The easiest way to think of a force is as a push or pull Forces start objects moving and keep them going. They slow down moving things or bring them to a stop. They change the direction or speed of movement. Think about a bicycle travelling over a level surface. To get it started you have to exert a pushing force on the pedals and you have to carry on pushing the pedals to keep it going. To slow the bicycle down or make It stop, you have to pull on the brakes. You can make the bicycle change direction by pushing and pulling the handlebars, and to make it go faster, you have to exert more force on the pedals. Forces bring about changes of shape and size. A piece of Plasticine can be moulded into a new shape by pushing and pulling it. Old motorcars can be squashed into very small blocks by pushing on them with a strong force, using a machine called a hydraulic ram.

5.2.3.1 The Pattern of SG in Physics Textbooks of Level 3

For the introduction of the concept "force", four steps are identified in the

217

development of SG, as shown in Figure 5. 13.

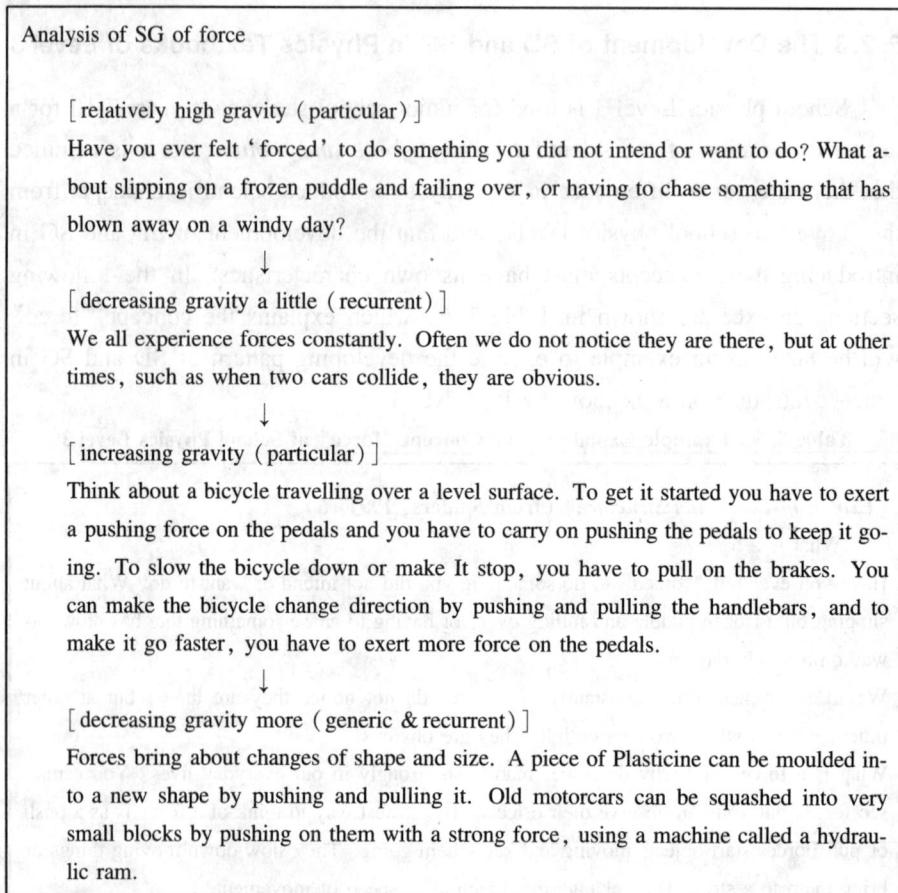

Analysis of SG of force

[relatively high gravity (particular)]

Have you ever felt 'forced' to do something you did not intend or want to do? What a-
bout slipping on a frozen puddle and failing over, or having to chase something that has
blown away on a windy day?

↓

[decreasing gravity a little (recurrent)]

We all experience forces constantly. Often we do not notice they are there, but at other
times, such as when two cars collide, they are obvious.

↓

[increasing gravity (particular)]

Think about a bicycle travelling over a level surface. To get it started you have to exert
a pushing force on the pedals and you have to carry on pushing the pedals to keep it going. To slow the bicycle down or make It stop, you have to pull on the brakes. You
can make the bicycle change direction by pushing and pulling the handlebars, and to
make it go faster, you have to exert more force on the pedals.

↓

[decreasing gravity more (generic & recurrent)]

Forces bring about changes of shape and size. A piece of Plasticine can be moulded into a new shape by pushing and pulling it. Old motorcars can be squashed into very
small blocks by pushing on them with a strong force, using a machine called a hydraulic ram.

Figure 5. 13   Analysis of SG of Force

In the first step, the SG of the meanings shown here is relatively strong because some particular examples of showing "felt forced to do something" are
provided, such as "slipping on a frozen puddle and failing over", "having to
chase something that has blown away on a windy day", and the interpretation of
their meaning is highly depending on specific contexts. In the second step, there
is a little decreasing of SG in that the recurrent activities implied by the present
tense and the generic participant "we" lift the meaning of this piece of experience somehow above the concrete particulars of specific contexts. That is, there
is a relatively low degree of SG to which the interpretation of the meaning

"force" is less dependent on its context. In the third step, the SG of the experience showing the function of "force" is strengthened in that the condensed abstract concept "force" is moving down to its concrete examples. The examples such as "To slow the bicycle down or make It stop" or "you have to pull on the brakes" are all particular instances for the abstract concept "We all experience forces constantly" in the above step. In the fourth step, the meaning about "force" is again lifted above the concrete particulars of specific contexts by generic entities "shape" and "size" and recurrent nature of processes expressed with the present tense and the modal verb "can", causing a weakening of SG.

The four steps, which realize the development of SG in the introduction of the concept "force", can be put in a form of wave, as Figure 5.14 shows.

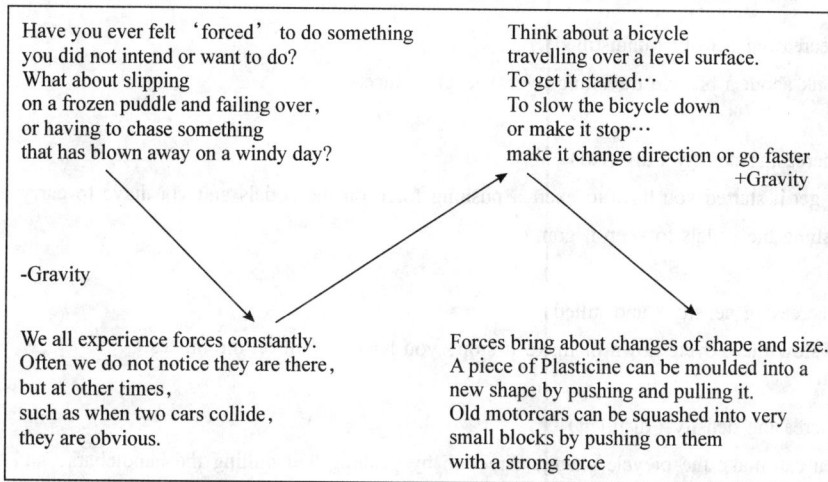

Have you ever felt 'forced' to do something
you did not intend or want to do?
What about slipping
on a frozen puddle and failing over,
or having to chase something
that has blown away on a windy day?

Think about a bicycle
travelling over a level surface.
To get it started···
To slow the bicycle down
or make it stop···
make it change direction or go faster
+Gravity

-Gravity

We all experience forces constantly.
Often we do not notice they are there,
but at other times,
such as when two cars collide,
they are obvious.

Forces bring about changes of shape and size.
A piece of Plasticine can be moulded into a
new shape by pushing and pulling it.
Old motorcars can be squashed into very
small blocks by pushing on them
with a strong force

Figure 5.14   Logogenetic Shunting (+ –SG)

As the wave of SG in Figure 5.14 shows, there are two characteristics about the development of SG in the introduction of the concept "force" at the school physics Level 3. First, there are two complete SG waves. The first step and the third step are at the tops of the two SG waves. The first step presents examples of "felt to do something", and the third step offers some instances of showing the function of "force". The second step and the fourth step, which describe the generic experience about "force", are at the bottoms of the two SG waves. Second, the explanation of the concept "force" begins with particular examples illustrating force and ends with the generic description of experience about "force".

5.2.3.2 The Pattern of SD in Physics Textbooks of Level 3

The development of SD for the introduction of the concept "force" at school physics Level 3 can be divided into eight steps to explain, as shown in Figure 5.15.

[relatively low density (undistilled)]

Have you ever felt 'forced' to do something you did not intend or want to do? What about slipping on a frozen puddle and failing over, or having to chase something that has blown away on a windy day?

↓

[increasing density (distilled)]

We all experience forces constantly. Often we do not notice they are there, but at other times, such as when two cars collide, they are obvious.

↓

[decreasing density (undistilled)]

Think about a bicycle travelling over a level surface.

↓

[increasing density (distilled)]

To get it started you have to exert a pushing force on the pedals and you have to carry on pushing the pedals to keep it going.

↓

[decreasing density (undistilled)]

To slow the bicycle down or make It stop, you have to pull on the brakes.

↓

[increasing density (distilled)]

You can make the bicycle change direction by pushing and pulling the handlebars, and to make it go faster, you have to exert more force on the pedals.

Forces bring about changes of shape and size.

↓

[decreasing density (undistilled)]

A piece of Plasticine can be moulded into a new shape by pushing and pulling it.

↓

[increasing density (distilled)]

Old motorcars can be squashed into very small blocks by pushing on them with a strong force, using a machine called a hydraulic ram.

Figure 5.15   Analysis of SD of Force (from Spiders, 1991: 6)

In the first step, there is a relatively low SD because the experience is construed in the indistilled form. Before explaining the concept "force", some concrete examples showing "felt forced to do something" are given and expressed into everyday language. In the second step, the concept "force" appears in its distilled form directly as a technicality. It condenses a large range of meanings as realized by the following examples, which causes a relatively strong SD. In the third step, the SD of the concept "force" is weakened in that this dense concept is unpacked into everyday language with concrete examples "Think about a bicycle travelling over a level surface". In the fourth step, SD is strengthened again by the distilled expression of "pushing force". It is used as a technicality, which condenses the meaning shown in the following experience "pushing the pedals to keep it going". In the fifth step, there is a decrease of SD. The undistilled expression "To slow the bicycle down or make it stop, you have to pull on the brakes" construes a particular event, which is unpacking the condensed meaning of "pulling forces" in the above step. In the sixth steps, SD is increasing again, with the undistilled meaning of a specific case "You can make the bicycle change direction by pushing and pulling the handlebars" is packed into its corresponding technical term "forces". In the seventh step, there is a decrease of SD again, with the experience "A piece of Plasticine can be moulded into a new shape by pushing and pulling it" in its undistilled expression to unpack the condensed meaning of "Forces bring about changes of shape and size" in the above step. In the eighth step, the SD is strengthened with the distilled technicality "force" adopted again in illustrating its function of changing shape.

The eight steps, which realize the development of SD in the introduction of the concept "force", can be put in a form of wave, as Figure 5. 16 shows.

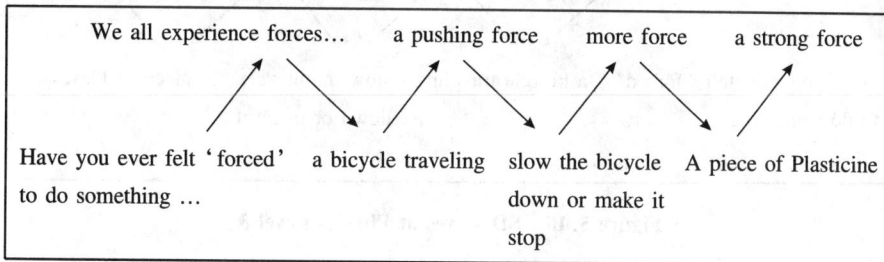

Figure 5. 16   Logogenetic Shunting (+ − SD)

221

As the wave of SD in Figure 5.16 displays, some features also characterise the development of SD at school physics Level 3. First, there are six complete SD waves. Second, the series of SD waves begin from concrete examples in un-distilled everyday language and end with the distilled technicality. Third, the whole pattern of this series of SD waves is as follows: down-up-down-up-down-up-down-up.

5.2.3.3 The Relationship Between SG and SD in Physics Textbooks of Level 3

The relationship of negative relevance between SG and SD at school physics Level 3 can be shown in Figure 5.17 and Figure 5.18.

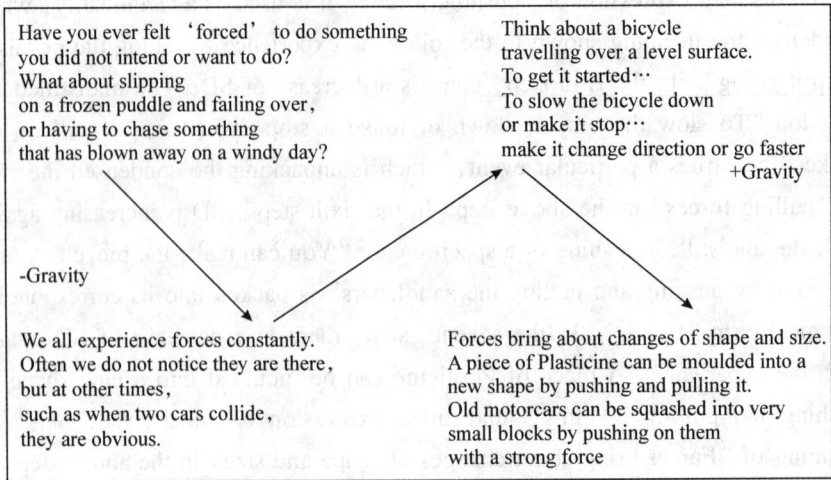

Have you ever felt 'forced' to do something you did not intend or want to do? What about slipping on a frozen puddle and failing over, or having to chase something that has blown away on a windy day?

Think about a bicycle travelling over a level surface. To get it started··· To slow the bicycle down or make it stop··· make it change direction or go faster +Gravity

-Gravity

We all experience forces constantly. Often we do not notice they are there, but at other times, such as when two cars collide, they are obvious.

Forces bring about changes of shape and size. A piece of Plasticine can be moulded into a new shape by pushing and pulling it. Old motorcars can be squashed into very small blocks by pushing on them with a strong force

Figure 5.17   SD waves at Physics Level 3

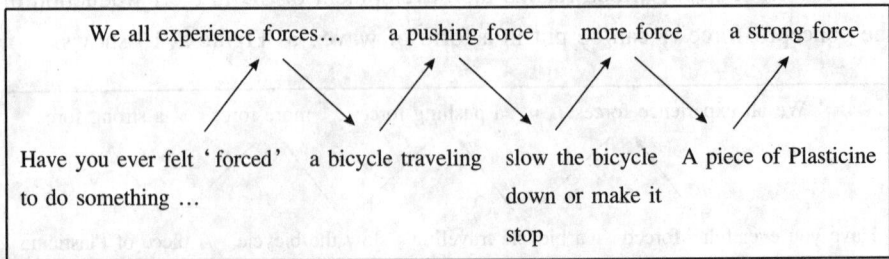

We all experience forces...   a pushing force   more force   a strong force

Have you ever felt 'forced' to do something ...   a bicycle traveling   slow the bicycle down or make it stop   A piece of Plasticine

Figure 5.18   SD waves at Physics Level 3

As Figure 5.17 and Figure 5.18 illustrate, the relationship between SG and

SD is not so directly relevant. First, more steps are needed for the analysis of SD development than SG. The steps of SG development can be divided according to features of a much larger linguistic cluster, and those of SD development are usually decided by characteristics of a smaller group of linguistic samples. Second, the larger linguistic cluster as a step in SG development should be divided into several smaller groups used as steps in SD development. In addition, there is some overlapping between the steps of SG and SD. The second step in SG and SD is about the same experiences, which is at the bottom of SG and the top of SD, that is, the lowest SG and the highest SD.

5.2.4 The Developing Patterns of SG and SD in Physics Textbooks

The developing pattern of SG and SD in introducing technical concepts at each level of school physics is investigated to throw some light on knowledge building, which shows both some similarities and some variations, as Figure 5.19 shows.

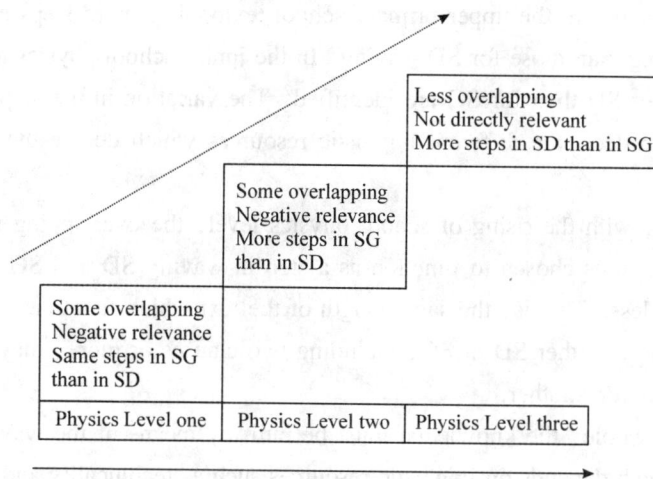

Figure 5.19   The Development of SD and SG Across School Physics Levels

The developing pattern of SG and SD in the introduction of the technical concept "force" shows some similiarities in building knowledge at each level of school physics.

First, there must be some steps for the successful waving of SD and SG. The top of SD which is realized by a technicality, or the bottom of SG which is characterized by nomimalization or abstract concepts, is the site for creating knowledge.

Second, there are some overlapping in the linguistic expressions chosen to function as a step in waving the SD and SG. That is, the same length of the text, which may be one clause, two clauses or more, is used as steps for analyzing both SD and SG.

Third, the degree of the SG shown by the step is in negative relevance to that of the SD expressed by the same step, but the degree in each is not necessarily the same.

However, the analysis shows that there are some differences in the development of SD and SG in the introduction of technical concepts across the three levels of physics textbooks.

First, the steps needed for the successful waving of SD do not necessarily correspond to those for the successful waving of SG. In the lower primary school textbooks, the steps for the successful waving of SD and SG match with each other completely. In the upper primary school textbooks, more steps are needed for SG waving than those for SD waving. In the junior school physics textbooks, more steps for SD than for SG are identified. The variation in the steps between SD and SG reflects the different linguistic resources which decide the degree of SD and SG.

Second, with the rising of school physics level, the overlapping in the linguistic expressions chosen to function as a step in waving SD and SG is becoming less and less. That is, the same length of the text which functions as one step in the waving of either SD or SG, including two clauses or more, may be acting as more steps for another.

On the whole, the knowledge must be built by means of the waving of SD and SG, which depends on linguistic resources such as technicality and grammatical metaphor to fulfill its realization.

5.3 Summary

Based on the analysis tool of SG and SD from a linguistic perspective, this chapter has presented a comprehensive picture of the development of SG and SD at all the three levels of physics textbooks and the different patterns of SG and SD at each level of physics textbooks.

Through a quantitative analysis of those linguistic variables concerned with SG and SD, that is, deixis, arguability, iconicity and technicality, it is found that SG tends to be weaker and SD tends to be stronger from lower-level textbooks to higher-level textbooks, which signifies that the physical knowledge is built across schooling in a direction from simple and common-sense to abstract and scientific.

Through a qualitative analysis of the developing patterns for SG and SD in the introduction of the concept *force* at each level of physics textbooks, some similarities and variations are discovered in building knowledge at each level of school physics.

Chapter 6 Conclusion

In this study, knowledge building in physics textbooks from the lower primary school level through the upper primary school level to the junior school level is investigated from an integrated perspective of SFL, SF-MDA and Bernstein's SE including Bernstein's theory of knowledge structure and semantics in LCT. Based on the physics textbooks corpus, an empirical analysis is done in terms of genre, field, multimodality, SG and SD. In this chapter, the major findings of the study will be summarized, the significance of the research will be examined, the limitations of the study will be enumerated, and finally suggestions for future work will be presented.

6.1 Summary of the Findings

This study embarks with an illumination of some key notions and theories pertinent to the analysis of this research, with an aim to set up the theoretical framework for this project. Then it proceeds to explore the features of knowledge building across three levels of school physics in terms of genre, field, multimodality, SG and SD.

As has been designated at the outset, this research adopts an integrated perspective of SFL, SF-MDA and Bernstein's SE on the variations of knowledge building and the development of SD and SG across school physics.

Based on these theoretical foundations, an empirical study with qualitative analysis is conducted in this research to investigate the patterns of knowledge building and the development of SD and SG across three levels of physics textbooks from the lower primary schools through the upper primary schools until the junior schools. Based on the statistic results and qualitative analysis, this research has engendered the following major findings:

First, the analysis of genres presents us three important points about knowl-

226

edge building in physics textbooks.

(1) There is a distinctive distribution of genre types across the three levels of physics textbooks. Macrogenres are favorite ones, which agrees with Christie's findings (1997). One type of macrogenres is *experimental proce-dures*, which are found in all the three levels of physics textbooks, and another type of macrogenres is the *picture commentary*, which characterizes the first level of physics textbooks. *Stories* occur across the three levels of textbooks with a de-creasing tendency.

(2) The macrogenres *experimental procedures* vary in schematic structures for different levels of physics textbooks. The third stage in macrogenre *experi-mental procedures* varies with different levels of physics textbooks: *Theoretical summary* for textbooks of Level 1, *Theoretical summary* or *Theoretical explora-tion* for textbooks of Level 2, and *Theoretical exploration* for textbooks of Level 3. In addition, in the second stage *Experiment*, the sub-stages *Steps* and *Results* are not completely same. The sub-stage *Steps* in physics Level 1 are concerned only with doing, those in physics Level 2 with doing in some texts and with do-ing and thinking in others, while those in physics Level 3 with both doing and thinking. The sub-stage *Results* in physics Level 1 are developed into *Results processing*.

(3) Story genres, which are not typical ones in science, are found in phys-ics textbooks of Level 2 and Level 3. This suggests that school science is some-how different from canonical science. In fact, scientific knowledge is recontextu-alized in school science to meet the requirements of students and this knowledge recontextualization is reflected in the use of genres.

Second, the empirical study of entities, a main component of field, reveals significant features of knowledge building in physics textbooks. As the results show, all the three levels of physics textbooks take the same five types of entities as top-occurring ones in construing knowledge: concrete everyday entities, ge-neric entities, technical entities, pronouns and metaphoric process entities in the descending order of frequency. For each kind of entities, its occurrence tends to change across these school physics sub-fields. Generally speaking, as the school physics sub-fields develop from the lower level to the upper level, there is a de-crease of the occurrence of common-sense entities and an increase of the occurrence of uncommon-sense entities, with the exceptions of their specific types. This similarity and variation of entities across three school physics sub-fields prove that each level of school physics field functions as a sub-field and that they all belong to the large school physic field.

Third, the empirical analysis of processes shows a similar result to that of entities. On the one hand, there are some similarities in the use of processes for all the three levels of physics textbooks in constructing knowledge. Material, relational and mental processes are occurring often in all these textbooks. On the other hand, as an independent sub-field, each level of school physics uses each type of processes differently in number. More material processes and few relational and mental processes are characteristics of the lower-level primary school physics sub-field, and vice versa for the higer-level school physics sub-field. There is a regular occurrence across the three levels of physics textbooks, which reflects the accumulative nature of knowledge building along the three school physics sub-fields.

Fourth, the analysis of taxonomic relations between technical terms in each school physics sub-field presents a picture of the development of the scientific concepts *force and motion* across the three school physics fields, that is, more complex taxonomic relations exist in the higher-level school physics. The taxonomic relations between technical terms in lower primary school sub-fields are quite simple in that few concepts are introduced and no causation category exists. As physics is getting into its upper primary school sub-field, the taxonomic relations between technical terms are becoming complex with more concepts introduced and more causation categories occurring. In junior school sub-fields, the taxonomic relations between technical terms are more complex in that new concepts continue to be introduced and previous concepts at the upper primary school physics are further elaborated. This leads to more relations of causation. Again, this analysis reflects the accumulative nature of knowledge building along the three school physics sub-fields.

Fifth, the analysis of visual images also reveals the variations in ways of knowledge building across three levels of physics textbooks.

Besides language, other semiotics, such as visual images and mathematical symbols, also make their indispensable contributions to knowledge building.

They construe their own special meanings and complement with language. There-fore, a framework is necessary for analyzing these extra-linguistic meaning-crea-ting resources and to explore the interactive device between written language and visual images. This study adopts some theories of SF-MDA: O'Halloran's SF Model for mathematical symbolism and mathematical images (see Table 3.13 and Table 3.14), the framework for non-mathematical ones by Martin and Rose (see Figure 3.11), and adapts Unsworth's system for ideational interactions be-tween language and images (see Figure 3.12).

A multimodal analysis of ideational meanings offers a new understanding of knowledge building. The results reveal that both the ideational meanings con-strued by visual images and the intersemiotic meanings between language and im-ages are getting from simple to more complex across three levels of physics text-books.

Sixth, both a quantitative and a qualitative exploration of SD and SG in physics textbooks from the perspective of SFL presents us a more general under-standing of ways of physical knowledge building. The developing patterns of SD and SG display both similarities and differences across the three levels of physics textbooks.

Through a quantitative analysis of those linguistic variables concerned with SG and SD, that is, deixis, arguability, iconicity and technicality, it is found that SG tends to be weaker and SD tends to be stronger across the three levels of physics textbooks, which signifies that the physical knowledge is built across schooling in a direction from simple and common-sense to abstract and scientific.

A qualitative analysis is given of the developing patterns for SG and SD in the introduction of the concept *force* at each level of physics textbooks. The find-ings suggest that the SD and SG waving is necessary for knowledge building and that linguistic resourses, such as technicality and grammatical metaphor, function to fuilfull its realization.

6.2 Significance of the Research

This research is of theoretical and practical significance, which may be highlighted as follows.

First, this study adopts an integrated perspective of SFL and SE on knowledge, thus presenting a more complete picture about knowledge building in physics textbooks. In SFL, knowledge is seen as meaning which is realized by means of linguistic resources. In SE, knowledge is considered as distributed social goods and should be explored into the structures of itself. In addition, an investigation model of LCT's SD and SG from the linguistic perspective may bridge the gap between SFL's and Bernsteinain approaches to knowledge.

Second, the investigation of knowledge building in physics textbooks throw some light on what kinds of linguistic resources influence the nature of knowledge. The linguistic patterns, which are explored empirically and qualitatively in terms of genres, field and and multimodality, show ways of knowledge building from a new perspective. The detailed and specific analysis of the development of technical terms, which is based on the linguistic model of LCT's SD and SG, expands the scope of SFL and Bernstein's SE and in turn of discourse analysis.

Third, the adapted model of entity classifying and the revised system of taxonomic relations offered in this study prove useful. The methods and specific procedures for the application of the model are specified. This provides readers with specific ways for field and ideation analysis in scientific discourse.

Fourth, the critera for distinguishing grammatical metaphor and technicality presented in this research are also significant for scientific discourse analysis.

Grammatical metaphors and technicalities construe important entities in scientific discourses. There is a close relationship between them, that is, grammatical metaphors help to create technicalities, but the technicality is not equal to the grammatical metaphor. The distinction between them is sometimes not very clear since some grammatical metaphors stand for an instant technicality and some grammatical metaphors die immediately to evolve into a technical term. Therefore, to distinguish an instant grammatical metaphor and a distilled grammatical metaphor (technicality) in discourse analysis is necessary and important.

In this study, some criteria for distinguishing an entity realized by a grammatical metaphor from the one realized by a technicality are pointed out as follows: if a grammatical metaphor occurs with a classifier, in a definition, with a focus, with an elaboration or without introduction, it can be taken as a technicality.

230

Fifth, a linguistic perspective of SD and SG is given. An exploration of SD and SG from a linguistic perspective is pioneered by Martin, and this project expands this model to the discourse level for explaining patterns of knowledge building in physics textbooks.

6.3 Limitations and Suggestions for Future Work

Due to restrictions in both theory and practice, the study is not devoid of limitations, which can be seen in the following two aspects.

First, this research has made strenuous efforts to support the theorization with an empirical study of nine physics textbooks in terms of entities and processes so as to minimize the inevitable subjectivity and speculation of qualitative study. Considering the various style of textbooks by authors who do not receive linguistic training of how to write science for students, the samples for the current study are probably not large enough. For further researches, a bigger and more comprehensive corpus covering more physics textbooks is in need to reveal more about knowledge building across school years.

Second, this research has made some tentative efforts to integrate the theories and methodologies of SFL, SF-MDA and Bernstein's BS to investigate the development of knowledge building in physics textbooks. So far, the integration of SFL, SF-MDA and SE in exploring knowledge building is still at a preliminary level. A more comprehensive integration of these three promising approaches to knowledge building may provide deep and new insights into the nature of knowledge.

Appendix

Data Samples

1 Physics Textbooks of Level 1

Push and pull (from Riley, 2001)

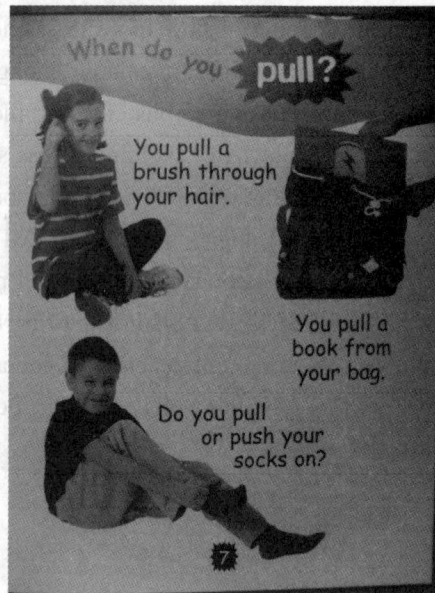

Using a **force**

You use a force every time you move something, change its direction or change its shape.

A push is a force (see page 6).

A pull is a force (see page 7).

You use pushing and pulling forces to twist and turn things, too.

26

Jessica tries to bend some things.

She uses pushing and pulling forces.

She sorts the things into groups.

Try to bend a collection of things. Sort them into groups as well.

Make a table of your results.

27

Bend	Do not bend
straw	brick
string	
ribbon	screw
card	rock

Forces and motion (**from Royston, 2002**)

What Is a Force?

A force makes things move. These people are moving a piano. One man is pushing it. The other man is pulling it.

4

Pulls and pushes are forces. This girl is pushing down on the pedals to make the bicycle move forward.

5

Friction

Friction is a force that slows things down. The boy pushes the toy and then lets go. The toy moves quickly at first. Then it slows down and stops.

The toy slows down because the wheels rub against the ground. The rubbing is called friction. The wheels on the toy are **rough.** They cause more friction than smooth wheels.

22

23

Start science：forces and motion （**from Nunn，2003**）

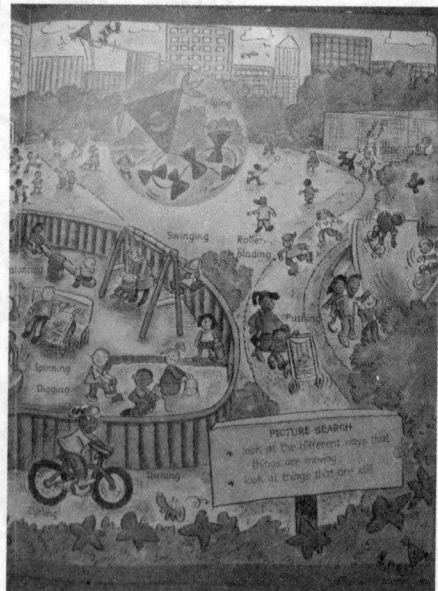

Pushing and pulling

Moving things can go in any direction – backwards and forwards, up and down or round and round. The force that moves them either pushes or pulls. This boy is really pushing the ball with the bat.

Opposite forces

When you walk, two **opposite** forces work together. You push down on the ground and the ground pushes up on your foot with the same amount of force. The arrows show the direction of the forces.

Upthrust

The boat is pushing down on the water. It **floats** because the water is pushing it back up with the same amount of force. This force is called **upthrust**.

Wind

Wind is really moving air. Air pushes against the kite and keeps it flying above the ground.

ELASTIC FORCE

Hold the end of the elastic and bounce the ball.

The force of the ball falling pulls against the elastic and stretches it. The elastic then pulls the ball up as it springs back into shape.

MAGNETISM

Magnets pull objects made of certain kinds of metal towards them with a force called **magnetism**.

START AND STOP

Try pushing and pulling a ball or a toy with wheels to make it move, stop and change direction.

2 Physics Textbooks of Level 2

Motion (from Farndon, 2003)

FRICTION

Not all forces make things move; some bring them to a halt. A moving object's momentum should mean it carries on moving at the same speed unless some force slows it down. Theoretically, it could go on moving forever.

Yet most things do slow down eventually. Nobody can throw a ball more than a few hundred feet, for instance. Nor has anybody yet made a perpetual motion machine—a machine that goes on turning forever under its own momentum.

Racing cyclists try to cut friction with the air by wearing shiny clothes and streamlined helmets.

20

The reason is that forces slow things down. The main stopping force is friction. Friction is the force between two things rubbing together, and it occurs in almost every situation where things move.

When two solids rub together, jagged places on each surface catch together. These jagged places are clearly visible ridges and snags. But there are often microscopic jagged places even on apparently smooth surfaces. Sometimes the friction can be caused by the attraction between tiny molecules in each surface.

When a ball flies through the air, the friction is created by constant collisions between the ball and air molecules. The ball falls back to the ground as this friction slows it down enough for gravity to pull it down.

Friction tends to make things hot, because much of the energy of a moving object's momentum is converted into heat as the object slows down. Friction can also create noise, as the energy is turned into sounds, such as rubbing and scratching noises.

Sometimes friction is helpful. Without friction, people could not walk on the pavement without their feet sliding as if on ice. Friction makes car tires to grip the road. If tires didn't grip, cars could never brake or even turn corners.

In the real world

Stopping distances from different speeds.

CAR STOPPING DISTANCES

Often, friction is a problem. It impairs the efficiency of car engines, turning motion into heat. It also makes it hard to slide a heavy object such as a washing machine across a floor.

The amount of friction between two surfaces depends on the two materials and how hard they are pushed together. The amount of friction between two materials is given a rating called the coefficient of friction. Rubber sliding on concrete has a coefficient of 0.8, which is high. Teflon sliding on steel is 0.04, which is very low.

FRICTION 21

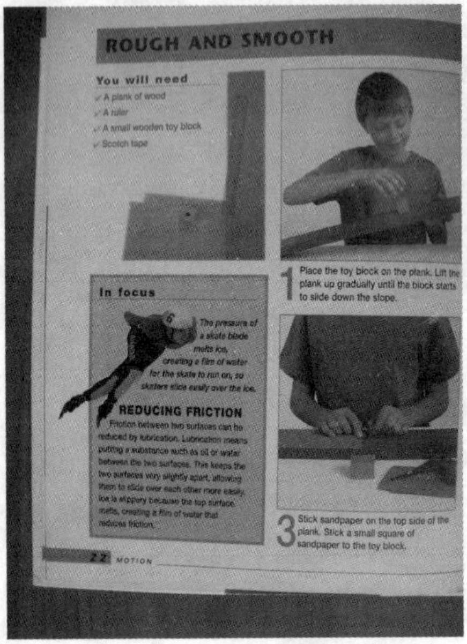
ROUGH AND SMOOTH

You will need
✓ A plank of wood
✓ A ruler
✓ A small wooden toy block
✓ Scotch tape

1 Place the toy block on the plank. Lift the plank up gradually until the block starts to slide down the slope.

In focus

The pressure of a skate blade melts ice, creating a film of water for the skate to run on, so skaters slice easily over the ice.

REDUCING FRICTION
Friction between two surfaces can be reduced by lubrication. Lubrication means putting a substance such as oil or water between the two surfaces. This keeps the two surfaces very slightly apart, allowing them to slide over each other more easily. Ice is slippery because the top surface melts, creating a film of water that reduces friction.

3 Stick sandpaper on the top side of the plank. Stick a small square of sandpaper to the toy block.

22 MOTION

2 Measure the height of the plank at the point where the block starts to slide.

What is happening?
The greater the friction between two surfaces, the greater force is needed to overcome it and make the objects move. Because the block and plank are smooth, the friction between them is low. So, as the measurement in Step 2 shows, the toy block slides when the slope is gentle and the force of gravity pulling the block down the slope is weak. Putting sandpaper on each surface increases the friction. The grains of sand on each surface interlock and stop them sliding together. So the slope must be much steeper and the force of gravity greater to overcome the friction and make the block slide.

Place the toy block on the plank at the same point as in Step 2, with the sandpaper side facing down. Lift the plank up gradually until the block begins to slide down the slope. You may find the brick never slides, but simply tips over. Measure the height of the slope when the block just begins to slide or tip over.

FRICTION 23

What are forces and motion **(from Sarah: 2002)**

Levers
Some machines, such as levers, make it easier to lift heavy objects. Levers work best when they are placed over an object that serves as a fulcrum. Levers pivot or tilt around the fulcrum point.
You could use a lever to help you lift an object, such as a big rock, in the following way.

1. Place a plank (the lever) under the rock. Place another rock (the fulcrum) under the plank, making sure it is near the big rock.
2. Push down on the long end of the plank. The big, downwards movement of the lever at this end lifts the big rock at the other.

You can see levers at work in scissors, some weighing scales, and claw hammers, which are used to pull nails out of wood.

Cranes act as a lever to lift and move loads.

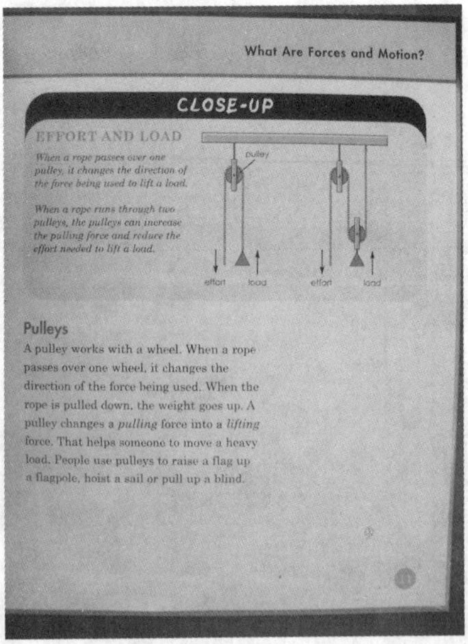
What Are Forces and Motion?

CLOSE-UP
EFFORT AND LOAD
When a rope passes over one pulley, it changes the direction of the force being used to lift a load.
When a rope runs through two pulleys, the pulleys can increase the pulling force and reduce the effort needed to lift a load.

Pulleys
A pulley works with a wheel. When a rope passes over one wheel, it changes the direction of the force being used. When the rope is pulled down, the weight goes up. A pulley changes a *pulling* force into a *lifting* force. That helps someone to move a heavy load. People use pulleys to raise a flag up a flagpole, hoist a sail or pull up a blind.

Science: *forces and motion* (from Wilson, 2001)

3 Physics Textbooks of Level 3

About science (from Shadwick & Barlow, 2003)

Science Australia（Janet，1999）

Exploring：forces and structure（Spiders，1991）

References

Abdi, R. , Rizi, M. T. and Tavakoli, M. 2010. The Cooperative Principle in Discourse Communities and Genres: A Framework for the Use of Metadiscourse [J]. *Journal of Pragmatics*, 42(6): 1669-1679.

Achugar, M. and Schleppegrell, M. J. 2005. Beyond Connectors: The Construction of Cause in History Textbooks [J]. *Linguistics and Education*, 16(3): 298-318.

Ainsworth, S. 1999. The Functions of Multiple Representations [J]. *Computers and Education*, 33(2): 131-152.

Ainsworth, S. 2006. Deft: A Conceptual Framework for Considering Learning with Multiple Representations [J]. *Learning and Instruction*, 16(3): 183-198.

Alison L. 1993. Lexico-grammatical Features of Geology Textbooks: Process and Product Revisited [J]. *English for Special Purposes*, 12(3): 197-218.

Allinson, G. R. , Sturm, H. and Mallinson, L. M. 1952. The Reading Difficulty of Textbooks for High-school Physics [J]. *Science Education*, 36 (1): 19-23.

Alvermann, D. E. 2002. Effective Literacy Instruction for Adolescents [J]. *Journal of Literacy Research*, 34(2): 189-208.

Arnheim, R. 1969. *Visual Thinking* [M]. Berkeley: University of California Press.

Arnheim, R. 1974. *Art and Visual Perception* [M]. Berkeley: University of California Press.

Arnheim, R. 1988. *The Power of the Centre: A Study of Composition in the Visual Arts* [M]. Berkeley: University of California Press.

Askehave, I. and Swales, J. 2001. Genre Identification and Communicative Purpose: A Problem and a Possible Solution [J]. *Applied Linguistics*, 22(2): 195-212.

Baldry, A. (Ed.). 2000. *Multimodality and Multimediality in the Distance Learning Age* [C]. Campobasso, Italy: Palladino Editore.

Baldry, A. P. and Thibault, P. 2006. *Multimodal Transcription and Text Analysis* [M]. London: Equinox.

Barthes, R. 1967. *Elements of Semiology* [M]. London: Cape.

Barthes, R. 1977. *Image, Music, Text* [M]. New York: Noonday Press.

Bazerman, C. 1988. *Shaping Written Knowledge: The Genre and Activity of the Experimental Article in Science* [M]. Wisconsin: The University of Wisconsin Press.

Bazerman, C. 1990. Discourse Analysis and Social Construction [J]. *Annual Review of Applied*

Linguistics, 11: 77-83.

Bernstein, B. 1990. *The Structuring of Pedagogic Discourse* [M]. London: Routledge.

Bernstein, B. 1996. *Pedagogy, Symbolic Control and Identity: Theory, Research, Critique* [M]. London: Taylor & Francis.

Bernstein, B. 1999. Vertical and Horizontal Discourse: An Essay [J]. *British Journal of Sociology of Education*, 20 (2): 157-173.

Bernstein, B. 2000. *Pedagogy, Symbolic Control and Identity: Theory, Research, Critique* (2nd Edn.) [M]. Oxford: Rowman & Littlefield.

Bhatia, V. K. 1993. *Analysing Genre — Language Use in Professional Settings* [M]. London: Longman.

Bhatia, V. K. 1997a. Applied Genre Analysis and ESP [A]. In T. Miller (Ed.), *Functional Approach to Written Text: Classroom Applications* [C]. 134-149. Washington D. C. : United States Information Agency.

Bhatia, V. K. 1997b. Introduction: Genre Analysis and World Englishes [J]. *World Englishes*, 16(3): 313-319.

Bhatia, V. K. 1999. *Analysing Genre: An Applied Linguistic Perspective* [C]. The 12th World Congress of Applied Linguistics, Tokyo.

Bloor, M. and Bloor, T. 1993. How Economists Modify Propositions [A]. In W. Henderson, T. Dudley-Evans and R. Backhouse (Eds.), *Economics and Language* [C]. 153-169. London/New York: Routledge.

Brookes, D. T. and Etkina, E. 2007. Using Conceptual Metaphor and Functional Grammar to Explore How Language Used in Physics Affects Student Learning [J]. *Physical Review Special Topics Physics Education Research*, 3 (1): 1-16.

Brookes, D. T. and Etkina, E. 2009. "Force," Ontology, and Language [J]. *Physical Review Special Topics-Physics Education Research*, 5(1): 010110-1-13.

Brown, V. 1993. Decanonizing Discourses: Textual Analysis and the History of Economic Thought [A]. In W. Henderson, T. Dudley-Evans and R. Backhouse (Eds.), *Economics and Language* [C]. 64-84. London: Routledge.

Burnheim, C. 2010. *Changing Autonomy in Australian Universities* [D]. Unpublished PhD Thesis. Melbourne: University of Melbourne.

Carroll, L. 1972. *The Annotated Alice* [M]. New York: Penguin books.

Chen, R. 2010. *Knowledge and Knowers in Online Learning: Investigating the Effects of Online Flexible Learning on Student Sojourners* [D]. Unpublished PhD thesis. Sydney: University of Wollongong.

Chisholm, R. M. (1989). *Theory of Knowledge* (3rd Edn.) [M]. Englewood Cliffs, NJ: Prentice Hall.

Christie, F. 2002. *Classroom Discourse Analysis: A Functional Perspective* [M]. London: Continuum.

Christie, F. and Martin, J. R. (Eds.). 1997. *Genre and Institutions: Social Processes in the Workplace and School* [C]. London: Cassell.

Christie, F. and Derewianka, B. 2008. *School Discourse: Learning to Write Across the Years of Schooling* [M]. London: Continuum.

Coffin, C. 1997. Constructing and Giving Value to the Past: An Investigation into Secondary School History [A]. In F. Christie and J. R. Martin (Eds.), *Genre and Institutions: Social Processes in the Workplace and School* [C]. 196-230. London: Cassell.

Coffin, C. 2004. Learning to Write History: The Role of Causality [J]. *Written Communication*, 21(3): 261-289.

Collins, A. M. and Loftus, E. G. 1975. A Spreading-activation Theory of Semantic Processing [J]. *Psychological Review*, 82(6): 407-428.

Crismore, A. and Farnsworth, R. (1990). Metadiscourse in Popular and Professional Science Discourse [A]. In W. Nash (Ed.), *The Writing Scholar: Studies in Academic Discourse* [C]. 118-136. Newbury Park, CA: Sage.

Crystal, D. 1988. On Keeping One's Hedges in Order [J]. *English Today*, 4(3): 46-47.

Curtis, F. D. 1938. *Investigations of Vocabulary in Textbooks of Science for Secondary Schools* [M]. Boston: Ginn and Co..

Dahl, T. 2008. Contributing to the Academic Conversation: A Study of New Knowledge Claims in Economics and Linguistics [J]. *Journal of Pragmatics*, 40(7): 1184-1201.

Davidse, K. 1999. *Categories of Experiential Grammar* [M]. Clifton, Nottigham: Dept. of English Studies and Media Studies, Nottingham Trent University.

Davies, F. 1986. Structure and Language of Text-books Across the Curriculum [A]. In M. W. van Someren, P. Reimann, H. P. A. Boshuizen and T. de Jong (Eds.), *Learning with Multiple Representations* [C]. Amsterdam: Pergamon.

Derewianka, B. 1995. *Language Development in the Transition from Childhood to Adolescence: The Role of Grammatical Metaphor* [D]. Unpublished PhD thesis. Sydney: Macquarie University.

DiGisi, L. L. and Willett, J. B. 1995. What High School Biology Teachers Say About Their Textbook Use: A Descriptive Study [J]. *Journal of Research in Science Teaching*, 32(2): 123-142.

Doherty, C. 2007. *The Production of Cultural Difference and Cultural Sameness in Online Internationalised Education* [D]. Unpublished PhD Thesis. Brisbane: Queensland University of Technology.

Dolin, J. 2001. Representational Forms in Physics [A]. In D. Psillos, P. Kariotoglou, V.

Tselfes, G. Bisdikian, G. Fassoulopoulos, E. Hatzikraniotis and E. Kallery (Eds.), *Science Educaion Research in the Knowledge-Based Society* [C]. 359-361. Proceedings of the Third International Conference of the ESERA. Thessaloniki, Greece: Aristotle University of Thessaloniki.

Dondis, E. 1973. *A Primer of Visual Literacy* [M]. Cambridge, MA: MIT Press.

Doran, Y. 2010. *Knowledge and Multisemiosis in Undergraduate Physics* [D]. Unpublished Honours thesis. Sydney: University of Sydney.

Duke, N. K. and Kays, J. 1998. "Can I Say Once Upon a Time" Kindergarten Children Developing Knowledge of Information Book Language [J]. *Early Childhood Research Quarterly*, 13(2): 295-318.

Dyer, G. 1982. *Advertising as Communication* [M]. London: Methuen.

Eco, U. 1976. *A Theory of Semiotics* [M]. Bloomington: Indiana University Press.

Eggins, S. 1994. *An Introduction to Systemic Functional Linguistics* [M]. London: Pinter.

Eggins, S., Wignell, P. and Martin, J. R. 1993. The Discourse of History: Distancing the Recoverable Past [A]. In M. Ghadessy (Ed.), *Register Analysis: Theory and Practice* [C]. 75-109. London: Pinter.

Eugene L. C. 1993. Do Middle School Life Science Textbooks Provide a Balance of Scientific Literacy Themes [J]? *Journal of Research in Science Teaching*, 30 (7): 787-797.

Exline, J. D. 1984. National Survey: Science Textbook Adoption Process [J]. *The Science Teacher*, 51(1): 92-93.

Fahnestock, J. 1986. Accommodating Science: The Rhetorical Life of Scientific facts [J]. *Written Communication*, 3(3): 275-296.

Farndon, J. 2003. *Motion* [M]. New York: Marshall Cavendish Corporation.

Feldman, R. 2003. *Epistemology* [M]. Upper Saddle River, NJ: Prentice Hall.

Fiske, J. 1982. *Introduction to Communication Studies* (2nd Edn.) [M]. London: Routledge.

Freebody, P., Maton, K. and Martin, J. R. 2008. Talk, Text, and Knowledge in Cumulative, Integrated Learning: A Response to "Intellectual Challenge" [J]. *Australian Journal of Language and Literacy*, 31(2): 188-201.

Freedman, A. 1993. "Show and Tell? The Role of Explicit Teaching in the Learning of New Genres" [J]. *Research in the Teaching of English*, 27(3): 222-251.

Gee, J. P. 1990. *Social Linguistics and Literacies: Ideology in Discourses* [M]. London: The Falmer Press.

Gee, J. 2002. Millenials and Bobos, Blue's Clues and Sesame Stree: A Story for Our Times [A]. In D. Alvermann (Ed.), *Adolescents and Literacies in a Digital World* [C]. 51-67. New York: Peter Lang.

Goldman, A. I. 1986. *Epistemology and Cognition* [M]. Cambridge, MA: Harvard University

Press.

Gombrich, E. 1960. *Art and Illusion: A Study of the Psychology of Pictorial Representation* [M]. London: Phaidon Press.

Gonzalez, F. , Prain, V. and Waldrip, B. 2003. *Using Multi-modal Representations of Concepts in Learning Science* [C]. European Science Education Research Association Conference, Noordwijkerhout, the Netherlands.

Good, R. 1993. Editorial: Science Textbook Analysis [J]. *Journal of Research in Science Teaching*, 30(7): 619.

Gordon, W. 2007. Semiotic Mediation, Dialogue and the Construction of Knowledge [J]. *Human Development*, 50(5): 244-274.

Gosden, H. 1992. Discourse Functions of Marked Theme in Scientific Research Articles [J]. *English for Specific Purposes*, 11(3): 207-224.

Halliday, M. A. K. 1978. *Language as Social Semiotic: The Social Interpretation of Meaning* [M]. London: Edward Arnold.

Halliday, M. A. K. 1985. *An Introduction to Functional Grammar* [M]. London: Edward Arnold.

Halliday, M. A. K. 1987. Spoken and Written Modes of Meaning [A]. In R. Horowitz and S. Jay Samuels (Eds.), *Comprehending Oral and Written Language* [C]. 55-87. New York: Academic Press.

Halliday, M. A. K. 1989. Some Grammatical Problems in Scientific English [A]. In Webster, J (Ed.), 2004. *The Language of Science* [C]. 159-180. London, New York: Continuum.

Halliday, M. A. K. 1993a. *Language in a Changing World* [M]. Deakin, A. C. T. : Applied Linguistics Association of Australia.

Halliday, M. A. K. 1993b. Some Grammatical Problems in Scientific English [A]. In M. A. K. Halliday and J. R. Martin (Eds.), *Writing Science: Literacy and Discursive Power* [C]. 69- 85. London: Falmer Press.

Halliday, M. A. K. 1993c. On the Language of Physical Science [A]. In M. A. K. Halliday and J. R. Martin (Eds.), *Writing Science: Literacy and Discursive Power* [C]. 54-68. London: The Falmer Press.

Halliday, M. A. K. 1993d. Writing Science: Literacy and Discursive power [A]. In Webster, J (Ed.), 2004. *The Language of Science* [C]. 199-226. London, New York: Continuum.

Halliday, M. A. K. 1994. *An Introduction to Functional Grammar* (2nd Edn) [M]. London: Edward Arnold.

Halliday, M. A. K. 1995. Language and Reshaping of Human Experience [A]. In J. Webster (Ed.), 2004. *The Language of Science* [C]. 7-23. London, New York: Continuum.

Halliday, M. A. K. 1997. On the Grammar of Scientific English [A]. In J. Webster (Ed.),

2004. *The Language of Science* [C]. 181-198. London, New York: Continuum.

Halliday, M. A. K. 1998a. Language and Knowledge: The "Unpacking" of Text [A]. In J. Webster (Ed.), 2004. *The Language of Science* [C]. 24-48. London, New York: Continuum.

Halliday, M. A. K. 1998b. Things and Relations: Regrammaticising Experience as Technical Knowledge [A]. In J. R. Martin and R. Veel (Eds.), *Reading Science: Critical and Functional Perspectives on Discourses of Science* [C]. 183-235. London: Routledge.

Halliday, M. A. K. 1999. The Grammatical Construction of Scientific Knowledge: The Framing of the English Clause [A]. In J. Webster (Ed.) 2004, *The Language of Science* [C]. 102-134. London, New York: Continuum.

Halliday, M. A. K. 2001. *Language as Social Semiotic: The Social Interpretation of Language and Meaning* [M]. Beijing: Foreign Language Teaching and Research Press.

Halliday, M. A. K. 2002a. *Linguistic Studies of Text and Discourse* (J. Webster, Ed.) [C]. London, New York: Continuum.

Halliday, M. A. K. 2002b. The Construction of Knowledge and Value: Charles Darwin [A]. In J. Webster (Ed.), *Linguistic Studies of Text and Discourse* [C]. 168-194. London, New York: Continuum.

Halliday, M. A. K. 2004. *An Introduction to Functional Grammar* (2nd Edn.) [M]. Beijing: Foreign Language Teaching and Research Press.

Halliday, M. A. K. 2006. Some Theoretical Considerations Underlying the Teaching of English in China [J]. *The Journal of English Studies*, (4): 7-20.

Halliday, M. A. K. 2009. *The Essential Halliday* (J. Webster, Ed.) [C]. London: Continuum.

Halliday, M. A. K. and Hasan, R. 1976. *Cohesion in English* [M]. London: Longman.

Halliday, M. A. K. and Hasan, R. 1985. *Language, Context and Text: Aspects of Language in a Social-semiotic Perspective* [M]. Geelong: Deakin University Press.

Halliday, M. A. K. and Martin, J. R. (Eds.). 1993. *Writing Science: Literacy and Discursive Power* [C]. London: Falmer Press.

Halliday, M. A. K. and Matthiessen, C. 2004. *An Introduction to Functional Grammar* (3rd Edn.) [M]. London: Arnold.

Halliday, M. A. K. and Matthiessen, C. M. I. M. 2008. *Construing Experience Through Meaning: A Language-based Approach to Cognition* [M]. Beijing: The world books publisher.

Harris, R. 1995. *Signs of Writing* [M]. London: Routledge.

Hasan, R, 1977. Text in Systemic-functional Model [A]. In W. Dressler (Ed.), *Current Trends in Text Linguistics* [C]. 228-246. Berlin: Walter de Gruyter.

Hasan, R. 1984a. The Structure of the Nursery Tale [A]. In L. Coveri (Ed.), *Linguistica Testuale* [C]. 95-114. Rome: Bulzoni.

Hasan, R. 1984b. Coherence and Cohesive Harmony [A]. In J. Flood (Ed.), *Understanding Reading Comprehension* [C]. 184-219. Newark, DE: International Reading Association.

Hasan, R. 1985a. The Structure of a Text [A]. In M. A. K. Halliday and R. Hasan *Language, Text, and Context: Aspects of Language in a Socio-semiotic Perspective* [C]. 52-69. Geelong, Vic. : Deaking University Press.

Hasan, R. 1985b. The Identity of a Text [A]. In M. A. K. Halliday and R. Hasan (Eds.), *Language, Text, and Context: Aspects of Language in a Socio-semiotic Perspective* [C]. 97-119. Geelong, Vic. : Deaking University Press.

Hasan, R. 1995. The Conception of Context in Text [A]. In P. H. Fries and M. Gregory (Eds.), *Discourse in Society: System in Functional Perspective* [C]. 183-283. London: Greenwood Publishing Group.

Hasan, R. 1999. Speaking with Reference to Context. In M. Ghadessey (Ed.), *Text and Context in Functional Linguistics* [C]. 219-328. Amsterdam: Benjamins.

Hasan, R. and Williams, G. 1996. *Literacy in Society* [M] London: Longman.

Henderson, W. and Hewings, A. 1990. Language and Model Building [A]. In A. Dudley-Evans and W. Henderson (Eds.), *The Language of Economics: The Analysis of Economics Discourse* [C]. 43-54. London: Modem English Publications.

Henderson, G. 1999. Learning with Diagrams [J]. *Australian Science Teachers' Journal*, 45 (2): 17-25.

Hewings, A. , 1990. Aspects of the Language of Economics Textbooks [A]. In A. Dudley-Evans and W. Henderson (Eds.), *The Language of Economics: The Analysis of Economics Discourse* [C]. 109-127. London: Modern English Publications.

Hewitt, P. G. 1998. *Conceptual Physics* [M]. Reading, Mass. : Addison, Welsley.

Hoey, M. 1983. *On the Surface of Discourse* [M]. London: Allen & Unwin.

Kirszner, L. and Mandell, S. 1987. *The Writer's Sourcebook: Strategies for Reading and Writing in the Disciplines* [M]. New York: Holt, Rinehart, and Winston.

Humphrey, S. and Hao, J. 2010. Becoming a Researcher in Science: From Laboratory Report to Research Report in an Undergraduate Biology Degree [J]. *Linguistic and Human Sciences*, (in press).

Hussey, E. 1990. The Beginnings of Epistemology: From Homer to Philolaus [A]. In S. Everson (Ed.), *Epistemology* [C]. 11-38. Cambridge, England: Cambridge University Press.

Hyland, K. 1994. Hedging in Academic Writing and EAP Textbooks [J]. *English for Specific Purposes*, 13(3): 239-256.

Hyland, K. 1996. Writing Without Conviction? Hedging in Science Research Articles [J]. *Ap-*

245

plied Linguistics, 17(4): 433-454.

Hyland, K. 1998. *Hedging in Scientific Research Articles* [M]. John Benjamins, Amsterdam.

Hyland, K. 2002. What do They Mean? Questions in academic Writing [J]. *Text*, 22(4): 529-557.

Hyland, K. 2005. *Metadiscourse: Exploring Interaction in Writing* [M]. Continuum, London.

Inan, H. Z. 2010. Examining Language of Information Books for Children [J]. *Education*, 130 (3): 399-403.

Janet, M. 1999. *Science Australia* [M]. Australia: Curriculum.

Jetton, T. L. and Alexander, P. A. 1997. Instructional Importance: What Teachers Value and What Students Learn [J]. *Reading Research Quarterly*, 32(3): 290-308.

Jewitt, C. 2003. Re-thinking Assessment: Multimodality, Literacy and Computer-mediated Learning [J]. *Assessment in Education: Principles, Policy & Practice*, 10 (1): 83-102.

Kant, I. 1781. *Critique of Pure Reason* (W. S. Pluhar, Trans.) [M]. Indianapolis: Hackett.

Klein, P. 1971. A Proposed Definition of Propositional Knowledge [J]. *The Journal of Philosophy*, 68 (16): 471-482.

Klein, P. 1976. Knowledge, Causality, and Defeasibility [J]. *The Journal of Philosophy*, 73 (20): 792-812.

Kress, G. 1997. Visual and Verbal Modes of Representation in Electronically Mediated Communication: The Potentials of New Forms of of Text [A]. In I. Snyder (Ed.), *Page to Screen: Taking Literacy into the Electronic Era* [C]. 53-79. Sydney: Allen and Unwin.

Kress, G. 2000a. Design and Transformation: New Theories of Meaning [A]. In B. Cope and M. Kalantzis (Eds.), *Multiliteracies: Learning Literacy and the Design of Social Futures* [C]. 153-161. Melbourne: Macmillan.

Kress, G. 2000b. Multimodality: Challenges to Thinking About Language [J]. *TESOL Quarterly*, 3(4): 337-340.

Kress, G. 2003a. Genres and the Multimodal Production of "Scientificness" [A]. In C. Jewitt and G. Kress (Eds.), *Multimodal Literacy* [C]. 173-186. New York: Peter Lang.

Kress, G. 2003b. *Literacy in the New Media Age* [M]. London: Routledge.

Kress, G. and van Leeuwen, T. 1996. *Reading Images: The Grammar of Visual Design* [M]. London: Routledge.

Kress, G. and Hodge, R. 1979. *Language as Ideology* [M]. London: Routledge & Kegan Paul.

Kress, G. and van Leeuwen, T. 1990. *Reading Images* [M]. Geelong, Victoria: Deakin University Press.

Kress, G.. and van Leeuwen, T. 1995. Critical Layout Analysis [J]. *Internationale Schulbuchforschung*, 17(1): 25-43.

Kuhn, T. S. 1962. *The Structure of Scientific Revolutions* [M]. Chicago: The University of Chicago Press.

Kuhn, T. S. 1963. The Function of Dogma in Scientific Research [A]. In A. C. Crombie (Ed.), *Scientific Change* [C]. 347-69. London: Heineman.

Kuhn, T. S. 1970. *The Structure of Scientific Revolutions* (2nd Edn.) [M]. Chicago: University of Chicago Press.

Lai, L. 2011. *A Teleological Model of Genre Analysis: A Case Study of Corporate Website Genres* [D]. Unpublished PhD thesis. Xiamen: Xiamen Universtiy.

Langer, J. A. 2001. Beating the Odds: Teaching Middle and High School Students to Read and Write Well [J]. *American Educational Research Journal*, 38(4): 837-880.

Layton, D. 1991. Science Education and Praxis: The Relationship of School Science to Practical Action [J]. *Studies in Science Education*, 19(1): 43-79.

Lemke, J. L. 1982. Talking Physics [J]. *Physics Education*, 17(6): 263-267.

Lemke, J. L. 1988b. Text Structure and Text Semantics [A]. In R. Veltman, and E. Steiner (Eds.), *Pragmatics, Discourse, and Text: Systemic Approaches* [C]. 158-170. London: Pinter.

Lemke, J. L. 1994. Multiplying Meaning: Literacy in a Multimedia world [C]. National Reading Conference, Charleston SC.

Lemke, J. L. 1995. Intertextuality and Text Semantics [A]. In M. Gregory and P. Fries (Eds.), *Discourse in Society: Functional Perspectives* [C]. 85- 114. Norwood, NJ: Ablex Publishing.

Lemke, J. L. 1997a. Review of: Roy Harris. Signs of writing [J]. *Functions of Language*, 4 (1): 125-129.

Lemke, J. L. 1997b. *Evaluative Meaning in Multimedia Genres* [C]. International Congress of Systemic-Functional Linguistics, Toronto.

Lemke, J. L. 1998a. Metamedia literacy: Transforming Meanings and Media [A]. In D. Reinking, M. McKenna, L. Labbo and R. Kieffer (Eds.), *Handbook of Literacy and Technology: Transformations in a Post-typographic World* [C]. 283-302. New Jersey: Erlbaum.

Lemke, J. L. 1998b. Multiplying Meaning: Visual and Verbal Semiotics in scientific Text [A]. In J. R. Martin and R. Veel (Eds.), *Reading Science: Critical and Functional Perspectives on Discourses of Science* [C]. 87-113. London: Routledge.

Lemke, J. L. 2000. Multimedia Literacy Demands of the Scientific Curriculum [J]. *Linguistics and Education*, 10(3): 247-271.

Lemke, J. L. 2002. Travels in Hypermodality [J]. *Visual Communication*, 1(3): 299-325.

Lemke, J. L. 2003. Mathematics in the Middle: Measure, Picture, Gesture, Sigh and Word [DB/OL]. http://www-personal. umich. edu / jaylemke/papers/myrdene. htm, (June 6,

2010).

Lemke, J. L. 2004. Teaching all the Languages of Science: Word, Symbols, Images, and Actions [DB/OL]. http://www-personal. umich. edu/ ~ jaylemke/papers/barcelon. htm, (July 20, 2011).

Lemke, J. L. 2009. Multimodal Genres and Transmedia Traversals: Social Semiotics and the Political Economy of the Sign [J]. *Semiotica*, 173(1/4): 283-297.

Lin, C. -Y. 2010. ' ... that's actually sort of you know trying to get consultants in...' : Functions and Multifunctionality of Modifiers in Academic Lectures [J]. *Journal of Pragmatics*, 42 (5): 1173-1183.

Lindstrom, C. 2010. *Link Maps and Map Meetings: A Theoretical and Experimental Case for Stronger Scaffolding in First Year University Physics Education* [D]. Unpublished PhD thesis. Sydney: University of Sydney.

Lindwall, O. and Lymer, G. 2011. Uses of "understand" in science education [J]. *Journal of Pragmatics*, 43(2): 452-474.

Liu, Y. and O'Halloran, K. 2009. Intersemiotic Texture: Analyzing Cohesive Devices Between Language and Images [J]. *Social Semiotics*, 19(4): 367-388.

Liu, Y. and Owyong, Y. S. M. 2011. Metaphor, Multiplicative Meaning and the Semiotic Construction of Scientific Knowledge [J]. *Language Sciences*, 33|(5): 822-834.

Loi, C. K. and Evans, M. S. 2010. Cultural Differences in the Organization of Research Article Introductions from the Field of Educational Psychology: English and Chinese [J]. *Journal of Pragmatics*, 42(10): 2814-2825.

Loock, R. 2007. Appositive Relative Clauses and Their Functions in Discourse [J]. *Journal of Pragmatics*, 39(2): 336-362.

Love, A. 1991. Process and Product in Geology: An Investigation of Some Discourse Features of Two Introductory Textbooks [J]. *English for Specific Purposes*, 10(2): 89-109.

Love, A. 1993. Lexico-grammatical Features of Geology Textbooks: Process and Product Revisited [J]. *English for Specific Purposes*, 12(3): 197-218.

MacDonald, S. P. 1992. A Method of Analyzing Sentence-level Differences in Disciplinary Knowledge Making [J]. *Written Communication*, 9(4): 533-569.

Macken-Horarik, M. 2003. A Telling Symbiosis in the Discourse of Hatred: Multimodal News Texts About the "Children Overboard" Affair [J]. *Australian Review of Applied Linguistics*, 26(2): 1-16.

Macken-Horarik, M. 2004. Interacting with the Multimodal Text: Reflections on Image and Verbiage in Artexpress [J]. *Visual Communication*, 3(1): 5-26.

Martin, J. R. 1984. Language, Register and Genre [A]. In F. Christie (Ed.), *Children Writing: Reader* [C]. 21-29. Geelong, Vic: Deakin University Press.

Martin, J. R. 1989. *Factual Writing: Exploring and Challenging Social Reality* [M]. London: Oxford University Press.

Martin, J. R. 1992. *English Text: System and Structure* [M]. Amsterdam: Benjamins.

Martin, J. R. 1993a. Technicality and Abstraction: Language for the Creation of Specialised Texts [A]. In M. A. K. Halliday and J. R. Martin (Eds.), *Writing Science: Literacy and Discursive Power* [C]. 203-20. London: The Falmer Press.

Martin, J. R. 1993b. Technology, Bureaucracy and Schooling: Discursive Resources and Control [J]. *Cultural Dynamics*, 6(1): 84-130.

Martin, J. R. 1993c. Literacy in Science: Learning to handle text as technology [A]. In M. A. K. Halliday and J. R. Martin (Eds.), *Writing Science: Literacy and Discursive Power* [C]. 166-202. London: The Falmer Press.

Martin, J. R. 1993d. Genre and Literacy — Modelling Context in Educational Linguistics [J]. *Annual Review of Applied Linguistics*, 13: 141-172.

Martin, J. R. 1993e. Life as a Noun: Arresting the Universe in Science and Humanities [A]. In M. A. K. Halliday and J. R. Martin (Eds.), *Writing Science: Literacy and Discursive Power* [C]. 242-293. London: Falmer Press.

Martin, J. R. 1994. Macro-genres: The Ecology of the Page [J]. *Network*, 21: 29-52.

Martin, J. R. 1995. Text and Clause: Fractal Resonance [J]. *Text*, 15 (1): 5-42.

Martin, J. R. 1997. Analysing Genre: Functional Parameters [A]. In F. Christie and J. R. Martin (Eds.). *Genre and Institutions: Social Processes in the Workplace and School* [C]. 3-39. London: Cassell.

Martin, J. R. 1999. Mentoring Semogenesis: Genre-based Literacy Pedagogy [A]. In F Christie (Ed.), *Pedagogy and the Shaping of Consciousness: Linguistic and Social Processes* [C]. 123-155. London: Cassell.

Martin, J. R. 2001. From Little Things Big Things Grow: Ecogenesis in School Geography [A]. In R. Coe, L. Lingard and T. Teslenko (Eds.), *The Rhetoric and Ideology of Genre: Strategies for Stability and Change* [C]. 243-271. Cresskill, NJ: Hampton Press.

Martin, J. R. 2002a. Writing History: Construing Time and Value in Discourses of the Past [A]. In M. J. Schleppegrell and M. C. Colombi (Eds.), *Developing Advanced Literacy in First and Second Languages: Meaning with Power* [C]. 87-118. Mahwah, NJ: Lawrence Erlbaum Assoc.

Martin, J. R. 2002b. Meaning beyond the clause: SFL perspectives [J]. *Annual Review of Applied Linguistics*, 22: 52-74.

Martin, J. 2002c. Fair trade: Negotiating Meaning in Multimodal Texts [A]. In P. Coppock (Ed.); *The Semiotics of Writing: Transdisciplinary Perspectives on the Technology of Writing* [C]. 311-337. Turnhout: Brepols.

Martin, J. R. 2007. Construing Knowledge: A Functional Linguistic Perspective [A]. In F. Christie and J. R. Martin (Eds.), *Language, Knowledge and Pedagogy: Functional Linguistic and Sociological Perspectives* [C]. 34-64. London: Continuum.

Martin, J. R. 2010. Life as a Theme: Pitching Vertical Discourse in Powerpoint Slides [C]. 5ICOM, UTS.

Martin, J. R. 2011a. Bridging Troubled Waters: Interdisplinarity and What Makes it Stick [A]. In F. Christie and J. R. Martin (Eds.), *Disciplinary: Functional Linguistic and Sociological Perspectives* [C]. 35-61. London: continuum.

Martin, J. R. 2011b. Modelling Context: Matter as Meaning [C]. ISFC 38, University of Lisbon.

Martin, J. R. 2011c. Grammatical Metaphor [Z]. Sydney: University of Sydney.

Martin, J. R. and Matruglio. E. 2011. Flights of fancy: A Functional Linguistic Interpretation of Semantic Gravity and Semantic Density in Secondary School History Teaching [DB/OL]. http://www. griffith. edu. au/_data /assets / pdf_file /0017/221840 / Martin - and-Matruglio. RT-doc. pdf, (May 1).

Martin, J. R., Matthiessen, C. and Painter, C. 2010. *Deploying Functional Grammar* [M]. Beijing: The Commercial Press.

Martin, J. R. and Rose, D. 2003. *Working with Discourse: Meaning Beyond the Clause* [M]. London: Continuum.

Martin, J. R. and Rose, D. 2007. *Working with Discourse: Meaning Beyond the Clause* (2nd Edn.) [M]. London Continuum.

Martin, J. R. and Rose, D. 2008. *Genre Relations: Mapping Culture* [M]. London: Equinox.

Martin, J. R. and Rothery, J. 1986. *Writing Project Report* 1986 [M]. Sydney: University of Sydney.

Martin, J. R. and Veel, R. (Eds.). 1998. *Reading science: Critical and Functional Perspecgtives on Discourses of Science* [C]. New York: Routledge.

Martin, J. R. and White, P. R. R. 2005. *The Language of Evaluation: Appraisal in English* [M]. London: Palgrave Macmillan.

Martin, J. R., Wignell, P., Eggins, S. and Rothery, J. 1988. Secret English: Discourse Technology in a Junior Secondary School [A]. In L. Gerot, J. Olderburg-Torr and T. van Leeuwen (Eds.), *Language and Socialization: Home and School* [C]. 143-173. Sydney: Macquarie University.

Martinec, R. 1997. *Rhythm in Multimodal Texts* [M]. Ms: London School of Printing.

Martinec, R. 1999. Cohesion in Action [J]. *Semiotica*, 124(1/2), 161-180.

Martinec, R. 2000a. Rhythm in Multimodal Texts [J]. *Leonardo*, 33(4), 289-297.

Martinec, R. 2000b. Types of Process in Action [J]. *Semiotica*, 130(3/4), 243-268.

Martinec, R. and Salway, A. 2005. A System for Image-text Relations in New (and old) Media [J]. *Visual Communication*, 4(3): 337-371.

Maton, K. 2007. Knowledge-knower Structures in Intellectual and Educational Fields [A]. In F. Christie and J. R. Martin (Eds.), *Language, Knowledge and Pedagogy: Functional Linguistic and Sociological Perspectives* [C]. 87-108. London: Continuum.

Maton, K. 2008a. Grammars of Sociology [C]. International Basil Bernstein Symposium, Cardiff University.

Maton, K. 2008b. Knowledge-building: How Can We Create Powerful and Influential ideas? [C] *Disciplinarity, Knowledge & Language: An international symposium*, University of Sydney.

Maton, K. 2009. Cumulative and Segmented Learning: Exploring the Role of Curriculum Structures in Knowledge-building [J]. *British Journal of Sociology of Education*, 30(1): 43-57.

Maton, K. 2011. *Seeing Knowledge and Knowers* [Z]. Slides for the course of LCT. Sydney: University of Sydney.

Maton, K. and Matruglio, E. 2009. How do We Know: The Social Relation in School History Discourse [C]. *LCT-SFL Roundtable*, University of Sydney.

Maton, K. and Moore, R. (Eds.). 2010. *Social Realism, Knowledge and the Sociology of Education: Coalitions of the Mind* [C]. London: Continuum.

Maton, K. and Muller, J. 2006. A Sociology for the Transmission of Knowledges [DB/OL]. http://www. KarlMaton. com, (Dec 8, 2010).

4Matruglio, E., Maton, K. and Martin, J. R. 2011. Waves Through Time: Temporality and the Semantic Wave [R]. ASFLA, UNE.

Matthiessen, C. M. I. M. 1993. Register in the Round: Diversity in a Unified Theory of Register Analysis [J]. In M. Ghadessy [Ed.], *Register Analysis: Theory and Practice* [C]. 221-92. London: Pinter.

Matthiessen, C. 1995. *Lexicogrammatical Cartography: English Systems* [M]. Tokyo: International Language Sciences Publishers.

McCloskey, D. N. 1985. *The Rhetoric of Economics* [M]. Madison, WI: The University of Wisconsin Press.

Miller, C. R. 1984. Genre as Social Action [J]. *Quarterly Journal of Speech*, 70(2): 151-167.

Miller. C. R. 1994. Rhetorical Community: The Cultural Basis of Genre [A]. In A. Freedman and P. Medway (Eds.), *Genre and the New Rhetoric* [C]. 67-78. London: Taylor & Francis.

Moser, P. K. (1992). The Gettier Problem [A]. In Jonathan and E. Sosa (Eds.), *A Com-*

panion to Epistemology [C]. Malden, MA: Blackwell.

Muller, J. 2007. On Splitting Hairs: Hierarchy, Knowledge and the School Curriculum [A]. In F. Christie and J. Martin (Eds.), *Lanuguage, Knowledge and Pedagogy: Functional Linguistic and Sociological Perspective* [C]. 65-86. London, continuum.

Myers, G. 1989. The Pragmatics of Politeness in Scientific Articles [J]. *Applied Linguistics*, 10 (1): 1-35.

Myers, G. 1990. *Writing Biology: Texts in the Social Construction of Scientific Knowledge* [M]. Madison, Wis. : University of Wisconsin Press.

Myers, G. 1992a. Textbooks and the Sociology of Scientific Knowledge [J]. *English for Specific Purposes*, 11(1): 3-17.

Myers, G. 1992b. 'In this paper we report...': Speech Acts and Scientific Facts [J]. *Journal of Pragmatics*, 17(4): 295-313.

National Curriculum board. 2009. Shape of the Australian Curriculum: Science [DB/OL]. http://www. ag. gov. au/cca, (May 10).

Newton, 1962. *Mathematical Principles of Natural Philosophy* [M]. Berkekey: University of California Press.

Nielsen, A. , Ford, S. and Doherty, F. 1996. *Science and Life: Work, Leisure, Technology and the Environment* [M]. Melbourne, Australia: Oxford University Press.

Noth, W. 1995. *Handbook of Semiotics* [M]. Bloomington: Indiana University Press.

Nunn, S. 2003. *Start Science: Forces and Motion* [M]. London: Chrysalis Books PLC.

O'Halloran K. L. 1996. *The Discourses of Secondary School Mathematics* [D]. Unpublished PhD thesis. Perth: Murdoch University.

O'Halloran, K. 1999. Interdependence, Interaction and Metaphor in Multisemiotic texts [J]. *Social Semiotics*, 9(3): 317-356.

O'Halloran, K. 2003. Intersemiosis in Mathematics and Science: Grammatical Metaphor and Semiotic Metaphor [A]. In A. -M. Simon-Vandenbergen, M. Taverniers and L. Ravelli (Eds.), *Grammatical Metaphor* [C]. 337-365. Amsterdam, John Benjamins.

O'Halloran, K. L. (Ed.) 2004. *Multimodal Discourse Analysis: Systemic Functional Perspectives* [C]. London: Continuum.

O'Halloran, K. L. 2005. *Mathematical Discourse: Language, Symbolism and Visual Images* [M]. London: Continuum.

O'Halloran, K. 2007. Mathematical and Scientific Forms of Knowledge: A Systemic Functional Multimodal Grammatical Approach [A]. In F. Christie and J. R. Martin. *Language, Knowledge and Pedagogy: Functional Linguistic and Sociological Perspectives* [C]. 205-236. London, Continuum.

O'Halloran, K. L. 2007b. Systemic Functional Multimodal Discourse Analysis (SF-MDA) Approach to Mathematics, Grammar and Literacy [A]. In A. McCabe, M. O'Donnell and R. Whittaker (Eds), Advances in *Language and Education* [C]. 77-102. London: Continuum.

O'Halloran, K. L. 2008. Systemic Functional-multimodal Discourse Analysis [SF-MDA]: Constructing Ideational Meaning Using Language and Visual Imagery [J]. *Visual Communication*, 7(4): 443-475.

O'Toole, M. 1992. A Functional Semiotics for the Visual Arts [A]. In J. Andrew (Ed.), *Poetics of the Text: Essays to Celebrate Twenty Years of the Neo-Formalist Circle* [C]. 57-78. Amsterdam: Rodopi.

O'Toole, M. 1994. *The Language of Displayed Art* [M]. London: Leicester University Press.

O'Toole, M. 1995. A Systemic-functional Semiotics of Art [A]. In M. A. K. Halliday, P. H. Fries and M. Gregory (Eds.), *Discourse in Society: Systemic Functional Perspectives: Meaning and Choice in Language: Studies for Michael Halliday* [C]. 159-179. Norwood, NJ: Ablex.

O'Halloran, K. 1999. Towards a Systemic Functional Analysis of Multisemiotic Mathematics Texts [J]. *Semiotica*, 124 (1/2): 1-29.

O'Halloran, K. L. 2000. Classroom Discourse in Mathematics: A Multisemiotic Analysis [J]. *Linguistics and Education*, 10(3): 359-388.

Osborne, J. and Dillon, J. 2008. *Science Education in Europe: Critical Reflections (A report to the Nuffield Foundation)* [M]. London: The Nuffield Foundation.

O'Toole, M. 1990. A Systemic-functional Semiotics of Art [J]. *Semiotica*, 82(3/4): 185-209.

Painter, C. and Martin, J. R. 1986. Introduction [A]. In C. Painter and J. R. Martin (Eds.), *Writing to Mean: Teaching Genres Across the Curriculum* [C]. 1-10. Bundoora, Vic. : Applied Linguistics Association of Australia.

Parkinson, J. and Adendorff, R. 2005. Science Books for Children as a Preparation for Textbook Literacy [A]. *Discourse Studies*, 7(2): 213-236.

Pindi, M and Bloor, T. 1987. Playing Safe with Predictions: Hedging, Attribution and Conditions in Economic Forecasting. In T. Bloor and J. Norrish (Eds.), *Written Language* [C]. 55-69. London: CILT/ BAAL.

Rounds, P. L. 1982. Hedging in Written Academic Discourse Precision and Flexibility (Mimeo). Unpublished Paper. Ann Arbor: University of Michigan.

Ravelli, L. 1985. *Metaphor, Mode and Complexity: An Exploration of Co-varying Patterns* [D]. Unpublished Honours thesis. Sydney: University of Sydney.

Read, H. H. and Watson, J. 1968. *Introduction to Geology* (2nd Edn.) [M]. London: Macmillan.

Reid, T. 1764. In D. Brookes (Ed.), *An Inquiry into the Human Mind on the Principles of*

Common Sense [C]. University Park, PA: Pennsylvania State University Press.

Reid, T. 1785. In D. Brookes (Ed.) *Essays on the Intellectual Powers of Man* [C]. Edinburgh: Edinburgh University Press.

Richgel, D. J. 2002. Informational Texts in Kindergarten [J]. *Reading Teacher*, 55(6): 586-596.

Riley, P. 2001. *Push and Pull* [M]. London: Franklin Watts.

Roth, W., Pozzer-Ardhenghi, L. and Han, J. 2005. *Critical Graphicacy: Understanding Visual Representation Practices in School Science* [M]. Dordrecht: Springer.

Royce, T. 1998. A Metafunctional View of Intersemiosis in the Economist Magazine: A Framework for Analysis [A]. In T. D'Haen and C. C. Barfoot (Eds.), *Language and Beyond* [C]. 157-176. Amsterdam: Editions Rodopi.

Royce, T. 1999a. Synergy on the Page: Exploring Intersemiotic Complementarity in Page-based Multimodal Text [A]. In N. Yamaguchi and W. Bowche (Eds.), *JASFL Occasional Papers* [C]. 25-49. Tokyo: Japan Association of Systemic Functional Linguistics.

Royce, T. 1999b. *Visual-verbal Intersemiotic Complementarity in The Economist Magazine* [D]. Unpublished PhD thesis. England: University of Reading.

Royce, T. 2002. Multimodality in the TESOL Classroom: Exploring Visual-verbal Synergy [J]. *TESOL Quarterly*, 36(2): 191-205.

Royce, T. 2007. Inter-semiotic Complementarity: A Framework for Multimodal Discourse Analysis [A]. In T. D. Royce and W. L. Bowcher (Eds.), *New Directions in the Analysis of Multimodal Discourse* [C]. 63-109. Mahwah, NJ: Lawrence Erlbaum Associates.

Royston, A. 2002. *Forces and Motion* [M]. Chicago: Heinemann Library.

Rozeboom, W. W. (1973). Why I Know so Much More Than You Do [A]. In R. M. Chilsom and R. J. Swartz (Eds.), *Empirical Knowledge: Readings from Contemporary Sources* [C]. 75-92. Englewood Cliffs, NJ: Prentice-Hall.

Russell, B. 1940. *An Inquiry into Meaning and Truth* [M]. London: George Allen & Unwin.

Russell, T. and McGuigan, L. 2001. Promoting Understanding Through Representational Redescription: An Illustration Referring to Young Pupils' Ideas About Gravity [A]. In D. Psillos, P. Kariotoglou, V. Tselfes, G. Bisdikian, G. Fassoulopoulos, E. Hatzikraniotis and M. Kallery (Eds.), *Science Education Research in the Knowledge-Based Society* [C]. 277-284. Netherlands: Kluwer Academic Publishers.

Saint-Martin, F. 1987. *Semiotics of Visual Language* [M]. Bloomington: Indiana University Press.

Salager-Meyer, F. 1994. Hedges and Textual Communicative Function in Medical English Written Discourse [A]. *English for Specific Purposes*, 13(2): 149-170.

Sarah, E. 2002. *What are Forces and Motion* [M]. London: Franklin Watts.

Schank, R. C. and Abelson, R. P. 1977. *Scripts, Plans, Goals and Understanding* [M]. Hillsdale, NJ: Lawrence Erlbaum Associates.

Sellars, W. 1963. *Science, Perception and Reality* [M]. New York: Humanities Press.

Sellars, W. 1975. Epistemic Principles [A]. In H. Castañeda (Ed.), *Action, Knowledge, and Reality* [C]. Indianapolis: Bobbs-Merrill.

Shadwick, B. and Barlow, S. 2003. *About Science* 2 [M]. Marrickville NSW: Science Press.

Shalem, Y. and Slonimsky, L. 2010. Seeing Epistemic Order: Construction and Transmission of Evaluative Criteria [J]. *British Journal of Sociology of Education*, 31(6): 755-778.

Shea, N. 1988. *The Language of School Science Textbooks* [D]. Unpublished Honours thesis. Sydney: University of Sydney.

Spiders, E. 1991. *Exploring: Forces and Structure* [M]. England: Sussex.

Spor, M. W. and Schneider, B. K. 1999. Content Reading Strategies: What Teachers Know, Use, and Want to Learn [J]. *Reading Research and Instruction*, 38(3): 221-231.

Sriniwass, S. 2010a. *Knowledge Construction in the Genre of Chemistry Textbooks: A Systemic Functional Linguistic Perspective Part* 1 [M]. Saarbrucken, Germany: VDM Publishing House (Verlag).

Sriniwass, S. 2010b. *Knowledge Construction in the Genre of Chemistry Textbooks: A Systemic Functional Linguistic Perspective Part* 2 [M]. Saarbrucken, Germany: VDM Publishing House (Verlag).

Stake, R. E. and Easley, J. A. 1978. *Case Studies in Science Education* [M]. Urbana: University of Illinois Center for Instructional Research and Curriculum Evaluation.

Sutton, C. 1989. Writing and Reading in Science [A]. In R. Millar (ed.), *In Doing Science: Images of Science in Science Education* [C]. P. 137-159. London: The Falmer Press.

Swales, J. M. 1981. *Aspects of Article Introductions* (Aston ESP Research Report 1) [R]. Birmingham, England: University of Aston.

Swales, J. M. 1986. A Genre-based Approach to Language Across the Curriculum [A]. In M. L. Tickoo (Ed.), *Language Across the Curriculum* [C]. 10-22. Singapore: Regional English Language Center.

Swales, J. M. 1988. Discourse Communities, Genres and English as an International Language [J]. *World Englishes*, 7(2): 211-20.

Swales, J. M. 1990. *Genre Analysis: English in Academic and Research Settings* [M]. Cambridge: Cambridge University Press.

Swales, J. M. 1993a. The Paradox of Value: Six Treatments in Search of the Reader [A]. In W. Henderson, T. Dudley-Evans and R. Backhouse (Eds.), *Economics and Language* [C]. 223-239. London: Routledge.

Swales, J. and Feak, C. 1994. *Academic Writing for Graduate Students: Essential Tasks and*

Skills [M]. Ann Arbor, MI: University of Michigan Press.

Swales, J. M. 1995. The Role of the Textbook Writing Research in EAP [J]. *English for Specific Purposes*, 14(1): 3-18.

Swales, J. M. 2004. *Research Genres: Exploration and Applications* [M]. Cambridge, UK: Cambridge University Press.

Tadros, A. 1985. *Prediction in Text* [M]. Birmingham, UK: The University of Birmingham, English Language Research.

Tadros, A. A. 1989. Predictive Categories in University Textbooks [J]. *English for Specific Purposes*, 8(1): 17-31.

Talmy, L. 1988. Force Dynamics in Language and Cognition [J]. *Cognitvie Science*, 12(1): 49-100.

Tang, G. 1991. The Role and Value of Graphic Representation of Knowledge Structures in ESL Learning: An Ethnographic Study [J]. *TESL Canada Journal*, 9(1): 29-41.

Tann, K. 2010. *Semogenesis of a Nation: An Iconography of Japanese Identity* [D], Unpublished PhD thesis. Sydney: the University of Sydney.

Taylor, C. B. 1979. *The English of High School Textbooks* [M]. Canberra: Australian Government Publishing Service.

Thibault, P. 2000. Multimodal Transcription of a Television Advertisement: Theory and Practice [A]. In A. Baldry (Ed.), *Multimodality and Multimediality in the Distance Learning Age* [C]. 311-385. Campobasso, Italy: Palladino Editore.

Thompson, S. 1994. Frameworks and Contexts: A Genre-based Approach to Analysing Lecture Introductions [J]. *English for Specific Purposes*, 13(2): 171-186.

Tobin, K. 1990. Research on Science Laboratory Activities: In Pursuit of Better Questions and Answers to Improve Learning [J]. *School Science and Mathematics*, 90(5): 403-418.

Torr, J. and Jenni, H. 1997. Literacy and the Language of Science in Year 1 Classrooms: Implications for Children's Learning [J]. *Australian Journal of Language and Literacy*, 20(3): 222-251.

Tower, C. 2002. "It's a snake, you guys!": The Power of Text Characteristics on Children's Responses to Informational Books [J]. *Research in the Teaching of English*, 37(1): 55-88.

Tufte, E. 1983. *The Visual Display of Quantitative Information* [M]. Cheshire, Connecticut: Graphics Press.

Unsworth, L. 1992. Evaluating Reading Materials [A]. In B. Derewianka (Ed.), *Language Assessment in Primary Classrooms* [C]. 224-248. Sydney: Harcourt Brace Jovanovich.

Unsworth, L. 1996. *How and Why: Recontextualizing Science Explanations in School Science Books* [D]. Unpublished PhD thesis. Sydney: University of Sydney.

256

Unsworth, L. 1997. Scaffolding Reading of Science Explanations: Accessing the Grammatical and Visual Forms of Specialised Knowledge [J]. *Reading*, 31(3): 30-42.

Unsworth, L. 1999a. Developing Critical Understanding of the Specialised Language of School Science and History Texts: A Functional Grammatical Perspective [J]. *Journal of Adolescent and Adult Literacy*, 42(7): 508-521.

Unsworth, L. 1999b. Explaining School Science in Book and Cdrom Formats: Using Semiotic Analyses to Compare the Textual Construction of Knowledge [J]. *International Journal of Instructional Media*, 26(2): 159-179.

Unsworth, L. (Ed.). 2000. *Researching Language in Schools and Communities: Functional Linguistic Approaches* [M]. London: Continuum.

Unsworth, L. 2004. Comparing School Science Explanations in Books and Computer-based Formats: The Role of Images, Image/Text Relations and Hyperlinks [J]. *International Journal of Instructional Media*, 31(3): 283-301.

Unsworth, L. 2006a. Image/Text Relations and Intersemiosis: Towards Multimodal Text Description for Multiliteracies Education [C]. The 33rd International Systemic Functional Congress, Brazil.

Unsworth, L. 2006b. Towards a Metalanguage for Multiliteracies Education: Describing the Meaningmaking Resources of Language-image Interaction [J]. *English Teaching: Practice and Critique*, 5 (1): 55-76.

van Dijk, T. A. and Atienza, E. 2011. Knowledge and Discourse in Secondary School Social Science Textbooks [J]. Discourse Studies, 13(1): 93-118.

van Leeuwen, T. 1999. Speech, Music, Sound [M]. London: Macmillan.

Varttala, T. 1999. Remarks on the Communicative Functions of Hedging in Popular Scientific and Specialist Research Articles on Medicine [J]. English for Specific Purposes, 18(2): 177-200.

Veel, R. 1997. 'Learning How to Mean — scientifically Speaking: Apprenticeship into Scientific Discourse in the Secondary School' [A]. In F. Christie and J. R. Martin (Eds.), Genre and Institutions: Social Processes in the Workplace and School [C]. 161-95. London: Continuum.

Veel, R. 1998. The Greening of School Science [A]. In J. R. Martin and R. Veel (Eds.), Reading Science [C]. 114-51. London: Routledge.

Veel, R. and Coffin, C. 1996. Learning to Think Like an Historian: The Language of Secondary School History [A]. In R. Hasan and G. Williams (Eds.), Literacy in Society [C]. 191-231. Harlow, Essex: Addison Wesley Longman.

Wade, S. E. and Moje, E. B. 2000. The Role of Text in Classroom Learning [A]. In M. L. Kamil, P. Mosenthal and P. D. Pearson (Eds.), The Handbook of Research on Reading

[C]. 609-627. Mahwah, NJ: Lawrence Erlbaum Associates.

Webber, P. 1994. The Function of Questions in Different Medical English Genres [J]. *English for Specific Purposes*, 13(3): 257-68.

Wellington, J. and Ireson, G. 2008. *Science Learning and Science Teaching* [M]. New York: Routledge.

White, R. 2001. The Revolution in Research on Science Teaching [A]. In V. Richardson (Ed.), *Handbook of Research on Teaching* (4th Edn.) [C]. 457-471. Washington, DC: American Educational Research Association.

Wignell, P. 1994. Genre Across the Curriculum [J]. *Linguistics and Education*, 6(4): 355-372.

Wignell, P., Martin, J. R. and Eggins, S. 1993. The Discourse of Geography: Ordering and Explaining the Experiential World [A]. In M. A. K. Halliday and J. R. Martin (Eds.), *Writing Science* [C]. 36-165. London: The Falmer Press.

Wilson, C. 2001. *Science: Forces and Motion* [M]. London: Kingfisher publications.

Winter, E. 1992. The notion of Unspecific Versus Specific as One Way of Analysing the Information of a Fund-raising Letter [A]. In W. C. Mann and S. A. Thompson (Eds.), *Discourse Analysis: Diverse Analyses of a Fund-raising Letter* [C]. 131-170. Amsterdam: Benjamins.

Wolff-Michael Roth, G., Michael, B. and Michelle, K. M. 1999. Differences in Graph-related Practices Between High School Biology Textbooks and Scientific Ecology Journals [J]. *Journal of Research in Science Teaching*, 36(9): 977-1019.

郭建红. 2010. 论科技英语名词化隐喻:语篇功能和认知效果[J]. 外国语文 (2):76-78.

姜亚军,赵刚. 2006. 学术语篇的语言学研究:流派分野和方法整合[J]. 外语研究 (6):1-5.

李努尔. 1992. 科技英语的语域特征[J]. 外国语 (2) : 21-24.

林芳. 2012. 英汉科技语言中的语法隐喻现象及其类型对比[J]. 新疆大学学报(社会科学版), (4): 135-139.

唐青叶. 2007. 详略度、精密度与经验识解[J]. 外语教学 (4): 26-30.

汪燕华. 2010. 多模态话语中的图文关系[J]. 外国语文 (5): 73-75.

王晋军. 2003. 名词化在语篇类型中的体现[J]. 外语学刊 (2): 74-78.

杨蕾,延宏. 2012. 科技英语模糊限制语的语用特征[J]. 山西财经大学学报 (2): 68-68.

杨信彰. 2007. 系统功能语言学与教育语篇分析[J]. 四川外语学院学报 (6): 17-20.

杨信彰. 2009. 多模态语篇分析与系统功能语言学[J]. 外语教学 (4): 11-14.

杨信彰. 2011. 英语科技语篇和科普语篇中的词汇语法[J]. 外语教学 (4) : 18-21.

佚名. 2012. "国外中学物理教材评述" [DB/OL]. http://www.360doc.com /content /11/ 0313 /18 / 4165914 _100787855. shtml, 2012- 6-2 (1 月 3 日).

姚银燕, 陈晓燕. 2012. 英语学术书评语篇让步语义资源的介入意义[J]. 外语教学理论与实践 (1)：39-46.

曾蕾. 2007. 从语法隐喻视角看学术语篇中的"投射"[J]. 外语学刊 (3)：46-49.

曾蕾, 梁红艳. 2012. 学术语篇体裁结构与时态组合模式的元功能研究[J]. 外语教学 (1)：30-33.

张德禄. 2012. 论多模态话语设计[J]. 山东外语教学 (1)：9-15.

张德禄, 王璐. 2010. 多模态话语模态的协同及在外语教学中的体现[J]. 外语学刊 (2)：97-102.

赵英玲. 1999. 英语科技语体中的模糊限制语[J]. 外语与外语教学 (9)：15-17.

朱永生. 2007. Bernstein 的教育社会学理论对系统功能语言学的影响[J]. 外语教学 (4)：6-10.

朱永生. 2007. 多模态话语分析的理论基础与研究方法[J]. 外语学刊 (5)：82-86.

图书在版编目(CIP)数据

中小学物理教科书的知识建构/赵清丽著. —厦门:厦门大学出版社,2013.11
ISBN 978-7-5615-4842-4

Ⅰ. ①中… Ⅱ. ①赵… Ⅲ. ①物理课－教材建设－研究－中小学
Ⅳ. ①G633.72

中国版本图书馆 CIP 数据核字(2013)第 279039 号

厦门大学出版社出版发行

(地址:厦门市软件园二期望海路 39 号 邮编:361008)

http://www.xmupress.com

xmup @ xmupress.com

三明日报社印刷厂印刷

2013 年 11 月第 1 版 2013 年 11 月第 1 次印刷

开本:720×970 1/16 印张:17.25 插页:2

字数:300 千字 印数:1~1 000 册

定价:49.00 元

本书如有印装质量问题请直接寄承印厂调换